C. Haq.

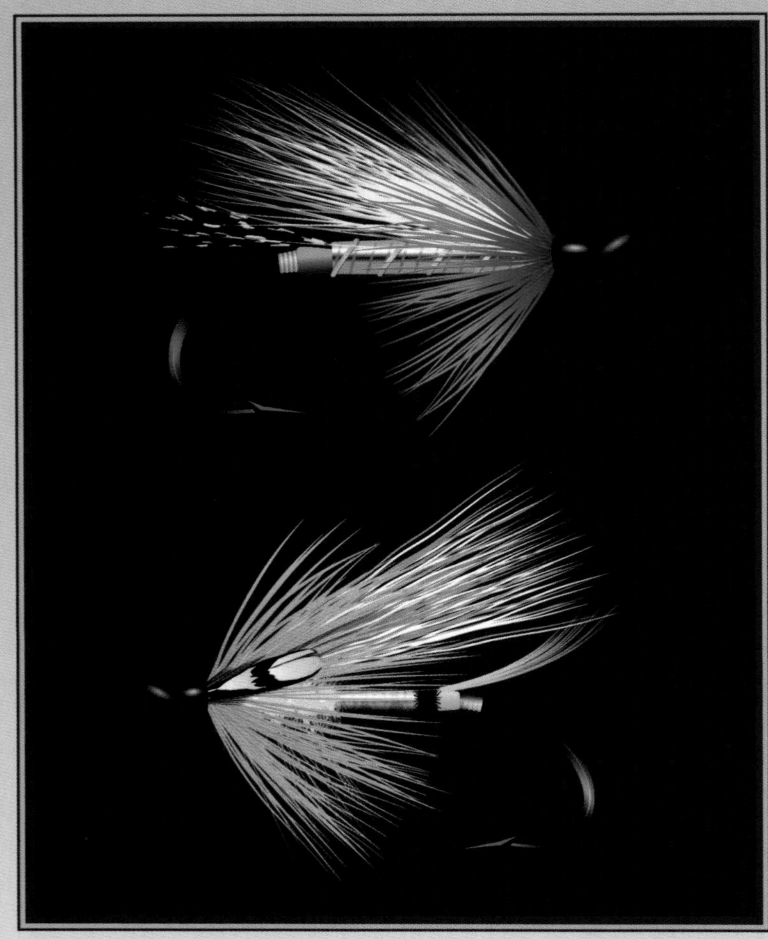

First published in Great Britain by Merlin Unwin Books, 2004

ISBN 1-873674-56-2

Published by
Merlin Unwin Books
Palmers House
7 Corve Street, Ludlow
Shropshire SY8 1DB, U.K.

British Library Cataloguing-in-Publication Data:
A catalogue record for this book is available from the British Library

Book design by Chris Mann
Printed in China by Leo Paper Products

Contents

Introduction and Acknowledgments

For many years it has been my habit, at the end of a day, to pick up one of the selection of books that I always keep at my bedside, and to read for a while before I settle down to sleep. One of the books that I have been reading recently is called *Once a Flyfisher* by Laurence Catlow. It is a diary of the author's fishing year, yet it is not a day-to-day account of fish caught or the techniques used to achieve success. Certainly fish are caught (most of the time) and often the fly is named but this is not the real stuff of the book. At the heart of the book is Laurence's attempt to make sense of why he fishes, what drives his passion for fishing and to put the pleasures of flyfishing into the context of his life. As I look at the open copy of the book lying on the desk next to my computer, I also reflect that the book is almost as much about the pleasures of owning and drinking good wine as it is about fishing. This makes me feel very well-inclined towards Laurence! I too love good wine and it makes me far more prepared to believe that here is a man who can get to the heart of the matter. W.C. Fields once commented in his misogynistic way that any man that hated kids and dogs couldn't be all bad. So it is with Laurence: any man that loves both flyfishing and good wine shows, by my definition anyway, a discerning palette in his choice of pleasures and has, I believe, found a small part at least of the answer to the big question about life, the universe and everything.

Where is all this preamble leading, I hear you ask – what has this all to do with a book about salmon and steelhead flies? Among the philosophical musings contained within *Once a Flyfisher*, Laurence tries to analyse what it is about catching a trout that gives him so much pleasure and comes to the conclusion that a trout is a treasure, the capture of which enables the fisherman to possess and become one with a small part of the mysterious universe around us. So, I think, is it with flies. Certainly the prime purpose of a fly is to deceive a fish, but it is not the only purpose it has. A fly is also a treasure which brings us pleasure beyond and independant of its success or otherwise in taking fish. A fly is a thing of beauty in its own right, an object that has a value beyond its narrow purpose. How else can we explain the endless fascination that flies have for flyfishers?

It is almost certain that a few flies containing a combination of the most successful 'trigger factors' would be all that we need to catch fish. All that we need perhaps, but not all that we want. There is, amongst fishermen for salmon and steelhead, a widespread feeling that the flies used must somehow be worthy of the opponent – a small treasure used to catch a greater treasure.

Among the hundreds of new flies devised every year is enshrined the hope that we have found the answer to the perennial search – the perfect fly! And yet one must ask if this is true, do we really want to find the perfect fly? I think not. What we really want is a fly which will work tomorrow and catch us two or three fish, not twenty-two or thirty-two, each day for the whole season. To catch twenty or thirty fish would be to devalue the treasure and reduce to the commonplace an experience that should remain a special thrill. Here therefore is a book containing many flies which will serve in this quest. I trust that you will find them effective and that you will be successful and catch fish – but not too many please God!

here are two opposing schools of thought about the importance of fly patterns – those who think that fly patterns are totally unimportant, and those who think that fly choice is critical. Those who think that fly choice is unimportant will point to the fact that the position, depth and speed of the fly in the water are the factors that determine if a fish will take the fly or not. Those who think that fly choice is critical will point to the fact that even if the speed and depth of the fly are correct, fish will still ignore one fly and then take another. Both schools are of course correct! It is however interesting to note that fishermen who maintain that fly choice is nearly irrelevant still select the flies that they will use very carefully indeed – when an angler says that fly selection is not critical, he does not mean that you can tie any old pattern on to the end of the leader. In fact most anglers will probably concede that both sets of factors are equally important. To be successful you need both the correct choice of fly and to fish it at the correct depth and speed. It is also of interest to note that when talking about fly patterns it very often seems that colour is the main criterion. This ignores the fact that the type or style of fly is at least as important as the colour. The style of fly determines how the fly will swim and react in the water currents – is it mobile, do the fibres of the wing and tail flutter attractively or will it be little more than a lifeless blob? The answers to these questions depend very much upon the water conditions that prevail. A fly that performs well in fast flowing water and heavy currents may well be a lifeless, sinking lump in slack water and light currents. Thus a wide range of fly types have been developed, each of which is adapted to be at its best in a particular set of circumstances.

Where does this leave colour choice then? Well, given that a style of fly is well adapted to the water conditions in which it is used, the colour of the fly then becomes important. The colour of the water, the colour of the bed of the river, the brightness and cast of the ambient light will all have a considerable influence upon the way that a particular colour will appear in the water. It is often said that fish 'like' a particular colour – we do not understand this to mean that fish like a colour in the way that a human might like red, or yellow or pink for that matter – we do not mean that fish have the ability to make critical, aesthetic choices. We simply mean that, on the pragmatic level, given the choice of a fly that is predominantly green or one that is predominantly red, it is observable that they may prefer the green one, for example. At that time, on that day, in those conditions.

The other problem with colour choice is that we have absolutely no idea how the fly actually appears to the fish! It is simply observable that one colour may be more attractive to fish than another in certain conditions.

It is well known that insects, for example, are attracted to certain plants by the colours of the flowers, it is not surprising therefore that they swarm all over bright scarlet red flowers. Not all is at it seems, however – many of the bright red flowers are also beacons of brightness at the untra-violet end of the spectrum. The insects are attracted not by the bright red that we see, but by the bright ultra-violet that they see! Which explains why they are also attracted to flowers that seem very non-descript to our eyes. Colour is important, but not always for reasons that seem obvious to us.

We should also consider one of the great mysteries of fly fishing. Why is it that a particular fly may be very successful for one angler, but absolutely useless for another? One of the most long-lived and popular trout flies from Scotland is the Peter Ross. This fly has a long and distinguished history and always takes fish – but not for me! I have never, ever caught a fish on a Peter Ross and I, personally, do not believe that it is possible to catch a trout on a Peter Ross. If I tie a Peter Ross on my leader I prove my point over and over again by not catching trout – but why? I believe that confidence in a fly pattern is critical to its success and I think I know why. If I believe in the fly that I am using, I will fish it properly. I will do the right things because I fully expect to get a take at any time. I will cast to the right place, I will take the trouble to mend the line to ensure the right presentation, I will be patient enough to allow the fly to fish at the right speed. In other words, I will do all the things that I should do to maximise my chances of taking a fish. Lo and behold what is the result? – I catch a fish. Which has the effect of confirming my judgement about the fly and will increase my confidence the next time I use it.

Compare this with my performance when I am using a fly in which I have no confidence. I expect it to fail and, by my actions, will almost certainly ensure that it does. I will be impatient and fish far too quickly, I will hardly be able to wait to lift the fly out of the water to cast again and after doing this for a few minutes will have my judgement confirmed that the fly is useless! I will simply go through the motions with no belief that I will catch a fish.

How can we summarise all these factors then to form a coherent view of fly choice? To me it seems that the so-called controversy between those that insist that fly choice is irrelevant and those that say it is critical is in fact no argument at all. To say that fly choice is unimportant is to say that as long as a house has good foundations it doesn't matter what it looks like. Conversely the other view is to hold that the outward appearance is everything and that it doesn't matter if the house then falls down! The fact is that no sensible person would hold either of these views, in practice, if not in what they say. Those who say presentation is everything do not use any old fly that comes to hand. They choose flies very carefully in order to be able to present them correctly. They say that colour doesn't matter but then restrict themselves to three or four colours that they know will work in most circumstances. Those who profess to hold that fly choice is the most important thing, nevertheless go to great lengths to present them at the correct depth and speed.

Perhaps the most important point is that the angler must believe that the fly will work. Only in this state of mind will he then fish in a way that will maximise his chances of success. Presentation is important: the fly must be delivered at the correct depth and at the correct speed. But the fact that a fly must be correctly presented does not mean that the choice of fly is unimportant. It simply means that until the fly is correctly presented, other factors are almost irrelevant. The form and style of fly, the key to its performance in the water, is one of the most important factors in determining if the presentation is correct – they are simply two elements in an interlinked equation. The fly must be of a type and size which, because of its characteristics, allows the angler to present it correctly. When this is achieved the colour of the fly will then play its role.

Simply presenting a fly correctly is in itself no guarantee of success. Just as choosing the correct style of fly is no guarantee unless you can put it in the right place. Success comes when the right combination of presentation, fly style and fly colour is achieved.

It is no accident that most anglers will have a particular fly pattern that they know will work in a particular set of water conditions. They will then have a range of colour variants of this pattern from which they can choose, to suit the conditions of the day. It does not matter at all that this fly choice might not be my fly choice, or yours for that matter!

In the following pages I have assembled a huge range of hairwinged flies that meet all the right criteria. They have all been successful on their day, some in a wide variety of conditions, others work in a more restricted way. All are worth examining to see if they provide the combination of factors that could make them the fly for you.

Introduction

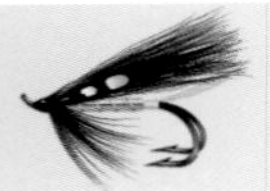

What exactly is a hairwing fly? At its simplest level it is fly that is winged with hair, as opposed to feather fibres. This simple definition, however, in no way reflects the wide range of hair flies that have been developed over the years. Even the word 'hairwing' is not strictly correct because I have included flies in which the hair is mainly in the tail of the fly. And in the case of tube flies, to describe the fly as being 'winged' at all is probably pushing the boundaries of the word. Rather the word 'hairwing' should be taken to mean flies which are constructed mainly out of hair. This does not mean that feathers are never used in the construction of hairwing flies, in many cases hair and feather is combined, sometimes very effectively.

Many of the flies in this book are well-known patterns which have been around for years and reference to which can be found in other publications. I have included popular flies such as these for two reasons. Firstly, it is often the case that as time goes by, the dressing detail changes and it is no bad thing to see how they started out. Secondly, they form the basis of a wide range of variants, many of which I have illustrated. These long-lived patterns have not stood the test of time by accident – they are still around because they work. Such patterns still form one of the most important starting points for the development of new flies.

Other flies are very new, forming the basis of developing trends that will no doubt spread and extend over the years. Typical examples of this category would include the Scandinavian Fatback or Templedog styles of tube fly. Furthermore there is the spreading use of extremely mobile fox hair as a winging material in preference to marabou. The use of hair hackling, as in the 'Hairy' flies created by Gordon Mackenzie, is another example of a hair-tying technique that might not be familiar to every reader, but is certainly worth examining.

ACKNOWLEDGMENTS

I wish to record here my thanks to all the fishermen and flytyers who have helped in many ways with the production of this book. Flytyers from many countries around the world have supplied me with superb examples of their art and have also shown patience and understanding as I pestered them to explain the how, when and why of the thinking behind the patterns. Steelhead anglers from the USA and Canada have taken the time and effort to try to educate me in the mysteries of steelhead fishing and have been unfailingly courteous when I returned with requests for yet more information about fishing techniques, fly patterns and rivers. The enthusiasm that these fishermen have for all aspects of steelhead fishing and their great regard and respect for their quarry should be an example to us all.

I have quoted widely from Merlin Unwin's other publications, particularly *Trout & Salmon Flies of Ireland*, *Trout & Salmon Flies of Scotland* and *Trout & Salmon Flies of Wales*. Special thanks are due to the authors of these books, Peter O'Reilly, Stan Headley and Moc Morgan.

As you will notice from the text I have also taken a lot of information from *Trout & Salmon* and *Fly Fishing & Fly Tying*. Special thanks are due to the publishers and editors of both of these magazines.

Special thanks are also due to Gordon Mackenzie, Steve Schweitzer, Martin Jorgenson, Davie McPhail, Tim Gaunt-Baker, Peter O'Reilly and Gerald Bartsch. From North America I have drawn heavily on the patterns of Dave McNeese, Warren Duncan, Fulsher & Krom, Bill McMillan, Frank Amato, Trey Combs, Randall Kaufmann, Troy Bachman, Brian Silvey, John Shewey, Steve Gobin, Garry Miltenberger and many more.

I also wish to express my thanks once more to Merlin Unwin and his team. They are a joy to work with and have made my task as an author much easier than it might otherwise have been. Finally, I would like to make it clear that although I have had the privilege of receiving information from many sources, responsibility for any errors, omissions or misunderstandings lies entirely with me.

Chris Mann, April 2004

The History and Development of the Hairwing Fly

When was the first hairwing salmon fly devised? Many students of the subject have mused on this topic over the years and theories abound. One of the greatest problems for any historian is where there is a lack of recorded evidence. In these circumstances, one is left to surmise. However educated and informed such interpolation may be, it is no substitute for hard evidence. But just because we may not be able to find written recorded evidence does not mean that things did not occur. One must appreciate the nature of the world preceding the printing press. In 15th century Britain, few people could read or write. The written word was the preserve of the clergy and lawyers and a few scribes in the employ of the nobility. Books were laboriously written by hand: each one an undertaking of perhaps months and sometimes years. They were incredibly expensive. The few books that were produced were concerned mainly with religion and theology; law; science and philosophy. Very little was written that concerned everyday life, even that of substantial land-owning families. A very few books were written on the sports of the aristocracy, but these concerned themselves mainly with the chase and other chivalrous pastimes. Fishing with rod and line was not a sport that concerned the rich and was probably deemed to be just a means of providing food.

In historical times – before the age of industry, pollution and excessive exploitation by large urban populations – the runs of salmon on the rivers throughout western Europe must have been phenomenal. They must have provided a rich source of food for the population at large. It is quite inconceivable that they didn't and yet hardly a mention of this is to be found in the written record. It is from this premise that I shall stick my neck out and posit my own firm conviction that hairwinged lures were probably used for fishing from much earlier times than we have written evidence for, possibly from the earliest days of fly fishing.

The first printed work on angling in the English language was *The Treatyse of Fysshynge wyth an Angle*, printed in 1496 as an appendix to an edition of the Boke of St. Albans. Authorship of the Treatyse has traditionally been accorded to one Dame Julyana Bernes who was reputedly the Prioress of Sopwell Priory near St. Albans, in Hertfordshire. There is some evidence to suggest that this might have been a total fabrication by the printer, Wynkyn de Word, though I am not qualified to enter into the controversy. For anyone interested in this subject, I recommend *Dame Juliana*, by Fred Buller and Hugh Falkus, which was published in 2001 by the The Flyfishers Classic Library. This book is not only a beautiful re-print of the Treatyse itself (with an inter-linear text in modern English), but also presents opposing views concerning its origins, with Fred Buller and Jack Heddon taking opposite sides of the argument. The twelve flies listed in the Treatyse are all feather winged trout flies. Other texts appeared in the 16th and 17th centuries, mostly based on the Treatyse, but none of them mention hairwing flies. It would be easy to suppose that this lack of written evidence was positive proof that hairwing flies did not exist. If they had existed, they would have been mentioned, surely? To show just how misleading this kind of thinking can be we only have to look at the 19th century. At this time we know that flies winged with hair were most certainly being used – we can also look through the major literature: Bainbridge, Blacker, Scrope, Knox, Francis, Kelson, Hale etc. and find almost no mention of hairwing flies! I believe that there are two main reasons for this omission. Firstly, some of the books are very specialised in subject, referring mainly to the flies used on a single river (e.g. Scrope and Knox). Secondly, most of the other books were written by authors who had a particular view of fly development (Bainbridge, Blacker, Kelson, etc.) and thus had no interest in giving a wider picture of the generality of angling practice.

To summarise, the written history of salmon flies and fishing is completely arbitrary. Books were written by a few people with the education and leisure to write them, as well as the money to have them published. They were also written from a partial point of view and were aimed at a particular privileged readership and not the general populace.

Any transatlantic argument attempting to show that the British invented hairwing flies ahead of the North Americans would be silly. Since we have Aelian's account of flyfishing in Macedonia in the 3rd century, there were probably hairwing flies in use 1700 years ago! Regardless of the earliest origins, the widespread use and development of hairwing flies for salmon fishing must be properly accorded to the North Americans. It was certainly they who raised the hairwing fly to the pre-eminent position it occupies today.

The earliest specific reference to hair winged flies that I can find is that noted by Buckland and Oglesby in *A Guide to Salmon Flies*. Here, the authors refer to Morgan, who in 1770, stated that hair, squirrel hair, spaniel tail and cat's whiskers were being used to wing flies. In 1800, Samuel Taylor in *Angling in All its Branches* mentions that a salmon fly "may be forked (winged), if thought proper, with two or three hairs of a squirrel." Let us start from here then. We have written evidence that by 1800 hairwing flies were being used for salmon. We need another 50 years, however, until we find mention of a specific pattern. In Ireland, the 'Erris' series of flies were originated by Pat Hearn, of Ballina, around 1850. Of these, the Owenmore is the best known.

Owenmore

The Erris flies have a wing structure which is termed 'maned': the wing consisted substantially of bunches of mohair (angora goat) which were tied in at intervals along a multi-segmented body. An overwing of golden pheasant tail fibres and bronze mallard was usually added, so these flies are not pure hairwings. Maned flies did not retain their popularity very long, the main reasons being that they were complicated to tie and because the wing fibres tended to collapse together in the water due to the fine texture of the mohair.

Why weren't these maned flies developed further and the design problems overcome? From this remove in time, it's hard to tell but I believe that they were simply swamped by the rising fashion tide of the complex featherwing flies. They were, perhaps, a good idea that simply came at the wrong time. An interest in the maned structure for salmon flies was rekindled only much later in the 20th century. The steelheaders were the first to revive this kind of fly, although they probably didn't know of the precedent. In the 1960s and 1970s many flies, such as the Steelheader Bucktail and Paint Brush were dressed in two versions: one in which the wing hair was applied conventionally and a second version in which the wing was split into two bunches of hair, mounted separately. Curiously enough, this style of dressing seems to have fallen from favour again amongst steelhead fly tyers, just at the time when maned flies have been re-discovered by the salmon fishermen of the Canadian east coast. As you will see in the section on North American flies (see page 83), new maned flies have now been developed in which the design problems have been overcome by the careful choice of wing materials and the potential advantages of this construction may at last be realised.

The practise of mounting hairwings as a series of small bunches, spread out along the back of the fly has a lot to recommend it. Firstly, it enables the tyer to achieve a dense silhouette without bulk. Secondly, it allows the fly to have a small, neat head – the windings only have to cover the last bunch of hair. Thirdly, it allows the prismatic mixing of wing colours that remain translucent and not collapse into a dense clump. Lastly, the series of hair bunches mounted along the hook shank provide an inherent stability in the water so that the fly swims on an even keel. The Matuka style from New Zealand (highly regarded in many other countries throughout the world) achieves exactly the same effect using a feather wing. There is no reason why flies tied in this style have to have a complex body construction. The hair bunches can be mounted almost one behind another with perhaps only one turn of the body material between them.

Other early hairwing flies such as the Nora Criena, the Mohair Canary, the Silver Canary and the Goshawk also had their home in Ireland. All of these are hairwing offspring of the Parson flies and retain many of the features, such as the use of golden pheasant toppings, so typical of these brilliant early Irish flies. The dressings illustrated in Plate 1 are from E. J. Malone, described in his *Irish Trout and Salmon Flies* (1984). We don't have dates for these flies but their derivation from the Parson series and the use of mohair for the wing material makes it likely that they date to before 1900. Following on from my point that books often don't reflect the actuality of angling, it is interesting to note that as late as 1984 Malone mentions only four other hairwing dressings – versions of the Blue Charm and Silver Doctor, together with a Green Stoat tube and a yellow fly from Northern Ireland called the Goat.

After these flies the development of the hairwing seems to come to almost a dead stop. Whilst it is certainly true that hairwing flies were being used here or there, nothing further appears in the literature until the 1930s. In the intervening years, salmon fly development was almost exclusively the story of the complex feather winged classics. It is actually extraordinary that the use of such flies should have continued as long as it did. In Kelson's time and earlier it was still believed that salmon ate butterflies and other insects when they entered the rivers. By the turn of the 19th century, however, this was known not to be true. Why then did it take so long for the design of flies to reflect this knowledge?

To quote an article by Colonel Esmond Drury (inventor of the General Practitioner) in the *Journal of the Flyfishers' Club* in 1960: *"The extraordinary fact is, not that Kelson held these beliefs, but that succeeding generations of salmon fly-fishermen have apparently accepted the products of ignorance and misconception without question .."*

It is true that by the 1920s the classic featherwing had been simplified somewhat. Nevertheless, they still retained many of the features of the earlier flies: complex tails, multi-part bodies with joints that were butted with herl

Silver Canary

Goshawk

Nora Criena

Canary

PLATE 1: Early Irish Hairwings

and so on. The wing construction itself had been simplified and was generally reduced to an underwing of mixed fibres with an overwing of bronze mallard. The golden pheasant topping was also often retained. Other than the occasional hairwing conversion of a classic featherwing pattern and the gradual simplification of the tying style, the development of the salmon fly in Europe reached a hiatus in the early years of the 20th century. Few really new ideas were developed and new flies that were to have a lasting influence were very few and far between. There were, of course, some honourable exceptions, such as the General Practitioner, and a trend towards sparse, small dressings for low water use. Generally speaking, however, if we want to see any real salmon fly development in the early 20th century, we must turn our attention from the Old World to the New where the true hairwing revolution was to take place.

Most writers on the subject, such as Bates and Fulsher & Krom, seem to take the view that the early North American fishermen replaced the feathers of the classic European flies with hair of various sorts because they were unable to obtain the original materials. Superficially, this theory seems logical. The importation of exotic feathers from Europe and Asia would have been expensive and troublesome. But why did the North Americans switch to hair instead of finding more obvious feather substitutes from the indigenous birds of the New World? A brief survey of the extensive avian fauna of North America shows any number of plumages suitable for fly tying. The list is very extensive indeed and ranges from duck, geese and turkey through jays, bluebirds, robins, kingfishers and woodpeckers to humming birds. Other common sources of suitable feathers would have included various quail, grouse, cranes and birds of prey such as kites, hawks and eagles. Many of these species are very colourful and could well have provided substitutes even for exotic plumage such as chatterer, kingfisher and Indian crow. So why didn't North American fly tying mirror that of the other side of the Atlantic, using locally available plumage as substitute? Unfortunately, there comes a point at which logic and research cannot provide the answers. We must simply note that New World versions of the classic built wing salmon flies, using feather substitutes obtainable in North America, do not seem to have come into being. At least, if they did, nobody has told us about them!

There was little written about fly fishing in North America until the beginning of the 20th century. Anecdotal evidence suggests that immigrants from the British Isles to Newfoundland in the 18th century fished for sport as well as for food. The flies that they used were made from the common materials that they found around them, including hair from their domestic animals. In *Atlantic Salmon Flies and Fishing*, Bates mentions something that the angling historian, Herbert Howard, had seen in a family Bible from Newfoundland. The bible belonged to a family named Stirling and it contained a note, dated 1795, which made reference to a hairwing fly called the Red Cow which had caught salmon.

Red Cow

In those pre-Kelson days there would have been no thought of fancy flies with complex construction and exotic feathers. The fly would probably have had a body of dubbed under-fur and the wing and throat would have been of the longer guard hairs.

One of the earliest and best-known North American salmon flies was the Night Hawk, devised by Stanford White. White was shot dead in 1906 so the Night Hawk is certainly older than this. In its original form the fly had a wing of black feathers. A hairwing version, using black squirrel tail, may be nearly contemporary. With its silver and black colours this fly would certainly catch fish today.

Night Hawk - Stanford

The Red Abbey is another early pattern that dates from about 1913 and was very popular in the Restigouche area of Quebec. Bates notes that this was the fly used by Colonel Lewis Thomson when he first devised the 'Patent' (a dead drift, greased line technique) method of fishing.

Red Abbey

Herbert Howard also documents the development of the Rat series of hairwings and dates it to 1911, thus making the Rats some of the earliest hairwing flies on either side of the Atlantic.

The Rat series is one of the most important developments in hairwing salmon flies for they are still in regular use today in many countries. So widespread and popular are the Rats that many anglers are unaware of their venerable history and assume that they are a recent development. The first of the Rat flies were devised by Roy Angus Thomson in New Brunswick, Canada, in the autumn of 1911. The name comes from his initials. Originally, there were four flies in the series: the Rat, the Grey Rat, and the Silver and Gold Rats. There is some doubt as to whether the Rat or the Grey Rat was the very first. The form of the Rat series has had a lasting influence on hairwing design, particularly on the east coast of Canada. The wound collar hackle sloping back over a hair wing is typical of many Canadian hairwing patterns to this day and gives them a distinctive look which is not to be confused with hairwings from other countries. From the original Rats there have been many further variants since (Bates noted 31 in 1970), the most important of which are to be found in the section on the East Coast in the chapter on North America (see page 83).

As can be seen from the illustrations, a wound grizzle collar hackle and a red head are distinguishing features of this series – vaguely similar to the classic Doctor patterns. Jungle cock eyes are given as optional for most variants.

Perhaps only second to the Rat series in their influence (and also finding widespread use up to the present day) are the Cosseboom series, devised by John Cosseboom. The original Cosseboom was a bucktail streamer fly devised in about 1922 for

PLATE 2: The Original Rat Series

the Margaree River. A revised version, which is now known as the Cosseboom (or Cosseboom Special), dates from 1923. Bates notes over 30 variants of the original fly but the six shown in Plate 3 were the most effective and commonly used of the early ones. Cosseboom variants continue to proliferate and many more are discussed in the chapter on North America (see page 83). Jungle cock sides or eyes are given as optional on most of these patterns.

Both the Rat and Cosseboom series of flies have spread widely outside North America and have proved to be effective and popular, particularly in Iceland, Scandinavia and Russia. They are not so well known in Great Britain. Somewhat surprisingly, neither the Rats nor the

Cosseboom Special

Gold Cosseboom

Orange Cosseboom

Yellow Cosseboom

Red Cosseboom

Black Cosseboom

PLATE 3: The Original Cosseboom Series

Cosseboom appear to have had much influence on the steelhead fisheries of western USA and Canada. Why this should be so, is difficult to say. They have all the credentials which would lead one to believe that they would be very effective. Perhaps the only exception is the Steelhead Rat series from Mike Brooks, as detailed in *Steelhead Fly Fishing* by Trey Combs. These were based on the Pack Rat Atlantic salmon fly.

Of the other early hairwing patterns from the Atlantic coast of North America there are three black bodied, black winged flies that are important because they are forerunners of the Butt series of flies.

The Black Bear, a tying from Harry Smith of Maine, is considered by Bates to be one of the main influences on the Butt series. However, in *Modern Atlantic Salmon Flies*, Paul Marriner prefers the Black Bomber from Joe Aucoin of New Waterford, Nova Scotia, which dates to earlier than 1929, and the Black Spider, from Ira Gruber, dating to about 1935, as the more likely ancestors. Marriner points out that there is a major disparity between Bates's description of the Black Bear and the photograph of the fly in *Atlantic Salmon Flies and Fishing*. Having studied the photograph, I must say that I tend to agree with Marriner.

The Butt series of flies are basically black-bodied flies with butts (or more correctly 'tags' – see below) of a contrasting colour (normally green, orange or red). They are typical of eastern Canadian salmon flies. Since their inception, myriad variants have been devised. Many of the more modern versions feature a butt of fluorescent material. Paul Marriner notes that – strictly speaking – the word 'butt' is incorrect in naming these flies. In the dressing terminology of the classic salmon fly, a butt covers the tail windings of the dressing. In the modern versions of the Butt series, the 'butt' is actually behind the tail and should therefore be correctly described as a 'tag'. Marriner notes that in the original Black Spider, the butt was in front of the tail and thus the usage was correct. It is one of the delights of angling literature to find examples such as this, where an author has not only read the history but has really looked at it in detail and thought about what it really means.

Marriner's *Modern Atlantic Salmon Flies* concentrates on salmon flies for eastern North America, but is a book that I heartily recommend and which might give thought to many British salmon anglers.

The streamer or bucktail style of fly has a long and distinguished history on the east coast of the USA and up until the present day represents one the most commonly used styles of fly on rivers such as the Penobscot. The home of this style of fly is undoubtedly Maine where they were, and still are, extremely popular for land-locked salmon. Bates wrote extensively about streamers and bucktails in two of his books (*Streamer Fly Tying and Fishing* and *Streamers and Bucktails: The Big Fish Flies*). He considered them vastly underrated as salmon flies.

It should be noted that in the North American context, the word 'bucktail' usually denotes a fly in which the hair wing is considerably longer than the hook, often extending well beyond the tail of the fly. The winging material is normally of bucktail because of the required fibre length (hence the name), but other materials may be used. It's still a bucktail if the bucktail style is retained. Just to confuse things, the term 'bucktail' may also be used simply to describe a fly where the winging material is of bucktail even if it doesn't conform to the 'bucktail style'. It is, however, normally pretty clear from the context which is meant.

The Herb Johnson Special dates to around 1960 and was first intended for land-locked salmon. It made its name, however, when it was tried on the Miramichi and had sensational success. The original version of this fly had prominent painted eyes on a silver head but this seems to have disappeared on many modern tyings. In addition to the Herb Johnson Special, Bates further recommends the Grey Ghost as a darker fly and the Mickey Finn described below as a bright alternative.

Herb Johnson Special

Mickey Finn - Knight

The Mickey Finn is one of the best known of the bucktails, first popularised in 1932 by John Alden Knight. This fly started out by being named the Red & Yellow Bucktail, was later changed to The Assassin and was finally christened the Mickey Finn by Gregory Clark. It is still a widely used fly on the east coast of North America and in 1976 Trey Combs also noted it as a popular steelhead fly on the west coast fisheries, in his book *Steelhead Fly Fishing & Flies*.

On the west coast steelhead fisheries of North America, hairwings have always been popular. Perhaps the most surprising thing is that, contrary to the experience of the Atlantic salmon fisheries, hairwings have never quite attained absolute dominance over featherwings. This is primarily due to the long lasting influence of such individual fly tyers as Syd Glasso who re-cast the traditions of the beautiful Spey and Dee flies and who ensured their survival until the present day. It should be said that some of these modern Spey patterns are actually winged with hair rather than feather. They nevertheless still retain all the other characteristics of Spey flies and are covered exhaustively in *Shrimp & Spey Flies for Salmon & Steelhead*. Having said that, in the 1930s and 1940s many hairwing patterns were used for steelhead fishing. Some of these early steelhead flies were adaptations of British and east coast salmon patterns but it wasn't long before indigenous patterns began to make their mark.

Improved Governor

The Improved Governor is based upon the old British fly, The Governor, which was itself based on the classic Coachman design. The steelhead version was used on the Eel river as far back as 1910 or even earlier. It was originally winged with bronze mallard but the hairwing conversion probably dates to the 1930s.

Devised in 1930 for use on the Eel, the Nite Owl was designed by Lloyd Silvius, one of the doyens of steelhead fly fishing. It was one of the first steelhead flies to have been originally designed as a hairwing rather than being a conversion of a featherwing pattern. Its influence was immediate and in the next decade featherwing steelhead flies declined very much into the minority. The Nite Owl still finds use today and was noted by Trey Combs in 1976 as being one of the most popular steelhead flies of the time. A well-used variant is the Nite Owl Optic which has a weighted and eyed head as noted for the other optic flies mentioned below. Trey Combs also gives an alternative dressing which has a yellow floss or wool body, ribbed with oval gold tinsel.

Nite Owl - Silvius

The Montreal is another extremely old pattern whose origins can be traced back to Peter Cowan of the Bedford district of Quebec in around 1850. The original dressing had wings of grey feather strips combined with a claret body and hackle. The hairwing version appears to date from the early 1930s, probably having been influenced by the Nite Owl (see above). Just to complicate matters, the name was also (wrongly) attributed to another fly of the same style but which had a red body and hackle with brown winging. Both versions, illustrated below, were still in use at the end of the 1970s and are included in *Steelhead Fly Fishing and Flies* by Trey Combs in 1976.

Montreal #1

Montreal #2

The Coquihalla Orange and the Coquihalla Silver are flies from Major Thomas Brayshaw and were designed for use on the Coquihalla River in 1946 and 1947 respectively. These patterns are still in occasional use and are included in the pattern list in *Fly Patterns of British Columbia* by Arthur Lindgren, published in 1996. Three other related patterns, the Coquihalla Orange – Dark, the Coquihalla Orange – Light and the Coquihalla Red have feather overwinging, although hairwing variants exist in which the mallard overwing is replaced by bucktail. Brayshaw tied the original flies with many of the features of the classic fully dressed flies, such as butts, double ribbing, golden pheasant toppings and jungle cock cheeks. Whilst these adornments probably don't add much to the effectiveness of the fly (and are largely omitted in more modern examples), they are nevertheless beautiful examples of the flytyer's craft. With their predominantly orange/white colouring, I'm sure that these flies would be effective today. I have seen some superb looking examples of the Coquihallas tied in the Spey-style, with a long hackle over the front part of the body.

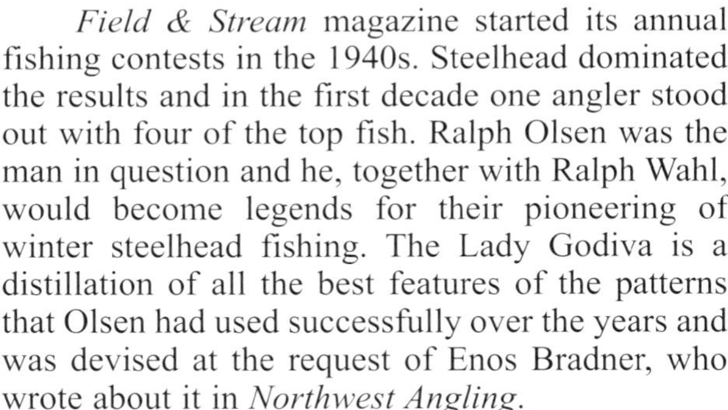

Field & Stream magazine started its annual fishing contests in the 1940s. Steelhead dominated the results and in the first decade one angler stood out with four of the top fish. Ralph Olsen was the man in question and he, together with Ralph Wahl, would become legends for their pioneering of winter steelhead fishing. The Lady Godiva is a distillation of all the best features of the patterns that Olsen had used successfully over the years and was devised at the request of Enos Bradner, who wrote about it in *Northwest Angling*.

Ralph Wahl was Olsen's long-time fishing partner and riverside companion. The Lord and Lady Hamilton flies, dating from the early 1940s for use on the Skagit for winter fishing, were his alternatives to Olsen's Lady Godiva as 'the perfect fly'. The names have nothing to do with British aristocracy but derive from a settlement on the Skagit, near to which many significant catches were made.

One of the most noticeable features of these early flies was the popular combination of a yellow body with red and white hackles and wings. The ubiquitous hot orange, which dominates the colouring of modern flies, was much less in evidence then. Yellow bodies are markedly less popular these days and when it is used it is almost always combined with black and orange. Is there a good reason for this, or is it just one of those fashion things? Certainly the flies with this coloration were very effective and caught many specimen fish. There is no denying that the coloration of flies probably has more to do with human notions of aesthetics than success or otherwise in catching fish. I believe that, in this case, it is simply that the combination of yellow, red and white is somehow less appealing to the human eye than black, orange and yellow. Other enduring flies which use the same colour combination include the Skykomish Sunrise and the Skykomish Yellow.

Among the best known of other early steelhead hairwings are the hairwing version of the Admiral, the Black Gordon, Al's Special, the Golden Demon, the Thor and the Stillaguamish Special. Most of these flies are simple in construction, with a wool or chenille body and a hair wing of bear or bucktail. All of them can still be effective today, especially if tied in a slightly more modern fashion, e.g. with more mobile and translucent dubbing for the body.

Admiral

Black Gordon

Al's Special

Golden Demon

Thor

Stillaguamish Special

PLATE 4: Early Steelhead Hairwings

The father and son team of Ken and George McLeod are the originators of three of the most enduring steelhead patterns of all time – the Skykomish Sunrise, the Purple Peril and the McLeod Ugly. Since its introduction in 1940 the Skykomish Sunrise has become the most popular steelhead fly pattern in the history of the sport. A later variant, the Skykomish Yellow, is identical except that the body is of yellow chenille instead of red. All of these patterns are still in everyday use on rivers throughout the North West. The Skykomish Sunrise and Purple Peril in particular have spawned a whole series of derivatives of which the Spey style versions are the most beautiful (see *Shrimp & Spey Flies for Salmon & Steelhead*).

Black Optic - Prey

The term 'Optic' is used to denote a steelhead fly featuring an extra large head with 'eyes'. Although he didn't invent it, this style of tying was brought to prominence in 1940 by Jim Prey. The head of an Optic may be produced by winding tying thread but more commonly the flies have

Purple Peril

McLeods Ugly

Skykomish Sunrise

Skykomish Yellow

PLATE 5: The Flies of Ken & George McLeod

weighted heads of brass or even lead in the form of beads. It is hard to tell whether these flies were effective because of their appearance, or if the weighting at the head end ensured that the fly fished at the correct depth, or gave the fly an attractive action in the water. Whatever the truth, the 'Optic' aficionados insisted that the eyes were necessary for the best results. For some reason, the Optic style went out of fashion quite quickly and by 1990 not one single Optic fly remained in the list of flies presented by Trey Combs in *Steelhead Fly Fishing*.

In *Steelhead Fly Fishing and Flies* (1976), Trey Combs details a steelhead pattern called the Black Bear, devised in the early 1950s by Al Knudson of Washington. It is one of the dark flies which he considers very effective for winter steelhead fishing. In *Steelhead Fly Fishing*, published in 1991, this fly remains on his list of preferred dark patterns, so it has obviously stood the test of time. Curiously, considering the name, the pattern is not winged with bear but with bucktail.

Black Bear - Knudson

Tube flies have never been popular in North America for either Atlantic salmon or steelhead. This is probably because they are usually associated with the use of treble hooks which were either illegal in many areas or were not used because of the likelihood of damage to fish which anglers wished to release. The notion that tube flies have to be fitted with treble hooks is now changing. Many Scandinavian rivers now have a ban on treble hooks and anglers are finding that tube flies can be just as effective when equipped with a double or a single hook of appropriate pattern.

In Europe, at least, the single hook has a bad reputation as a poor hooker and holder of salmon. Most salmon fishers, given the choice, will fish with an articulated treble hook attached to a tube or Waddington shank. However, if one studies the rationale proposed by writers such as Richard Waddington in support of their preference for articulated treble hooks, it quickly becomes clear that the comparisons they made were not with the smaller, single hooks as used in summer fishing, but with the extremely large 'meat hook' irons that were typical of many of the old classic featherwing patterns. Some of these flies would appear monstrous to modern eyes, with hook sizes as large as 8/0 not uncommon. One might imagine that leverage could be a problem in compromising the hook hold, leaving aside any problem of actually setting such large single hooks as compared with smaller double and treble hooks. In fact, many of the older generation of gillies and fishermen will tell you that, once in place, single irons do not come out very often and are in no way inferior to trebles in their ability to hold a fish. We simply have to look at the catch records of Victorian times to realise that the fishermen of the day did not lose salmon in great numbers. The problem is that few modern salmon fishers have much experience with very large single hooks and thus have no benchmark to make any comparisons. In *A Guide to Salmon Flies*, Buckland and Oglesby make the interesting comment that ultra-longshank streamer flies are still used successfully in America and are not subject to the opprobrium heaped upon large single salmon irons by modern received wisdom in Britain.

In Britain, in the 30 years leading up to the 1950s, many of the old classic featherwing patterns were converted into hairwing versions. The Blue Charm, the Doctors and the Thunder & Lightning are just a few of the patterns that found success in their new hairwinged garb. In 1970, Bates (and other writers of around that time) gave a long list of hairwing versions of classic British featherwing flies, such as the Dusty Miller, Black Dose, Blue Doctor, Dunkeld, etc. There is no way of dating these hairwing conversions accurately –

theoretically, they could have been tied at any time after the introduction of the original pattern. Most of them probably date to around the 1950s when the hairwing revolution from North America was starting to have a major influence in Britain. Some of the most popular of these conversions are shown in plate 6 below. A few of them, such as the Blue Charm, continue to be used today.

The Garry Dog is generally held to be one of the earliest British hairwing patterns but its date of origin is the subject of some dispute. Buckland & Oglesby assign it firmly to James Wright of Sprouston, on the river Tweed, in the middle of the 19th century. Other writers are not so sure and John Veniard, in *The Fly Dresser's Guide*, considers it to have been devised by James's son, John Wright, at

Blue Charm
Blue Doctor
Thunder & Lightning
Black Dose
Dunkeld
Dusty Miller

PLATE 6: Hairwing Conversions of British Classics

a date sometime before 1950. In *Atlantic Salmon Flies and Fishing*, Bates prefers Veniard's version of events but then gives a dressing that, in terms of its elements, certainly could have been an early pattern. It retains all the classic ingredients such as a tag, tail, butt, palmered body hackle and throat hackle. Ironically, the dressing given by Buckland & Oglesby is more abbreviated and modern looking. Whatever the date of its origin, the Garry Dog has proved to be an enduring pattern which has stood the test of time. It is still in the lists of the most commonly used salmon flies in Britain and is regularly used in many other countries.

Garry Dog - Wright

In the 1950s, we see the major developments that set the tone for the wide range of hairwing salmon flies that are in use today. A general dissatisfaction with the complicated fully dressed featherwings had been growing steadily since the turn of the 19th century. Anglers no longer believed that strict adherence to these complex recipes was necessary for success and that their lack of mobility was actually a distinct disadvantage. Casting around for new inspiration, British anglers began to look to North America as a source of new ideas. The huge number of hairwing patterns in use in North America and the strong promotion of their advantages by such influential writers as Lee Wulff had a major impact. Hairwings seemed to be everything that the classic featherwings were not. They were easy to tie, the materials were readily available and relatively cheap and they possessed a mobility and translucence that the classic featherwings did not. The new truth had arrived and the early days of the hairwing invasion saw British anglers reacting with all the single-minded zeal of the converted: all things feathered were bad, all things hair were good. This one-sided view, which reached its zenith in the 1980s, very nearly threw the baby out with the bath water. It continued until very recent times when the influence of the Irish shrimp flies and the resurgence of Spey flies in North America provided a counterbalance. Whether a salmon fly wing is made of feather fibres or of hair or fur does not of itself imbue the fly with an inherent superiority. It is the way that the materials are used that is important. A badly tied hairwing, with the wrong materials, can be more lifeless and ineffective than a featherwing. Likewise, a featherwing does not necessarily have to be stiff and opaque. One only has to look at Syd Glasso's Spey patterns, which use hackle tip wings, to realise this.

Fortunately, we now seem to have reached a rather more balanced view of salmon fly design. We use hairwings and featherwings and – sometimes – mixtures of the two. Different types and styles of fly are selected for different conditions and the materials of construction chosen as are most appropriate to the particular application.

Many of the hairwings in use in the 1950s were either North American patterns or adaptations based on North American ideas but gradually the development of British and North American hairwings began to diverge. Hairwings from North America tend to have cigar shaped bodies, whereas those from Britain tend to have parallel bodies tied as slimly as possible. Apart from the streamer or bucktail style of fly, most North American hairwings tend to have short wings tied very close to the body. In Britain, hairwings became increasingly sparse and long. The collar hackle, tied in front of the wing, is rarely seen on British flies, which instead tend to use a throat hackle swept well back.

ne of the most consistently successful colour schemes for salmon flies over recent years is the combination of black and yellow. When we look at the classic salmon flies to find antecedents, however, we find very few flies based on this colour combination. The Akroyd, one of the original Dee strip wing flies dating back to the middle of the 19th century,

has a split body with black at the front and yellow at the back. The renowned Jock Scott shares this construction, albeit in different materials. Other than these, the only other classic flies that are predominantly black and yellow are the Charlie together with the Black Dog and the little known Ray Mead (the latter two, both from Kelson). The Ray Mead is unusual in that the body is silver and yellow, the black and yellow combination occurring in the wing, which consists of alternate strips of married black and yellow swan. It seems unlikely that the Black Dog, Ray Mead or Charlie would have entered the consciousness of the flytyers who devised the following patterns, but the better-known Akroyd and the Jock Scott may well have had an influence. The Akroyd is a fly that continues to be used in many parts of the world and the Jock Scott, in its day probably the most successful salmon fly of all, still has an influence on modern fly design.

The Black Maria is based on an old Breton pattern and was recommended by Mrs. Robertson in her book about the river Slaney in Ireland, *Thrifty Salmon Fishing* (1945), for its effective simplicity. Buckland and Oglesby have it in *A Guide to Salmon Flies* within the selection from Crawford Little who notes that it is one of the black and yellow flies so effective on the river Spey. It reportedly took over 500 fish on the Knockando beat in one season.

Black Maria

The Tosh is one of the earliest British hairwings and is widely used both in Scotland and Ireland. It was first devised in 1957 by E. Ritchie of the Delfour beat on the River Spey. The original pattern was very simple – an unribbed black body, black hair wing and a yellow throat hackle. Modern versions usually add a silver tag and ribbing and a yellow tail.

The Tosh is one of the few native British patterns that was tied in the manner of an American bucktail, i.e. with a wing that is longer than the hook. Stan Headley, in *Trout & Salmon Flies of Scotland*, speculates that this fly might have been the forerunner of the famous Collie Dog (see page 24) quoting as evidence an illustration in John Ashley-Cooper's book *Great Salmon Rivers of Scotland* in which the wing is tied extremely long.

Tosh - Ritchie

The Hairy Mary is one of the earlier British hairwings, dating from the beginning of the 1960s, but it has retained its popularity and is still widely used in Scotland and Ireland. Both Stan Headley and Peter O'Reilly agree that it is pre-eminently a summer pattern. Early tyings had the hackle tied as a collar but on modern versions it is normally tied as a throat.

Hairy Mary- Reidpath

The Jeannie is a hairwing version of an old strip wing Dee fly dating from the middle of the 19th century which originally had a wing of bronze mallard. The design was attributed by Kelson to a Mr. W. Brown who is also credited with the Logie, illustrated further below. The Jeannie is still popular in both Scotland and Ireland and is used mainly in the summer in low-water conditions.

Jeannie - Brown

Modern Logie Hairwing

Original Logie - Hairwing

Details of other modern European flies which share the same basic colour combination including Kenny's Killer, the Black & Yellow, Gordon's Fancy and the Galway Black & Yellow can be found in the next chapter starting on page 29.

The Logie is another of the simple strip wing Dee patterns from W. Brown which converted extremely successfully into a hairwing and which is still widely used. The original pattern had a claret rather than a red body and jungle cock cheeks. Modern versions have replaced the claret with red, probably following the influence of Pryce-Tannatt who used ruby red silk. Brown's original claret-bodied version, in which the yellow is confined to the underwing, looks extremely handsome and is also shown below. This form of the fly can be extremely effective and deserves to be more popular. Stan Headley notes in *Trout & Salmon Flies of Scotland* that the featherwing version is also still in regular use.

In Britain, particularly in England and Scotland, hairwings became strongly associated with the tube style of fly, normally combined with a treble hook. In *A Guide to Salmon Flies*, Buckland & Oglesby give possible credit for the invention of the tube fly to Mrs. Winnie Morawski who worked for the Playfair company of Aberdeen in the 1950s. However, they then go on to say that tube flies were undoubtedly both illustrated and explained by Wanless in 1932 in his book. It is probable that because this book was about spinning rather than fly fishing that Wanless never got the credit that he deserved. Tube flies are far less popular in Ireland, where hairwings are more usually dressed on normal double or treble hooks, although single hooks are still used to some extent. Many of the modern British tube patterns are extremely simple, consisting of little more than bunches of hair of various colours, tied in around the tube. The combination of a hair wing with a collar hackle, so common among North American patterns, is rarely seen.

One of the reasons that tube flies have become so popular is that the weight of the fly can be varied simply by changing the type of tube on which it is tied. Lightweight flies can be tied on plastic tubes, medium weight flies on aluminium and heavyweight flies can be tied on copper or brass tubes. The tube design is also highly regarded by many modern anglers because it overcomes the supposed problem of leverage associated with long hooks. The hook is not attached to the body of a tube fly but is tied directly on to the leader and is only held in alignment with a flexible plastic sleeve. When a fish is hooked, this system allows the tube to become detached from the hook, sliding up the line out of the way and thus offering less chance of the hook being levered out of the fish's mouth.

The heavyweight tube tied on brass is extremely useful when you need to get down deep in fast water, it does however have the disadvantage that once the fly enters slacker water it will tend to hang downwards, presenting an unenticing image to the fish. An idea designed to overcome this is the conehead tube which has been developed in Scandinavia. The fly is tied on a conventional lightweight plastic tube but with the addition of a brass cone shaped head at the front of the fly. The cone provides the necessary weight to take the fly down in fast flows but has the advantage that in slacker water it will tend to make the fly sink nose first. Any pressure imparted by the water or by manipulating the fly line will produce an up and down undulating movement that is extremely attractive to all predatory fish. The idea of nose-weighting flies is not new, indeed stillwater trout fishermen have been using it for many years with patterns such as the Dog Nobbler. Salmon fishermen are notoriously conservative and are often slow to pick up on innovations made in other areas of the sport. We sometimes forget that salmon and trout are very similar predators and close cousins biologically. Before similarities are dismissed out of hand, it is worth bearing in mind that a great many trout are not caught on closely imitative food patterns, but on attractor patterns (lures if you will) that rely on the natural aggression of the fish to be effective. Is there a lesson to be learnt here?

A further development, which is again very popular in Britain but has not caught on so much in other countries is the Waddington mount. Devised by Richard Waddington, the mount consists of a doubled steel shank with a break in it towards the rear to enable a hook (usually a treble) to be attached. The idea was to produce a fly with a slimmer body than a tube fly, but with an articulated hook intended to reduce leverage and loss of fish once hooked. As with tube flies, this configuration also enabled a damaged hook to be changed without losing the whole fly. This may have been the intention, but is not so easy in practice because the normal style of dressing Waddingtons covers the split in the shank with the body dressing! Originally, it was intended that the hook be held in line with the shank by splicing a piece of monofilament to both hook and shank, thus further reducing the ease with which a hook could be changed. Nowadays, the alignment is normally maintained by using a flexible plastic or rubber sleeve or electricians tape. In an article in *Trout & Salmon*, a Scottish gillie named Wattie Burns proposed a very simple alternative system

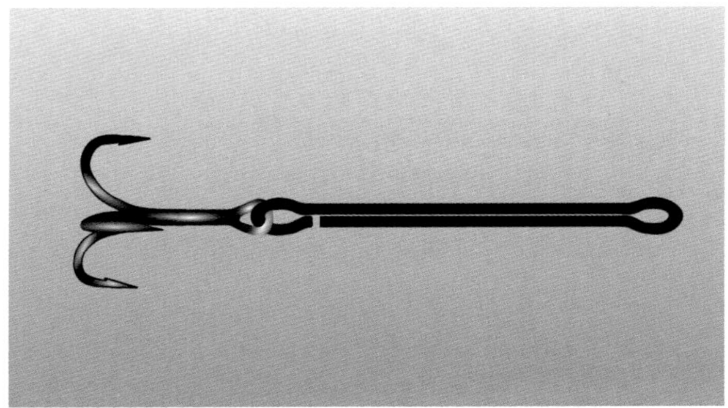

The Waddington Shank

that allows the hook on a Waddington to be changed quickly and easily. He suggested that the treble hook be tied directly to the leader, as in a tube fly, and not mounted on the Waddington shank at all. Instead, the leader is passed through the eye at the front of the shank, along the body and out through the rear eye. The hook is then tied onto the leader and a plastic tube pushed over the joint between hook and rear end of the shank to maintain alignment.

It should be noted that the Waddington shank was not necessarily conceived with hairwing dressings in mind. Indeed, many of the early Waddingtons were adaptations of classic featherwing flies, many of them with long heron hackles. In fact, modern Waddingtons are almost exclusively hairwings.

An interesting idea put forward by Terry Ruane in the July/August 1991 issue of *Fly Fishing and Fly Tying* was to straighten the eye of a Waddington shank, bringing it directly in line with the shank. The shank could then be set in the vice with the two parallel wires of the shank vertically above one another, and the fly tied in this position. Tied like this, one can mount a single or double hook in place of the treble and the fly dressed with a wing on top -as in a single hook dressing. The attached single or double hook than has the hook bend(s) underneath with respect to the dressing.

This, instead of the usual Waddington or tube format with the dressing 'all around' the shank/tube. I don't know if this idea has been widely tried, certainly I have not seen any examples of it. It does suggest itself as a possible approach for North American or Scandinavian fishers who might like to try Waddingtons, but who cannot or don't want to use treble hooks.

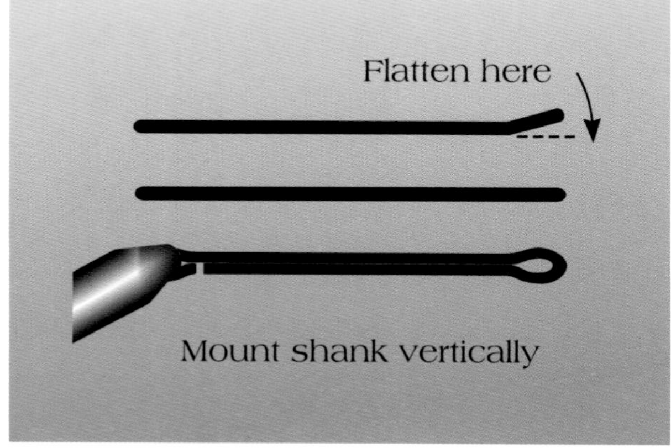

Modified Waddington Shank

A very neat method for adding weight to Waddington shanks was given by Andrew Graham-Stewart in the April 2000 issue of *Trout & Salmon*. He suggested that two copper rods are tied to the Waddington, nestling each side between the parallel shanks. This produces a rounder body cross section than the Waddington shank alone and adds weight without greatly increasing bulk.

An inherent problem with many standard British hairwings, particularly those tied on tubes, is a distinct lack of mobility in slow flowing water. Various methods have been developed to try and overcome this shortcoming. One of the most striking solutions was the use of extremely long hair: anything up to four or five times the tube body length. This style of tying became synonymous with the famous Collie Dog. As most fly tyers do not have ready access to a collie dog, this pattern is now usually tied using goat hair. The original dressing consisted simply of a long hank of black collie dog hair for the wing and a sparse black hackle (shown below).

The Sunray Shadow, devised by Ray Brooks for use on Norway's River Laerdal, is another very effective fly of this type. The original tying is shown below but other varaints can be found on page 40 and another variant, used in Iceland, can be found on page 67. At the start, these long-winged flies were generally held to be more effective on more northerly rivers and were used with great success in northern Scotland, Sweden, Norway and Russia. More recently, and with a modification to the fishing method, they have proved their worth on the more southerly rivers of Scotland, such as the Spey, Tweed and Teviot. This modified fishing method has proved particularly effective in low water conditions and involves the fly being cast square across the current on a floating or intermediate line and then retrieved back across the river with pace. In *Trout and Salmon Flies of Scotland*, Stan Headley quotes Alan Donaldson of the River Carron, saying that if the fish are not moving to this pattern, the fly is not being fished fast enough. I am not aware if flies of this type have been tried by West Coast steelheaders, but they might be well worth trying. Many experienced fishermen also rate these flies very highly as search patterns. If you want to know if there are any fish in a pool, try the Collie Dog fished fast, just under the surface.

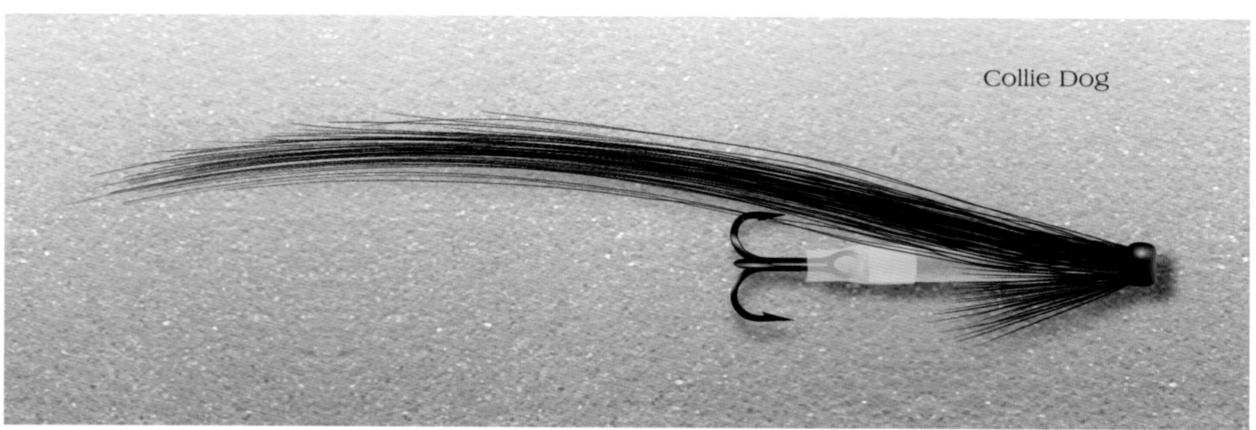

Collie Dog

Sunray Shadow - Brooks

Flies tied with these long wings do not necessarily have to be huge. One way of producing a fly with a long wing in relation to the body is to shorten the length of the tube, rather than extending the wing, producing what is known as a mini tube. Such flies can be tied on tubes as short as 6mm (0.25") with wings approximately 18mm to 25mm long (0.75" to 1"). For very small flies like these, the winging hair needs to be fine and flexible in order to maintain mobility. Mini tubes have become popular throughout Britain for low water, summer fishing, especially for grilse. An example from Davie McPhail is shown below.

Red Devil - McPhail

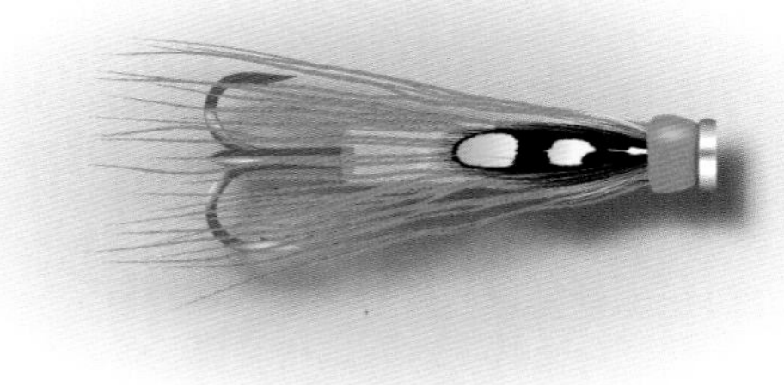

Incidentally, Davie believes that whilst these tubes dressed on a plastic tube will take some fish on the surface, it is far more effective to use heavier metal-bodied tubes fished on a floating line allowing them to skid round through the pool without mending the line.

One of the other most influential developments in hairwings to come from the British Isles is the use of long hair tails rather than long hair wings. One of the inherent problems with long hair wings is their tendency to wrap around the hook whilst casting. Mounting the long hair as a tail – i.e., *aft* of the hook – largely overcomes this problem. This device has proved extremely popular in the last few years, particularly for shrimp flies, the most widely known of which is the Ally's Shrimp. Because these long-tailed flies are generally classified as shrimps they are more comprehensively covered in *Shrimp & Spey Flies for Salmon & Steelhead*, but the Ally's Shrimp illustrated below shows the typical look and construction of such patterns.

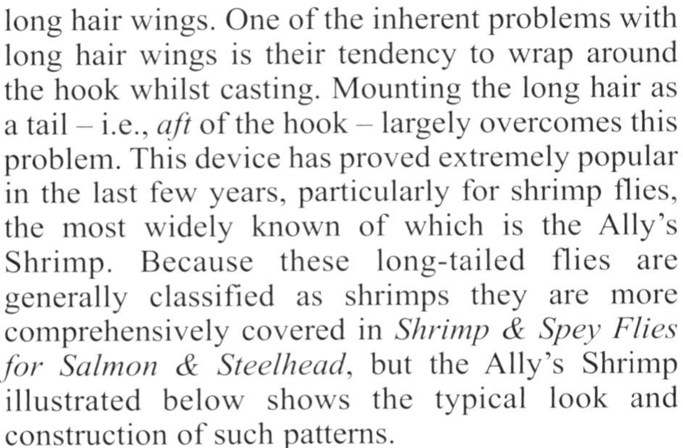

Ally's Shrimp - Gowan

In Scandinavia, particularly Sweden and Norway, hairwing patterns had become the norm by the 1970s. The flies used were typically hairwing versions of the classic British featherwings, such as Thunder & Lightning and Green Highlander, plus the more modern Stoat's Tail and a range of Cossebooms and Rats from

North America. It is, however, interesting to note that in *Atlantic Salmon Flies and Fishing*, published in 1970, Bates gives some eight flies from Scandinavia, all of them featherwings.

A typical hairwing conversion is that of the Green Highlander from Poul Jorgensen, given in his book *Salmon Flies* and illustrated below. This conversion retains almost all the features of the fully dressed fly. Other more recent conversions tend to be much simpler: most of them discarding the tag and butt, as well as the body hackling.

Green Highlander - Jorgensen

As in Britain, the standard hairwings and hairwing conversions were found to be effective in strong flows but were not so good in slack water. The Scandinavians came up with their own solution. They looked at the hair itself and decided that a winging material that would give movement and life even in slow water was badly needed. In the late 1970s, Haken Norling and Mikael Frodin, who were working as guides on the River Gaula in Norway, began to experiment with alternative winging materials. Almost everything was tried – marabou, rabbit and many types of soft fur. Of all the materials tried, soft fox tail proved to be the most effective. Many different styles were tried, most of them combining the mobile fox fur with strands of Flashabou and the standard patterns mentioned above were transformed into fox wings. These new flies proved to be very effective all over Norway and Sweden and the use of soft fox fur as a winging material has now spread widely to other countries.

The Black Doctor Flash is an example of this Scandinavian ultra-mobile hairwing form. It is derived from the classic Black Doctor featherwing. Many of the old classics have been similarly converted, but few have been as successful as this one. The pattern shown was given by Par Jansson in the July 1995 issue of *Trout & Salmon*, who noted that it was anglers on the Em and Morrum rivers in Sweden who replaced the red and blue swan feathers of the original with strands of Flashabou. The fly is extremely effective and has become a favourite on many Norwegian as well as Swedish rivers.

Black Doctor Flash

Another important development that further increased the mobility of hairwing tubes was the introduction of the 'fatback' style of tube fly. In this construction, the overwing hair is tied in at the head with main strands initially facing forwards and the untrimmed roots facing the rear of the fly. The hair is then doubled over backwards and held in its finished position with turns of thread, tight up to the bend in the hair. It is important to note that these turns of thread lie in front of the wing, not over it. If the hair is bound down to the tube, it will lie flat and the intended effect is lost. Tied properly, as intended, the hair should lie at a substantial angle away from the body of the tube, thus providing more mobility and action. The popularity of the modern fatback tube has now spread widely outside of Scandinavia and flies such as the Templedog are known throughout the salmon fishing world. The original Templedog, first tied in about 1986 for use on the River Em in Sweden by Hakan Norling, is shown in plate 7. Many other variants on this style can be found in the Scandinavian section of the book. Incidentally, the name is supposed to have arisen because the

Templedog original

Black Templedog Halfincher

PLATE 7: Templedog & Halfincher – Hakan Norling

original fly was tied with the hair from a recently deceased Shitzu dog which found its way by nefarious means into the hands of a flytyer (the Shitzu is an oriental dog breed, often found in temples in Tibet).

It should be noted that these Scandinavian tube flies have a distinct top and bottom orientation to them, as in a conventional single hook pattern. This is in marked contrast to the majority of British hairwing tubes that are usually tied in an 'all round' format. The standard Templedog, as tied by Hakan Norling, has a finished wing length that is considerably longer than the tube plus the hook. Some of these flies can be extremely long. A typical tying on a 25mm (1") tube may have a hair wing of about 75mm (3") long, while that on a 35mm (1.5") tube may be 100mm (4") long. The name Templedog has now come to mean a style of tying, rather than just a single pattern. There are now veritable packs of Templedogs.

One of Hakan Norling's own Templedog variations is called the Halfincher (so called because it was most often tied on a half inch long tube). It has an even longer wing in proportion to the body. Hakan often ties these flies with a free-swinging hook in order to avoid the problem of the hair wrapping around the hook. A blob of glue placed over the sharp crevices between the hooks of a double or treble can also be helpful and does not impair the hooking ability. Many of these flies have 'eyes' of Spectralite or holographic tape in preference to jungle cock.

In the April 1996 issue of *Trout & Salmon*, there is an article by Hakan Norling in which he makes some interesting points regarding tubes equipped with single hooks. Contrary to intuition, he finds that short shank single hooks are not the best choice and maintains that hooks with longer shanks retain a better hold.

In dressing any hairwing fly, the hair for the wing must be carefully chosen particularly when tying small flies. Many inexperienced fly dressers concentrate on the colour of the hair without being overly concerned about its texture and mobility. These qualities are far from being of secondary importance. Two flies that look very similar in the hand can appear and behave totally differently in the water, if different types of hair are used.

Bucktail is probably the best hair of all in terms of its ability to take up dye and to give a vivid colour image. However, bucktail is not the most mobile of hairs and, unless chosen very carefully, can often be too stiff for small flies. Bucktail's ability to produce strong colours when dyed is largely due to the opacity of the hair. This opacity is not always desirable and can be a disadvantage in many circumstances.

Polar Bear is very different and is highly regarded for its translucence and lustre. When dyed, however, it does not present the strength of colour obtainable with bucktail. If you are fishing in extremely bright conditions or, conversely, when light levels are low, this translucence is at a premium and many experienced anglers consider that polar bear is unmatchable in these conditions simply because it doesn't present an opaque image.

Fitch, stoat and other hairs obtained from the Mustelid family, together with squirrel hair, tend to be straight, fine and glossy. Wings made from these hairs have an attractive sheen, but their shininess and incompressibility make them quite difficult to tie in securely.

Calf tail varies a lot in texture and has a natural crinkle which can be both an advantage or disadvantage, depending on how and where it is used. The matt texture means that it ties in very securely and the natural curl renders it ideally suited to short, dense wings.

Badger hair is naturally cream in colour with black barring and white tips, although in use the cream colour at the base of the hair is often cut away giving the impression that the hair is dark at the roots. Grey squirrel is often used as a substitute because a good colour match can be obtained. The texture is, however, completely different. Badger hair is compressible and has an almost hollow feel to it. Badger hair will flare somewhat at the tying in point and seems to reduce in bulk when wet. Amongst commonly available hairs, racoon is probably the nearest match to badger in terms of its texture.

Goat hair is often used for large flies, simply because of the lengths in which it is obtainable. African or Angora goat can have guard hairs up to 150mm (6") in length and is generally glossier, smoother and more mobile than bucktail It also has a degree of translucence.

In recent years, fox hair has become very popular amongst European flytyers as an extremely fine, mobile winging material which is far stronger than the marabou (turkey) plumes which it now often replaces. Many different kinds of fox hair have become available, of which the most common are Arctic fox, Red fox, Grey fox and Silver fox. Arctic fox is the finest of these hairs and is naturally almost pure white, although a wide range of dyed colours are available. Grey fox hair is black and white barred with white tips and is best known as the winging material for the Rat series of flies. Selective breeding of all kinds of fox has produced a wide range of natural as well as dyed colours.

Icelandic horsehair is another new material, being marketed under the name of Arctic Runner. This is not the same as ordinary horsehair. It is as fine as Arctic fox – soft and mobile – but with a superb lustre. Icelandic horsehair has an underhair, generally between 20mm and 40mm (0.75" to 1.5") long, with longer guard hairs that can be 75mm (3") or longer depending upon where on the skin it is taken from.

European Hairwings & Tubes

The widespread use of the modern hairwing may have had its birth in North America but, after hairwings came back to Europe they took over to such an extent that between the 1950s and the 1990s the use of featherwing flies dwindled away almost to nothing. There were of course some exceptions, in Ireland the widespread use of shimp flies meant that hairwings never took over to the extent that they did in Scotland, and in Scandinavia a small band of dedicated enthusiasts kept the use of Spey and Dee flies alive, but this was very much an exception to the general trend. Why was this takover so complete? It is certainly the fact that there was a general feeling that the complexities of the classic salmon flies had little relevance to the riverbank experience of catching salmon. Salmon runs were decreasing markedly in this period for all manner of reasons. Netting of salmon in rivers had taken place for many years but the most far reaching new factor was the discovery of the high seas feeding grounds and the exploitation of the wild Atlantic salmon as a food source in quantities never before imagined. Faced with declining runs, anglers were keen to find flies that were perceived to be effective in a far wider range of conditions than the classic featherwings had been. The influence of angling writers such as Colonel Esmond Drury in England and Lee Wulff from the United States was also of importance. Simplicity was the new byword and hairwing flies embodied this principle. There was also the fact that the classic flies were difficult to tie and required materials that were becoming increasingly difficult to obtain even when they were not prohibited. In the U.K. a new generation of salmon fly fishers, many of whom had had their grounding in stillwater fishing for rainbow trout, came to salmon fishing far less wedded to the old traditions and for them the use of hairwing lures was normal. It is not suprising therefore that they took to the new doctrine enthusiastically and spread the gospel widely. All this would not have happened, of course, unless the new style of hairwing flies were effective – but effective they certainly were!

It is also worth remembering the context in which the hairwing revolution took place. Great advances had been made in tackle technology, particularly the introduction of plastic fly lines and modern rod materials. Fly lines became available in a wide range of tapers and different densities: from reliable floaters to very fast sinkers and with variations, such as sink tips. The introduction of carbon fibre meant that salmon fly rods could be lighter, longer and more efficient than any that had been available before. All these advances in fishing tackle enabled anglers to cast further and with less effort. It also enabled a new range of tactics and techniques, which would have been unachievable or much more difficult for earlier generations. No longer did salmon fishers simply cast down and across and let the fly swing in the current. They cast downstream, sometimes square, sometimes upstream, sometimes using weighted flies on floating lines, sometimes using light flies on sinking lines, sometimes they moved the fly quickly across the surface to produce a wake, sometimes they fished deep and slow. In these circumstances it is very difficult to separate the role played by fly design from that played by the wider range of more sophisticated fishing techniques that were being employed. Whatever the truth, the combination of the above factors certainly worked. Even with the declining numbers of fish in the rivers, a competent fisherman could catch salmon regularly. Not only that but, because of the simplicity of the hairwings, the ordinary fly tyer could experiment more easily than ever before, thus leading to an explosion in the number of new patterns and variants. I cannot be sure, but I'd guess that more new salmon fly patterns have been invented in the last ten years than in the previous one hundred! Amongst the flies on the following pages are some old standbys that still work, others are new takes on old classics and yet many more are completely new. All of them have proved their effectiveness and are worthy of consideration by fishermen all over the world.

GREAT BRITAIN & IRELAND

n Great Britain we have already seen that many of the earliest hairwing patterns were conversions of earlier classic featherwing flies. Some of these conversions, such as the Green Highlander, Blue Charm, Thunder & Lightning and the Jeannie continue to be used to this day. Other conversions that retain a degree of popularity include the Black Dose, the Whitewing and the Dunkeld.

Considered worldwide, the Green Highlander must surely be one of the most popular and widespread derivations of an old classic, fully dressed salmon fly. In various guises it is used in Scotland, Ireland, Sweden, Norway, the east coast of Canada and as a steelhead fly in the north-western USA and British Columbia in Canada. This is, perhaps, surprising because the Green Highlander – in its original featherwing form – was never one of the most popular flies in its native Scotland. The following illustration shows two versions from Scotland, one tied as a normal hairwing, the second as a tube fly.

The next fly is an interesting variant from Davie McPhail, tied in the Templedog style. This style of fly from Scandinavia is becoming increasingly popular in Scotland as the advantages of the unique action in the water are appreciated. The long teardrop shaped wing is built of multiple layers of different length hairs, which stand well out from the body of the fly. This style of fly is not easy to tie, but is well worth the effort to achieve the unique action.

Green Highlander Fatback Tube - McPhail

Fast Eddie - Headley

Fast Eddie Waddington

Four further green flies are also shown here which illustrate the point that green, which formerly was never widely used in Scotland, is now becoming more popular. The Green Mamba, from Robert Rattray, is a good early season fly, especially in clear water. A combination of green and yellow hair with an underwing of silver Flashabou and a body of pearl Lurex give a very bright, light image.

Green Mamba - Rattray

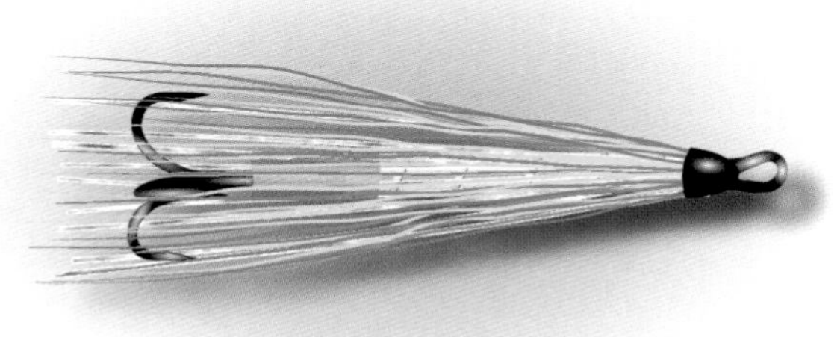

Fast Eddie is one of Stan Headley's flies. It was designed for the river Thurso and has proved to be effective both late spring and summer. The colours were suggested by Eddie McCarthy, the river Superintendent. A tube or Waddington version of this fly moves the orange throat hackle fibres into the wing.

Roy Arris gave the next two flies, which originate from the Tweed, in an article in the March/April 1995 issue of *Fly-Fishing & Fly-Tying*. Both were designed primarily for spring fishing, by Mick Williams, a professional fly-tyer from Carham Station near the Tweed. The Eternal Optimist is based on the Collie Dog style but is a combination of a pearl Mylar body with a dark green wing and yellow underwing. It certainly works, having taken a 28-pounder from the Tweed at Norham.

Although designed for spring fishing, the Eternal Optimist has since proved its effectiveness throughout the season, in a wide range of conditions, both in Scotland and overseas. It is one of three patterns recommended by Mick and described in an article in the February 2003 issue of *Trout & Salmon*.

Eternal Optimist - Williams

The Geordie Green has a green Mylar body and yellow winging. The fly illustrated is tied as a long-wing treble, a style of tying which Mick is convinced has more life and movement when fished on a sinking line compared to a heavy tube. Mick considers the Geordie Green to be the fly-fisher's alternative to the Yellow Belly Devon Minnow and it has shown itself to be effective in the same spring, high water conditions.

Geordie Green - Williams

The Whitewing is one of the classic salmon flies, generally credited to James Wright at about the middle of the 19th century. It is one of the few classic flies still used as a featherwing today, but tied as a tube fly it is now very popular on the river Tweed. It is recommended both for spring and autumn fishing and is often used for the last hour of daylight. The Tweed is one of the few rivers in Scotland where white-winged flies are regularly used.

Whitewing Tube

The Dunkeld started life as a strip winged salmon fly in the early part of the 19th century. These days, it is more generally known through Britain as a trout fly, but hairwing versions of the salmon fly still find use in both Scotland and Ireland. The Irish pattern comes from the river Moy where it is highly regarded for use at all times of the year in both clear and coloured water. A more complex version is described by Bates in *Atlantic Salmon Flies & Fishing*. This version retains many elements of the original and is shown on page 19.

A very similar fly from New Zealand – the Golden Demon – was popularised for steelhead fishing on the west coast of North America by Zane Grey (see page 16).

Dunkeld - Ireland

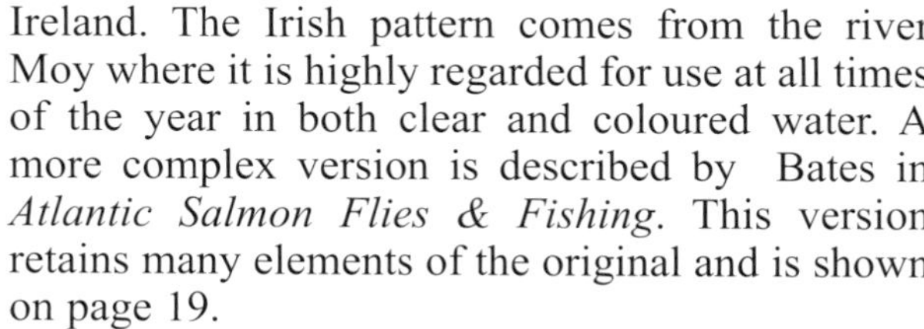

The classic Thunder & Lightning is credited by most writers to James Wright in the mid 19th century, although Francis Francis suggested that Pat Hearns of Ireland was the inventor. Whichever is true, it is still a widely used fly in hairwing adaptations. The following version is popular in Scotland and Ireland, but in recent times it is being overtaken by the Munro Killer which closely resembles it. It would be a shame if this lovely old fly disappeared, particularly when it works so well. Also shown is a simplified tube version, from Kevin Clayton of Co. Cork, Ireland, which is very effective on the river Lee.

Thunder & Lightning

Thunder & Lightning Tube

The Munro Killer is a much more recent pattern and, according to Stan Headley in *The Trout & Salmon Flies of Scotland*, is a strong contender for the title of 'Best Scottish Salmon Fly'. The very first version had a wing of brown bucktail dyed yellow, but this has since been replaced by un-bleached squirrel tail dyed yellow. An alternative, known in Ireland as the Dark Munro Killer, uses bleached squirrel dyed yellow and orange under black squirrel hair. Most anglers regard the Munro Killer as a summer and autumn pattern, but Stan Headley has had success with it as early as March on the river Thurso.

Munro Killer

Dark Munro Killer

The Gold Munro is a variant from Alan Donaldson. It is popular on the river Carron, but has taken fish all over Scotland. Stan Headley has noted a marked swing towards tinsel bodied salmon flies in Scotland over the last few years. This could be due largely to the advent of light-weight and durable, non-tarnishing Mylars, in a wide range of colours.

Gold Munro - Donaldson

The Berthdee Munro is a noticeably darker fly with a black throat hackle and was devised by a Mrs. Cormack and her brother Mr. Davies. It looks very much like a cross between a Tosh and a Munro Killer and must surely be a sound choice when a darker fly is needed.

Berthdee Munro - Cormack/Davies

The Willie Gunn was devised by Dusty Miller and named after a gillie on the river Brora. Extremely popular all over Scotland, the Willie Gunn has made its way successfully to the west of Ireland as well. With the same body and general coloration as the Munro Killer, the Willie Gunn has become the workhorse of spring and autumn fishing throughout Scotland. While the Munro Killer is seldom seen as a tube or Waddington, the Willie Gunn is rarely dressed on normal hooks.

In the July 2001 issue of *Trout & Salmon*, Crawford Little wrote that he would be hard pressed to say whether the Munro Killer or the Willie Gunn was his favourite black/orange /yellow fly and suggested that Willie Killer might be a more appropriate name!

The overall colour of a Willie Gunn can vary considerably depending upon the proportions of the constituent colours in the wing (indeed, the same is true of many other British tube flies). These days, the wing is usually tied with black over orange over yellow but the original fly had these three colours tied in as separate bunches. Other versions have a wing of mixed fibres. This may have been due to the fact that, when tied on a normal double or treble hook, separate bunches of hair are a nonsense. The Willie Gunn 'longwing', illustrated below, has such a mixed fibre wing.

Willie Gunn Tube

Willie Gunn Longwing

As with many widely used patterns, there are many variations of the Willie Gunn. I have illustrated a gold bodied version, which is particularly good for bright spring days. A version from Davie McPhail is tied as a long-winged double, with adhesive gold eyes added for extra impact (see above right).

Willie Gunn Gold

Willie Gunn Variant - McPhail

In the April 2000 issue of *Trout & Salmon*, Andrew Graham-Stewart gave another Willie Gunn variant in which the wing colours were purple over chartreuse green over orange. The fly illustrated below was tied by Kenny MacDonald, secretary of the Federation of Highland Angling Clubs.

Willie Gunn Variant - MacDonald

Another fly, closely related to the Willie Gunn, was devised by the late Bill Brown and was named the Rogie, after his nom-de-plume. This is a fly with the same wing ingredients as the Willie Gunn, but with a body of green Lurex. In the example that I have, the hair is not tied in all round but is restricted to the top and bottom of the fly. In this form, the green Lurex body is given full play (another very effective fly with a green Lurex body is the Green Brahan, see page 53). The Rogie is highly rated for spring fishing in the northern Scottish rivers.

Rogie - Brown

Robert Rattray's Chameleon is also reminiscent of the Willie Gunn and is recommended for use throughout Scotland in all water conditions. The wing fibres of black, yellow and red bucktail are mixed rather than being tied in discrete bunches, one over the other. A few strands of pearl Crystal Hair, tied in over the wing, adds a bit of sparkle. Although it is usually tied as a Waddington or tube from 25 to 75mm (1 to 3 inches) long, it also converts very well to a double or treble hook, as shown in the accompanying illustration. The name comes from the fact that the fly can look quite different by varying the proportions of the different component colours in the wing.

Chameleon - Rattray

Tosh, Gordon's Fancy, Black & Yellow. For this next fly you can take your pick of the names. Everything started simply enough: the original Tosh (see page 21) was a very simple fly with an unribbed black body, black hair wing and a yellow throat hackle. The problem started when tube and Waddington versions were introduced. The Tosh tube has a wing that consists of quartered bunches of black and yellow hair. The Gordon's Fancy usually has a wing consisting of one bunch of black and one of yellow hair, but sometimes it also has four bunches. The Black & Yellow can have two bunches of hair, sometimes four bunches or sometimes the colours are mixed. Confusing? Originally, the main difference was that the body of the Tosh was unribbed, whilst the other two flies had a silver rib. In recent times, however, the Tosh is also usually tied with a silver rib so any substantive difference between these patterns has largely disappeared.

Tosh - Modern Tying

Tied in Waddington format there is a theoretical difference between the Black & Yellow and the Gordon's Fancy. In the Gordon's Fancy, the yellow hair should be at the bottom. On the Black & Yellow, it should be at the top. Just to complete the confusion, I have also seen flies tied with a mixed fibre wing which were also called Tosh. Despite the confusion, a fundamental truth remains: these similar black and yellow patterns are extremely effective, particularly in the spring, and are widely used throughout Scotland.

Stan Headley also lists a gold-bodied Waddington variant of the Tosh, which is a very popular dressing for the river Dee. Unfortunately, this variant completely lacks the yellow component and thus can hardly be called a Tosh at all – Black & Gold would be a much more appropriate name.

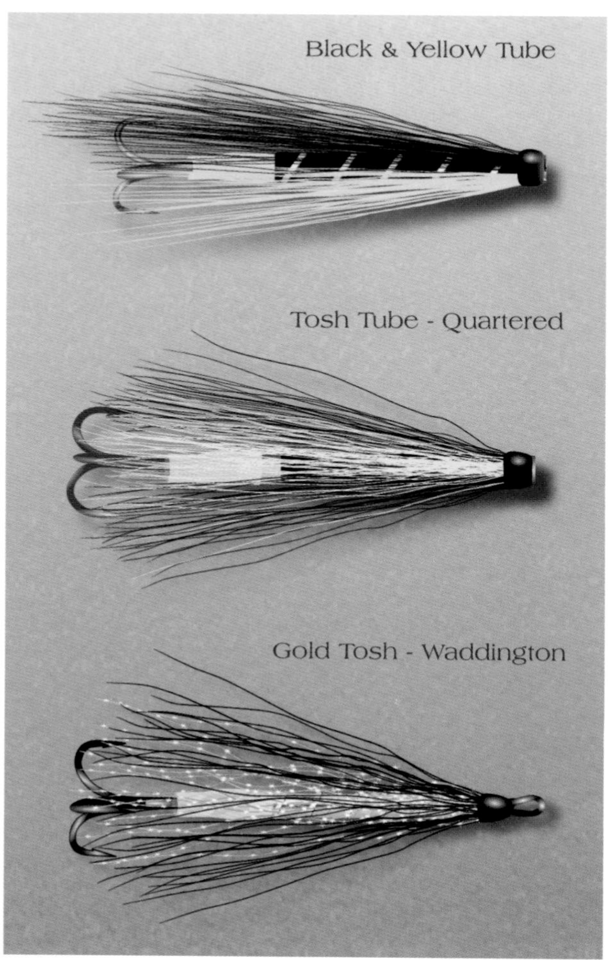

The Weasel, from Robert Rattray, is a similar pattern with predominantly black and yellow colouring. The ribbing on this fly is of flat silver and the dressing specifies that the black and silver bands on the body should be of equal width. The name comes from Rattray's black Labrador dog – the original source of the winging material. The Weasel is a summer and grilse pattern for low flows and is usually tied on low-water doubles in sizes 10 and 12.

The Black, Silver & Yellow Waddington, also from Robert Rattray, is recommended as a reliable year-round fly. Robert considers it particularly effective in large sizes for spring fish in the late evening.

Kenny's Killer is a very similar pattern to the Black, Silver & Yellow. Designed by Kenny Burns, of Gordonbush on the Brora, it has a reputation as one of the best grilse and sea-trout patterns and Stan Headley notes that it is extremely popular where both of these species are running. Crawford Little is credited with the gold-bodied version – the Gold Kenny's Killer. Stan Headley correctly notes that this configuration is almost identical to the Goldie, one of Bob Church's reservoir trout lures (the Goldie predates Little's pattern). Just to confuse things further, Little also suggested that an alternative name might have been the Gold Tosh. No, I don't think we need any more Toshes!

We continue the black and yellow theme with the Galway Black & Yellow, from Ireland. It hails from the famous Galway Weir Fishery and is much used when the grilse are running. In *Trout & Salmon Flies of Ireland*, Peter O'Reilly particularly recommends its use at dusk. The Galway Black & Yellow is almost identical to the Goldie, apart from the tail of golden pheasant topping. The tying style is quite different, however. The winging is much fuller and the throat hackle extends beyond the bend of the hook. Many Irish hairwings are dressed more fully than their Scottish counterparts, a trend that has been apparent for many years and which still continues. Considering that the majority of Irish fishing is for grilse, the fly sizes used in Ireland also tend to be a size or two larger. The recommended sizes for Kenny's Killer range from 8 to 12; for the Galway Black & Yellow, from 6 to 10.

Galway Black & Yellow

Peter Keyser is the originator of the Keyser Spey Fly. The name refers to its having been developed for the Delfur beat of the river Spey rather than any resemblance to the classic, long-hackled 'Spey Flies'. The shape of the wing is important and should achieve a shouldered, teardrop form by careful selection of a variety of hair lengths. This fly consistently produces fish on the Spey when other anglers are struggling.

Keyser Spey Fly - Keyser

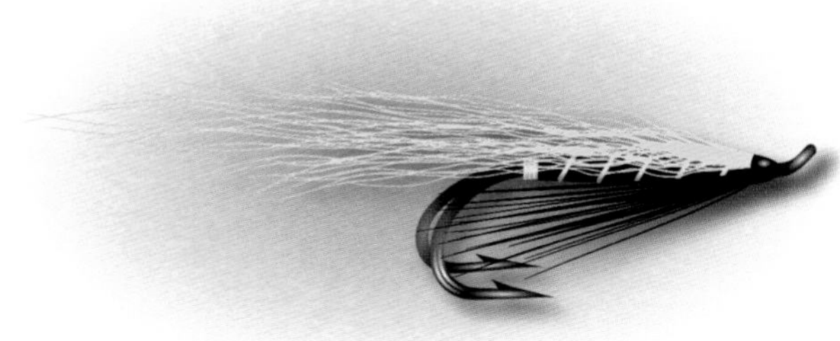

Moc Morgan, in *Trout & Salmon Flies of Wales*, also lists a black and yellow fly – the Leslie Peters – devised by an angler of that name for use on the river Usk. Moc notes that the bright yellow seal's fur body is in keeping with a long tradition of yellow-bodied Usk flies. The fly shown by Moc has, unusually, a head of yellow tying silk.

Leslie Peters

The Comet is a fly that is normally only seen as a tube or Waddington. It is slightly more complex than the normal tube in that it has a split two-part body and effectively three 'wings'. The first of these is tied in at the tail position, the second at the mid-body join and the third at the head. Each wing is of such a length that they all extend the same distance beyond the end of the tube. The Comet has been traditionally associated with the river Tweed where it is normally dressed on large brass tubes and is one of the preferred choices for the autumn runs. Tony Jones, a most experienced guide and angler who takes many parties of fishermen to the rivers of Norway, also reports that the Comet is very effective on the river Namsen. Having said that the Comet is regarded primarily as an autumn pattern, it is very similar in colour to the Tadpole (shown below), which is a mainstay of early spring fishing in the north of Scotland.

Two Comet conversions in the 'fatback' style from Davie McPhail are also shown below. These flies have proved to be extremely productive when the water is carrying some peat colouring.

The original Tadpole pattern is credited to Neil Graesser and had a long black wing; a yellow and red split body and a yellow tail. Crawford Little described a variant to the Graesser Tadpole in which the rear of the body (or butt) was of gold Mylar, with the yellow tail tied in between the body divisions. As this was given to him by a gillie on the river Tweed, he named it the Tweed Tadpole.

Stan Headley gives yet another Tadpole variation: the body in two halves, with silver tinsel at the rear and red floss in front. He recommends this variant for the dark, peat-stained waters that he fishes in the spring. All of the Tadpoles are dressed with a long wing, much in the style of a Collie Dog.

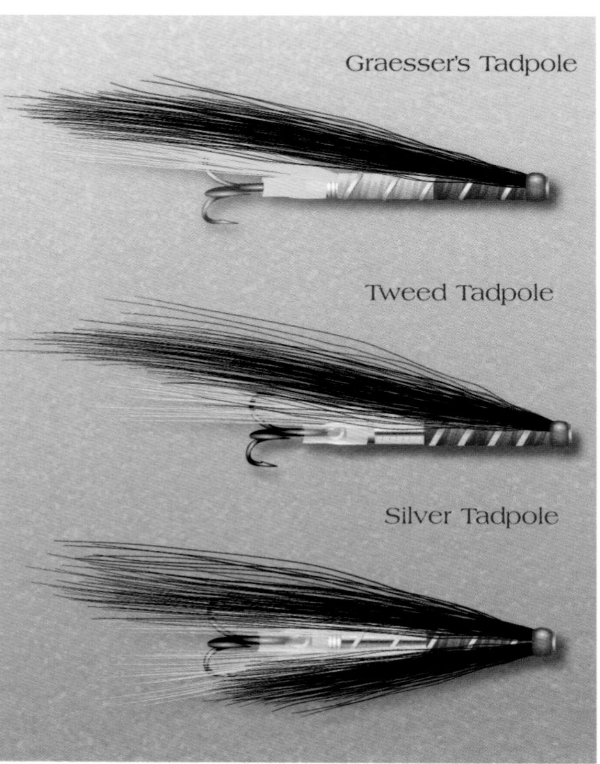

As we have seen, the Garry Dog is a hairwing with a long history and, in common with other long-lived flies, a wide range of variants have been developed. The first, from Davie McPhail, is tied without a tail and has a very sparse long wing.

Garry Dog Variant - McPhail

In order to keep the dressing as light as possible, the throat of blue dyed guinea fowl is replaced by a mixture of blue and black bucktail. Silver adhesive eyes give extra impact.

The next two variants, also from Davie McPhail, utilise the 'fatback' wing technique. The first has a silver tinsel body and uses red and yellow arctic fox for the wing. Red dyed jungle cock eyes complete the fly, which certainly has presence. Davie is a keen fan of dyed jungle cock eyes to provide a colour co-ordinated look to the fly. This technique is also often used by Scandinavian fly-tyers, but is rarely seen elsewhere. The second variant is much nearer the standard tying but has strands of gold Crystal Hair over the fox hair to complete the wing.

Garry Dog #1 - McPhail

Garry Dog #2 - McPhail

A further glittering variant is the Golden Garry, from Alan Donaldson. Tied as a tube or Waddington, it has a body of flat gold tinsel and red Crystal Hair added to the standard wing components. Recommended as a heavy water spring fly, it should also do well in peaty water conditions when real impact is required. The Silver Garry is the same, but with a silver body and pearl Crystal Hair, and is extremely effective for fresh springers.

The Northern Dog is another, brighter Garry Dog variant, again with added flash. The red wing component has been changed to orange. Stan Headley notes this as a good adaptation for the peat-stained waters of northern Scottish rivers and selects this as his first choice pattern when these rivers run black in the spring.

The Yellow Dog is taken from *A Guide to Salmon Flies* and the accompanying notes record the fly as being successful both as a deeply sunk pattern and fished near surface fly on a floating line. It is reportedly effective for both fresh run and resident fish in late autumn, so is perhaps a fly worth having to hand throughout the season.

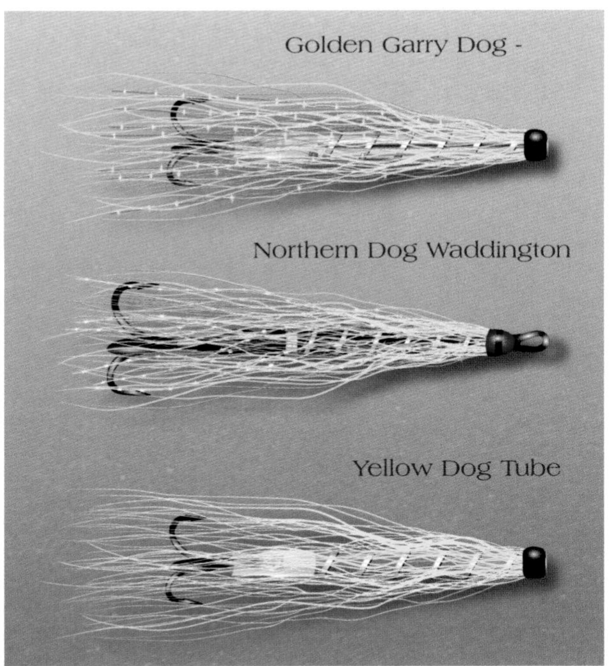
Golden Garry Dog -

Northern Dog Waddington

Yellow Dog Tube

The Heatherlie was devised by Tim Gaunt-Baker and two of his friends whilst fishing the river Spey. It is loosely based on the Garry Dog colour scheme, but with an added purple collar hackle. It was named after the hotel in which they were staying and has proved to be very effective. The combination of the fluorescent red front body segment and the purple hackle is very eye-catching and adds a distinct hot-spot at the front of the fly. Purple is little used in Scotland, but can be very good on its day and should be tried more often.

Heatherlie - Gaunt-Baker

Fished properly, the Collie Dog can be one of the most effective of all salmon flies. Even spring salmon in cold water will move to it enthusiastically. Some authorities recommend that the Collie Dog is best fished in fast, streamy water. It can also take fish from the slowest of water provided it is fished fast enough, with sufficient movement imparted to the fly by means of hand lining or leading with the rod tip.

A Collie Dog variant, shown below, which is quite popular in Ireland, sports a silver tinsel body and a red throat hackle.

The other Collie Dog variant shown at the bottom of the page comes from Alan Donaldson, of the river Carron in Sutherland. This is yet another example of a new fly or variant dressed with a Lurex body – in this case lilac and copper. The wing consists of two bunches of black goat hair with strands of fluorescent pink Twinkle in between.

Peaty Man - McPhail

The fly illustrated above is called the Peaty Man and is a pattern from Davie McPhail. As the name suggests, it was designed for use in heavily peat stained water. The glowing image presented by the combination of a Sunburst orange underwing and the flowing overwing of black goat hair is quite stunning and is Davie's recommended fly for such conditions. Sunburst orange is a

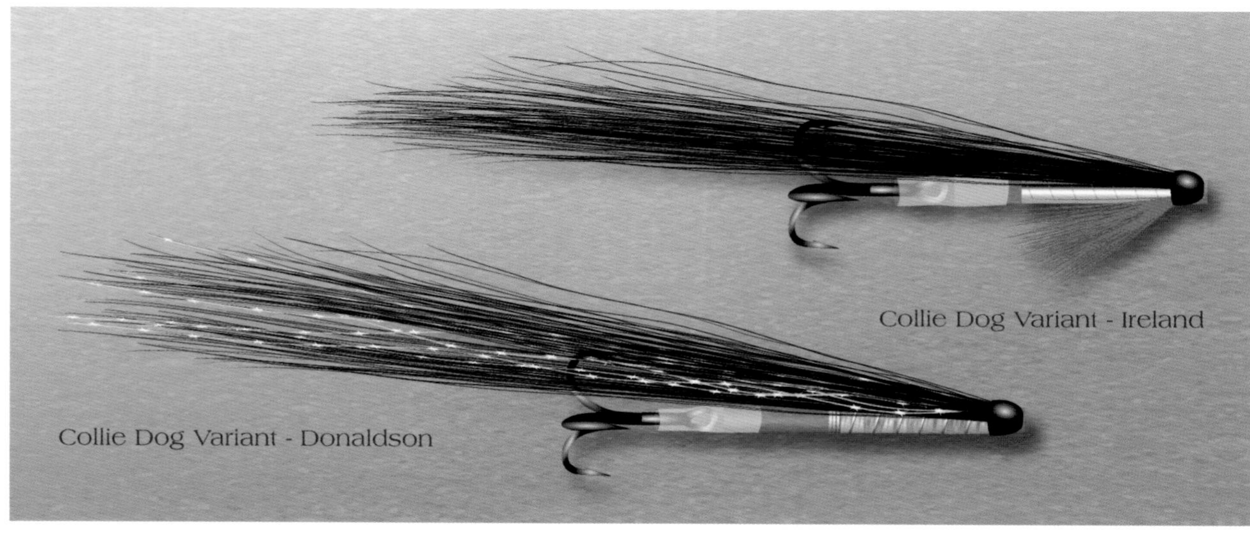
Collie Dog Variant - Ireland

Collie Dog Variant - Donaldson

specially dyed colour and is a brilliant light orange, shading to a rich golden yellow.

One of the noticeable stylistic differences between hairwings from opposite sides of the Atlantic is the way that the hair is tied in for the wing. In North America the hair is almost invariably stacked to even up the lengths; whereas the fashion in Britain is to use unstacked hair, with the goal of producing a tapered effect which will streamline into a teardrop shape when the fly is in the water. The following flies from Davie McPhail use this technique and are from the same series as the Garry Dog variant shown above. There is no doubt that, stylistically, long-winged flies of this type look their best tied on double rather than treble hooks, but Davie has a strong preference for doubles anyway. He maintains that flies tied on double hooks settle quickly in the water and swim on an even keel because the weight is concentrated below the shank. The Stoat's Tail uses holographic silver tinsel for the body rather than normal tinsel of the Silver Stoat to give more impact in the water.

Holographic Stoat's Tail - McPhail

Kerr's Sunburst

Another pattern from Peter Keyser is the Keyser Findhorn. In this pattern, the wing form is critical, being composed of unstacked fallow deer tail hair up to twice the hook shank length to give the desired teardrop form.

Keyser Findhorn Fly

The Kylie is another from Alan Donaldson and one which has proved to be an absolute star on peat-stained rivers. The name refers to the Kyle of Sutherland (not the diminutive Australian chanteuse), the estuary which disgorges the rivers Carron, Oykel, Shin and Cassley into the North Sea. Alan's own catch of over 100 fish to this fly in three seasons indicates just how effective it is. Also illustrated here is the Waddington or tube version (a long-tailed shrimp variant is shown in *Shrimp & Spey Flies for Salmon*).

Kylie - Donaldson

Kylie Waddington

The Purple McBain is one of the few salmon flies on the European side of the Atlantic which uses purple as the base colour. Devised by Gordon McBain, of Aberdeen, it is highly rated for the river Dee but has also been successful on many other rivers, particularly in spring. In an article on spring fishing in the March 1996 issue of *Trout & Salmon*, Bill Currie included a Waddington version of the Purple McBain among his recommended flies.

Purple McBain

The Rainbow Warrior is a fly from John Buckland which is included in Buckland & Oglesby's *A Guide to Salmon Flies*. It was devised about the time that the Greenpeace ship, Rainbow Warrior, was sunk in a New Zealand harbour. The construction of this fly is interesting because the winging is an update of that used for the old 'maned' flies such as the Owenmore (see page 6). Other multi-winged flies may be found in the North American chapter on pages 105 and 117. The front hackle can be varied from orange, blue and yellow.

Rainbow Warrior - Buckland

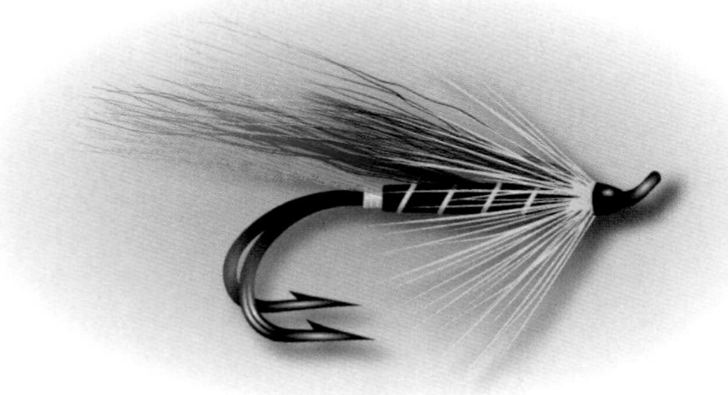

The next few flies are old patterns that continue to find a place in modern fly boxes. The feather wings of the original dressings have been simplified and replaced by hair. Watson's Fancy is a very old pattern which was originally a trout fly, tied with a black crow wing. The colour combination of black and red with a touch of yellow at the tail seems to have universal appeal and the Watson's Fancy continues to take fish both in Scotland and in Ireland where it is used as a late season grilse fly on the loughs. Bates also lists it in *Atlantic Salmon Flies & Fishing*.

Watson's Fancy

The Silver Wilkinson is a bright, silver-bodied pattern that is extremely popular in Ireland when tied as a shrimp fly. In Scotland it is mainly used as a summer fly tied on small doubles. Bill Pennington included the Silver Wilkinson as one of his fly choices in an article about the rivers of south-west Scotland (such as the Cree and Minnoch) in *Trout & Salmon*, December 1995. While the composition of the hairwing may vary, the silver body and magenta throat hackle are the Wilkinson's invariable distinguishing features. In the example shown, the classic underwing components of red, blue and yellow feather slips have been replaced by combed out strands of fluorescent floss. This adds colour with almost no bulk and allows the head to be kept small and neat.

Silver Wilkinson

Beltra Badger

Ballynahinch Badger

Silver Erriff

McDermott's Badger

Silver Badger

PLATE 8: Irish Badger Hair Flies

The Lemon & Grey in hairwing form is still very popular in the west of Ireland and particularly on the Moy where it is highly regarded for spring fish and fresh grilse. Its muted shades of yellow and grey are not exactly eye-catching to the angler, but salmon seem to think differently. Peter O'Reilly thinks that it is at its best in water with a bit of colour in it.

Lemon & Grey

Badger hair is an extremely popular wing material in Ireland where subdued flies are recommended for spring fishing and clear water. Success with these muted patterns is so consistent that perhaps anglers in other countries should take note. Badger hair is cream with black barring and white tips. Although slightly more wavy, white-tipped racoon has a similar texture and may make a better alternative than grey fox or grey squirrel where badger hair is no longer obtainable.

Five of the best of the Badger flies are shown in plate 8 above. Peter O'Reilly, author of *Trout & Salmon Flies of Ireland*, considers these patterns to be absolutely indispensable for any angler visiting Ireland.

The Ballynahinch Badger is, effectively, a badger winged Blue Charm and an alternative to the Hairy Mary. Very much an early season fly, it is one of the most effective flies for fresh salmon in clear water. Peter named this fly after the

Ballynahinch Castle Hotel, in Connemarra, where it was given to him by the manager, Michael Conneely.

The Beltra Badger is a fly devised for salmon fishing on Lough Beltra by Martin Maguire of Newport, Co. Mayo. Anyone contemplating spring fishing on Beltra should not be without one. For lough fishing it is usually dressed on a single hook but it is also very popular on the Delphi fishery tied on a size 10 double.

McDermott's Badger is attributed to the late Dr. Piggins of Burishoole and was named after Pat McDermott, gillie on the Newport River. A simple but elegant dressing, it catches an awful lot of spring fish.

The Silver Badger is the silver-bodied version of the Ballynahinch Badger. It is widely used in Connemarra and Mayo for fresh grilse and is particularly effective in low water when dressed on a size 10 double.

The Silver Erriff is very similar to the Silver Badger and can be regarded as a local variant for the river Erriff. The tag of silver tinsel and yellow floss is replaced with gold tinsel and the golden pheasant topping gives a bit more flash than the standard tying. It is recommended for all the rivers in the west of Ireland when the water is running clear.

Foxton Badger

Pringle's Badger

The Foxton Badger is named after Tom Foxton, a very successful angler on the river Slaney. It is basically a tube version of the Ballynahinch Badger but without the yellow tag or tail. It is extremely popular in April and is also used at Castleconnell and on the rivers of the west of Ireland. It is normally tied on brass, aluminium or plastic tubes between 12mm and 50mm (0.5" to 2").

Pringle's Badger is a pattern from Christopher Pringle, of Monaghan, and is used with success on the Slaney, Drowes, Erriff and Owenmore rivers. The sides are hackle tips in a choice of orange, red, yellow and blue, of which the most popular are orange and yellow. It is normally tied on a Waddington shank in sizes from 15mm to 50mm (0.75" to 2") long.

The Stoat's tail has been one of the mainstays of salmon angling in the British Isles for the last forty years. The original dressing has the wing made from the glossy black hair from the tip of a stoat's tail. The Stoat's Tail is a simple fly with a silver ribbed black body, GP crest tail, black wing and black throat hackle. Because stoat's tails are not always easy to come by, black squirrel hair is often substituted for the wing. Usually tied in small sizes on doubles and trebles, the Stoat's Tail is the quintessential small dark fly which can cover a multitude of fishing conditions.

Stoat's Tail

There are of course, many variants of the Stoat's Tail, the most popular of which are the Thunder Stoat and the Silver Stoat. The Thunder Stoat changes the ribbing from silver to gold and the throat hackle from black to orange, sometimes with blue guinea fowl over. Jungle cock eyes are also often added. In this form it is easy to see the amalgamation of the Stoat's Tail with the Thunder & Lightning. The most common Irish dressing of the Stoat's Tail has a tail of yellow hackle fibres over red and is also illustrated.

Thunder Stoat

Thunder Stoat - Irish

The Silver Stoat is the same as a standard Stoat's Tail, but with a body of silver tinsel. This is a very popular fly throughout Scotland and Ireland and is effective from May right through to the end of the season, particularly in times of low water.

Silver Stoat

A Silver Stoat tied with a golden pheasant topping tail, a wound throat hackle and jungle cock eyes becomes the Vambeck, a dressing from Louis Vambeck of Mullingar in Ireland. Looking at the dressing alone, one would think that this is the same fly, particularly as jungle cock eyes are an optional extra on the Silver Stoat anyway. Actually, the style of tying is very different. There is marked contrast between the sleek style of the Silver Stoat when compared to the fuller dressing of the Vambeck, with its fuller throat hackle – doubled and wound over the front part of the body – and the denser wing. The Vambeck has become one of Peter O'Reilly's favourite flies, bringing him three fish on one day when five other anglers on the beat caught nothing. It has been particularly successful late in the evenings and also for autumn fish.

Vambeck

A long-tailed Stoat variant from Robert Rattray is illustrated below. This fly has peacock sword fibres added to the wing which, incidentally, Stan Headley thinks may have been present in the original Stoat's Tail. The tail is over three times the length of the body and takes over the function of the wing without the danger of the fibres wrapping round the hook, a constant problem with long winged flies. Small and sparse, this pattern is well suited to floating line fishing for midsummer grilse in clear water conditions.

Stoat Long-Tail - Rattray

As the name would suggest, the Stinchar Stoat is a variant from the river Stinchar in the south-west of Scotland. The original tying had no body at all but later variations gained plain gold or copper bodies. It has to be said that it actually doesn't look much like a Stoat's Tail at all.

Stinchar Stoat

In the *Trout & Salmon Flies of Scotland*, Stan Headley also lists a Pearly Stoat from Stuart Topp and Davie Wood. This is a pearl-bodied variant that also incorporates pearl Crystal Hair in the wing. Tied sparsely, this is a very effective pattern for clear, low water conditions and is widely used on the rivers of south and east Scotland.

Pearly Stoat - Topp & Wood

The Thunderflash is a flashy derivation of the Thunder Stoat. Devised by Robert Rattray in 1995 for autumn fishing on the Spey, it proved to be immediately successful and took four fish on its first outing. It is usually tied on heavyweight doubles.

Thunderflash - Rattray

Bill's Stoat was devised by professional fly-tyer, Bill McLennan of Elgin. This is a black winged fly, which has a tail of red-dyed squirrel and blue-dyed squirrel for the throat hackle. Bill's Stoat is recommended to be effective for fresh run fish. Stan Headley comments that this fly has a typical 'Spey look'. Unbleached dyed squirrel is very popular on the Spey and flies tend to be more heavily dressed on that river than elsewhere.

Bill's Stoat - McLennan

Fluorescent Red Stoat

The Red Stoat complete our list of Stoat variants. Here, the yellow tail is replaced by red and the body is of silver tinsel. The version shown above uses fluorescent materials and was mentioned in an article by Alastair Gowans in the June 2002 issue of *Fly-Fishing & Fly-Tying* which discussed the use of fluorescents in modern salmon flies.

The next fly was included in the list of flies given by Eoin Fairgrieve for autumn fishing on the Tweed in an article in *Trout & Salmon* in October 2000. There was no name given, other than Templedog. Since this name refers to the tying style rather than a specific pattern, I have taken the liberty of calling it the Orange & Gold Templedog. This is yet another example of the fatback style of fly which continues to gain in popularity, particularly for high water spring and autumn fishing. The Templedogs were developed for use on the large, brawling Scandinavian rivers and are therefore ideally suited to heavy water conditions. The long wing, set at a distinct angle away from the body, provides a tremendously lively action in the water and will not collapse even in the fastest flows.

Orange & Gold Templedog

Looking at the illustration of the Kenyaman below, one might be excused for thinking that it was just another of the bushy, heavily dressed style of flies that seem to be so successful in Ireland, but which find little use in other countries. In fact, you would only be half right. The fly is successful in Ireland, but actually comes from Kenya. It was introduced to the Burishoole fishery, in Co. Mayo, in the 1950s. Peter O'Reilly has his own variant of this fly which has a silver tinsel body, a red feather slip tail, a black collar hackle and no wing.

Kenyaman

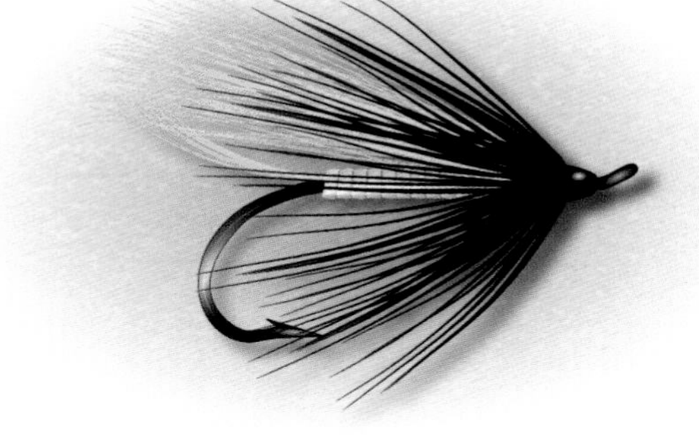

We have already seen that the use of green coloured flies is at last making headway in Scotland, particularly for spring fishing. Green has always been a more popular colour in Ireland, although there are only a limited number of flies.

The Galway Green is a simplified version of the Green Highlander and was introduced to the Galway Weir fishery by a Scot, Charlie Stevens. It has since established itself there as a favourite pattern for May and June.

Galway Green

The North Pole is a pattern from Davie McPhail which has an unusual combination of yellow and blue. The body is also unusual because it is made of wound strands of sparkling blue-green Reflections. In brown stained water the overall effect is green, but it has a more variable image than that produced by using unmixed wing of solid green. It is extremely well-suited to spring fishing in high water conditions as it has both colour and mobility.

North Pole - McPhail

The Canadian Green is a pattern from Warren Duncan, of New Brunswick, one of the doyens of hairwing fly-tyers. It is highly rated for fresh run fish on the Burishoole fishery in Ireland. The wound collar hackle, tied in after the wing, is typical of the form of many flies from the eastern provinces of Canada, such as the Cosseboom.

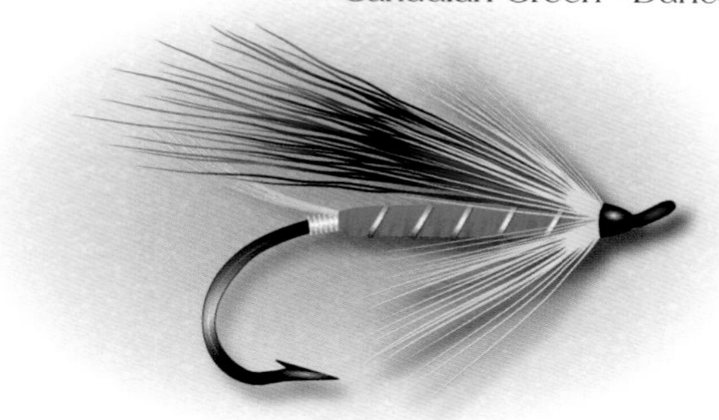
Canadian Green - Duncan

The Taylor Special is also from the other side of the Atlantic, in this case from Arthur Taylor of Maine. It is again an excellent fly for fresh-run fish. Peter O'Reilly recounts one morning on the Ridge Pool of the Moy when he hooked fish after fish while the other four rods struggled. In the end, feeling rather embarrassed by his good fortune, he removed it from his cast and gave it to one of the other fishermen who then caught a fish in very short order. A cursory examination shows that it could fit quite comfortably into the Rat series from Roy Thompson (see page 10), one of the signature pattern types of eastern North America. Apart from having the typical Rat form, green and yellow flies are much loved by Canadian anglers.

Taylor Special

The Moy Green is yet another green fly, devised by Chris Downey for the Moy. Once again, it is highly regarded for fresh fish in both clear and coloured water. It also works well in bright weather and in the still, calm evening at the end of a hot day. The green and orange combination is not particularly appealing to human eyes, but the fish seem to have few objections.

Moy Green

Botham's Fancy was devised and tied by Peter O'Reilly for Ian Botham, the England cricketer, for his visit to Ballynahinch in 1987. Flies like this – tied to commemorate some special occasion – are rarely successful in the long term and normally disappear without trace. Not so, this one! It was an immediate success and has remained effective ever since. It has also proved useful on the Erriff and the Moy for fresh grilse. Peter notes that it is sometimes, incorrectly, called the Ridge Pool Special.

Botham's Fancy

Claret & Jay

We have already seen the Goshawk: mentioned in the chapter on the history of hairwing flies as one of the earliest Irish hairwings, dating back to the 19th century. This is the modern hairwing version, still in use on the Moy and on many other waters all over Ireland. The combination of black, yellow and claret is unusual but seems to work very well, especially for resident fish. Claret remains an under-used colour in salmon flies, even though it has a long history of effectiveness. Many back-end flies which have red components would be well worth tying with claret instead.

Goshawk

The next three flies provide very good examples of just how good claret flies can be for salmon. All three are clearly related, but exactly which came first is very hard to say although the Irish Claret & Jay probably takes the honour. The Claret & Jay is an simplified hairwing version of the old classic Irish fly which probably dates from the first half of the 19th century. The underwing of golden pheasant tippet is typical of many Irish flies.

According to Stan Headley, the Irishman's Claret may be a derivative of the old Mallard & Claret. However, since its name indicates an Irish provenance, it may well be descended from the Claret & Jay instead. This would not be at all surprising because claret coloured flies are extremely popular and effective in the west of Ireland. The Claret Shrimp, Mourne Claret Shrimp, Claret Coolraw Killer, Howard's Claret Shrimp and the Claret & Jay are just some of the examples of claret flies in current use. Stan Headley finds the Irishman's Claret indispensable as a trout fly and also recommends it for salmon and seatrout, particularly on the rivers of west Scotland.

Irishman's Claret

The Dark Mackerel is an old trout pattern, dating back to before 1918, which was formerly widely used for loch fishing. It was brought back into current use with a modified body of red Lurex by David Leslie, for use on Loch Leven, one of the premier trout lochs in Scotland. Bill Currie popularised the fly for seatrout and it is now a commonly used pattern for both salmon and seatrout in the north and west of Scotland.

Dark Mackerel

Goat

Commenting on the Dark Mackerel in *Trout & Salmon Flies of Scotland*, Stan Headley relates that Charles McLaren (an icon among Scottish anglers) wouldn't use claret flies when seatrout fishing because they attracted too many salmon.

The Drowes Dawn is a modern tube fly, combining claret and yellow, that has been extremely effective on the Irish rivers Drowes and Slaney. The dark red hair is unusual and is obtained by dying brown bucktail red. A look at this fly suggests that it might be at its best towards the end of the season. In fact, it took a fish for its inventor, Hugh O'Conner, on January 1st – the opening day of the Drowes season.

Drowes Dawn - O'Connor

The Goat is an Irish hairwing with a long history. Peter O'Reilly suggests its inventor was the same unknown angler who devised the Foxford Shrimp. It is clearly based on the Lemon & Grey, but is regarded by many anglers as being more effective. The Goat is at its best in peat stained water or sunny conditions.

The Alistair is a fly from the river Helmsdale in northern Scotland. Although popular in Caithness and Sutherland, it is not widely used outside this area. For spring fishing it is normally used in tube or Waddington format. In summer, it is often fished on a riffling hitch, a technique that is still not widely used but which is becoming more popular. Davie McPhail informs me that small tubes fished in this manner are increasingly used on the rivers of south-west Scotland. The riffling hitch has been used for many years in North America, but seems to have caught on in Scotland only very recently.

Alistair

The Bourrach is a pretty little fly that has its home on the river Spey. It is regarded primarily as a summer fly for both grilse and salmon and ideally suited to fast, streamy water. Stan Headley notes that it has also taken spring salmon from the river Thurso, but on the Spey it is very much a summer pattern. The illustration follows the style of dressing as shown in *A Guide to Salmon Flies*, by Buckland & Oglesby. It is the dressing favoured by Crawford Little with an extremely sparse, long wing and tied on a low water double. Note that in this version the tail is a hackle tip, rather than a bunch of hackle fibres as is more usual.

Bourrach

The Orange Bourrach is a variant of the Bourrach with an orange wing instead of yellow. It seems to be more popular now than the original. The colour combination is again one that doesn't appeal to some people but the fly is nevertheless very effective. It just goes to show how misleading subjective human aesthetic judgements about fly colour can be. The only real arbiters are the salmon. They know what they like!

Orange Bourrach

The Orange & Blue is a back-end fly that is extremely effective when the river is cursed with autumn leaves. Its horribly contrasting colour combination would certainly stand out amongst the reds and russets. Stan Headley says that this fly is also known as Frank's Fancy and (with typical wit) commiserates with Frank on his poor taste! Poor taste or not, this fly once took five fish to one rod in an afternoon.

Orange & Blue

An Irish classic that is still used is the Black Goldfinch. This fly dates back to the middle of the 19th century and is one of a whole series of Irish flies with a wing of multiple golden pheasant toppings. In *Trout & Salmon Flies of Ireland*, Peter O'Reilly gives a featherwing dressing as well as a hairwing version. Kelson & Pryce-Tannatt specify a body hackle of yellow or golden olive but in *Irish Trout & Salmon Flies,* Malone gives one version with a claret hackle.

The Black Goldfinch is used on the Slaney for spring fish dressed on large irons in sizes 2/0 and 3/0. The hairwing version is much favoured on the Castleconnell fishery where it is dressed with a really bulky yellow bucktail wing with no red in it.

Black Goldfinch

The use of toppings (golden pheasant crest) as overwinging has definitely declined over the years but many very experienced anglers think that this is a feature of the old flies that should be retained. It actually seems to have a function rather than just being decorative. Even a hairwing enthusiast such as Lee Wulff thought it worthwhile to use toppings on many of his hairwing flies.

The combination of black and red has been around for a long time and is still widely used, particularly on the bodies of flies. The use of black and red in winging is not so popular but the following flies have proved to be very effective, particularly towards the end of the season when the fish seem to have a special predilection for red.

The Black & Red tube is a very straight forward pattern with a body of silver ribbed black floss and a wing consisting of bunches of black and red hair. If tied in the Waddington format, the black is tied in above the body and the red below.

A modification to the above fly with a gold rather than silver ribbing and the wing consisting of mixed black and red hair with some added silver Flashabou, is called the Moody Brag.

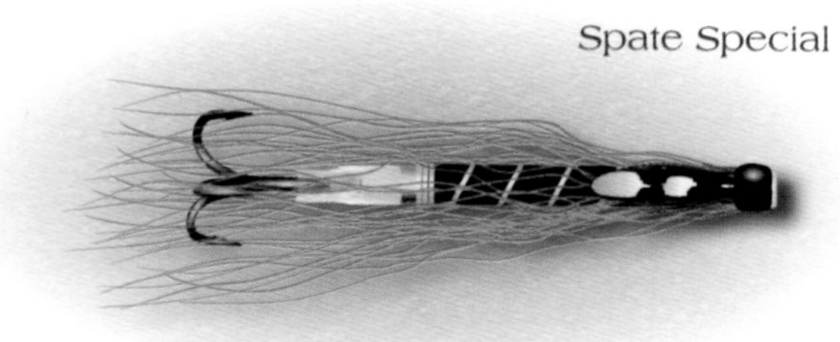

The Spate Special was designed to be effective in spate conditions where the river is high and the water carries colour. The pattern was taken from an article by Tim White in the November 1996 issue of *Trout & Salmon*. The recommended size of a 40mm to 50mm (1" to 2") brass tube, would normally be used only very late in the season or in early spring. Spate conditions, however, require a fly with enough weight to get down in the water and one with greater than usual visual impact to show up in the coloured water. A combination of orange with either a black, gold-ribbed body or a body of gold or silver Mylar was his chosen prescription.

The Glow Fly is also known by some as the Barbara Cartland for obvious reasons (for non-British readers, Barbara Cartland was a prolific celebrity romantic novelist who seemed to drift through life in a cloud of pink chiffon and dyed blond hair). It is a pattern from Alan Donaldson who says that it seems to arouse more suspicion and fear from anglers than it does from the salmon! Given enough water it works at all times of the season but is at its best in either very bright conditions or in poor light or coloured water. This is one to try when all else has failed or when you might otherwise think of the spinning rod.

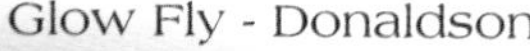

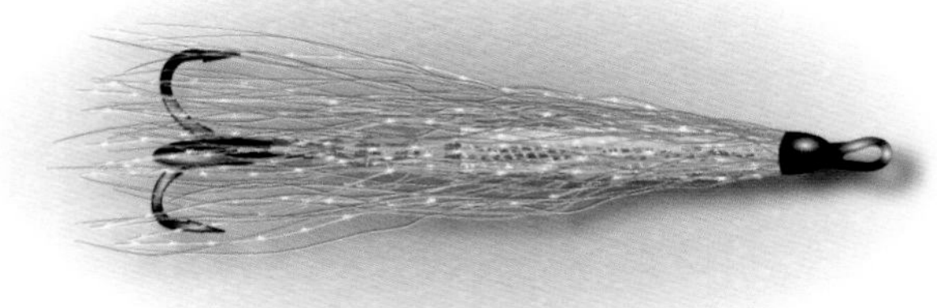

The Sheila is a pattern from Willie Mathieson which is popular all over the north-east of Scotland and particularly on the Beauly. Its gold, orange and black colours make it an ideal pattern for summer and autumn.

Sheila - Mathieson

The Black Brahan is an extremely popular pattern in Scotland, particularly in the north. It is regarded by many as an absolute necessity when the rivers are at low summer levels.

Black Brahan

The Green Brahan is very similar except that the body colour is changed to green Lurex instead of red. A second rib of fluorescent lime green floss follows the silver tinsel to give added impact. It is principally a summer grilse pattern and is mainly used in the north and east of Scotland. Stan Headley notes that it is also known as the Emerald Stoat (another Stoat!).

Green Brahan

The next series of flies were detailed in an article by Jimmy Younger in the May 2000 issue of *Fly Fishing & Fly Tying* about flies developed for use on Russia's Kola peninsular. The flies are all shown tied on single hooks, in keeping with the catch-and-release rules on the Russian rivers. These patterns are fished all through the season: in spring on sinking lines and short leaders; in summer on floating lines, very often riffle hitched. Sizes vary from 2 to 8.

The first is an interesting variant of the Sheila known as the Yokanga Gold. This fly was tied by a Norwegian camp manager for the Kola's Yokanga river. In its normal hairwing form it is identical to the Sheila apart from the addition of an underwing of gold Krystal Flash. A long fox winged version looks quite a bit different, however, and probably owes much of its inspiration to the Templedog. The extremely long wing is of Arctic fox with added strands of Krystal Flash.

Yokanga Gold

Yokanga Gold - Fox wing

Murmansk Killer

The Murmansk Killer is a Munro derivative, again with added flash. It has proved to be very effective in peat stained water and is particularly successful on the Varzuga. This fly looks like it would be well worth a try on Scottish rivers under the same conditions.

Among other flies which have become popular in Russia are the Ponoi Red and Green. These are basically derivatives of the Butt series of flies from North America, with the addition of a bit of sparkle in the wing. They are named after the river Ponoi. Both flies are at their best in clear water and have a good silhouette. They are darker than many other flies and offer a good alternative to present to fish which have moved to, but not taken, a flashier pattern such as an Ally's Shrimp.

Ponoi Red

Ponoi Green

The Copper Shrimp is another fly with its origins in North America. I am not absolutely sure but I believe this pattern was devised by Bill Hunter for the Miramichi or Restigouche rivers of eastern Canada. Although called a shrimp, the fly is tied in a fairly standard long hairwing format but with a wing tied underneath, as well as on top of the shank. The colours of orange, yellow and red, combined with a copper tinsel body make this a good late summer and autumn pattern which would also be worth a swim in coloured water conditions.

Copper Shrimp

As we have seen, the Templedog style of fly has become increasingly popular in Scotland in recent years. The next group of flies, which are all basically Templedog adaptations of well known patterns, are from Magnus Angus and are taken from an article in the March 2002 issue of *Fly-Fishing & Fly-Tying*.

The Willie Gunn Templedog was designed for a client who wanted a Templedog in the Willie Gunn colours. The wing colours are very similar to Davie McPhail's Peaty Man (see page 40) but in this case the body is in two halves: rear half, black floss; front half, black dubbing. The fly has taken fish on the Tay and the Tweed as well as from several Russian rivers.

The Black & Silver Templedog was designed primarily with Scottish rivers in mind but it has also been successful on rivers in both Norway and Russia. It is rather like a Templedog version of a Silver Stoat, a fly that is regarded as indispensable by many Scottish anglers.

The Green & Orange Templedog is based upon a green-bodied Willie Gunn or Rogie and is, in other respects, similar to the Willie Gunn Templedog shown above. It has proved effective in both Norway and Russia for spring fishing.

The Green Wing Templedog has much of the Green Highlander about it but the body is half holographic silver tinsel and half black dubbing.

Willie Gunn Templedog

Black & Silver Templedog

Green & Orange Templedog

Green Wing Templedog

PLATE 9: Templedogs - Magnus Angus

To give a better idea of the proportions and size of these flies, they are generally tied on tubes between 12mm and 38mm long (0.5 to 1.5"). The flies illustrated are tied on 38mm (1.5") tubes with a wing length of about 100mm (4"). The tubes used may be of aluminium, copper or brass.

Many experienced salmon anglers maintain a belief that the crest feather (topping) of the golden pheasant holds a singular attractiveness for salmon. I have already discussed the point that what might look attractive to the human eye may not necessarily impress the fish in the same way. The golden pheasant topping is surely a case where the judgement of both species happily coincide.

The following fly uses topping in a style of tying which can be applied to many flies, not just this particular pattern. The details of these flies were given by Mark Bowler, editor of *Fly Fishing & Fly Tying* in the April 2000 issue. Called Tall Tails, Mark relates that he first came across this type of fly in May 1994 on the river Tay when a lot of fish were caught on flies with long topping tails tied by Tom Heaps. The flies were of various patterns but every single one had the long tail.

The Kenmore Gold was devised by Mark Bowler together with Mark Wilton-Steer, owner of the Kenmore Hotel, and Chris Ponting. Named after the Kenmore Hotel, it has taken fish from the rivers Tay, Dionard, Ericht and Oykel. The tails on these flies are generally in the order of 60mm to 75mm long (or 2.5" to 3") for flies in sizes between 6 and 12. The technique also seems to give extra attraction to other patterns such as the Stoats Tail, Silver Stoat and 'Doctor' type flies for spring fish.

Kenmore Gold - Tall Tail

One of the most amusing and telling comments about salmon fishing and angler's attitudes to flies was made by Francis Francis. Commenting on changing fly patterns on the river Thurso, in northern Scotland, he noted of the salmon "they used to prefer a sober coloured fly, but of late they prefer more showy ones". Happily for the salmon anglers, the change in the salmon's preferences took place just at about the time that fishermen started to use the showy new flies! Bright flies have long been popular on the Thurso, of which the next fly is an example.

The Golden Demon (also known locally as the Thurso Demon) is a fly of venerable history. It was discovered by Zane Grey in New Zealand and popularised by him as a steelhead fly in the west of North America in the 1930s (see page 16). It is very much like a Dunkeld and originally was probably a hairwing variant of that fly (compare this with the hairwing Dunkeld on page 32).

Thurso Demon

Another new, bright little fly is The Editor, devised by Sandy Leventon, long-time editor of *Trout & Salmon* magazine. The fly has a pearl Lurex body and a rib of fluorescent green monofilament. The secret of this fly lies in the body, which positively gleams when wet. To achieve this effect the pearl tinsel must be underwound with a white material or floss – Sandy prefers fluorescent white Antron. Without this underbody, the pearl Lurex lacks the deep shine that seems essential to its success. For Waddington and tube versions, the body remains the same, with black winging above and below the body and the fly is finished with a collar hackle of dyed blue cock and jungle cock eyes. The Editor has taken fish on the Spey, Tweed, Tay and Nith, as well as some west coast spate rivers. Although Sandy didn't mention it when writing up this pattern, the general coloration is almost certain to make it an effective seatrout fly.

The Halpin is an Irish fly originating from the river Feale in north Kerry. It is regarded as an excellent late season fly by local anglers, who believe that the red colours provoke aggression in the cock fish. The Halpin has the look of a Black Doctor about it, particularly the red butt and head.

The next two flies were the subject of an interesting experiment by John Peaston, who wrote about it the April 1995 issue of *Trout & Salmon*. The flies were named Charlotte and Rebecca after two grandchildren, and were the only two flies that he used for a whole season of fishing. By the end of the year he had had his best season ever and had caught brown trout, rainbow trout, seatrout and salmon, all on the same two patterns.

Rebecca is a scarlet lady who has proved to be particularly seductive to salmon in coloured, spate water conditions. The red, orange and silver colour combination with just a few turns of black ostrich herl at the thorax is very striking.

Charlotte is less flashy but is still a sparkling fly, which seems better suited to clear water and early season fishing. The colours are yellow, blue and black with a gold tinsel body. Apart from taking salmon, Charlotte has also proved to be very attractive to seatrout.

The next three flies all have an element of blue about them. Many flies sport a blue throat hackle but the use of blue elsewhere, such as for bodies and wings, is much less common.

The Kerry Blue was devised by Harry Davis for use on the River Ewe and has become one of the standard dressings there. The Ewe also has (or had, unfortunately) really good runs of sizeable seatrout and the Kerry Blue has proved equally attractive to them.

Kerry Blue - Davis

Lady Ewe - Mateer

Dave Mateer was the originator of the Lady Ewe – also designed for use on the river Ewe. It was inspired by the Kerry Blue and, not unexpectedly, its blue and silver colour scheme has proved effective for both salmon and seatrout.

Jamie's Fancy is a fly designed by Willie Mathieson for the river Beauly. In 1995 this fly took 35 fish between February and May, proof enough that it works. Although differently arranged, the combination of yellow, blue and black is not a long way away from the Waddington version of John Peaston's Charlotte.

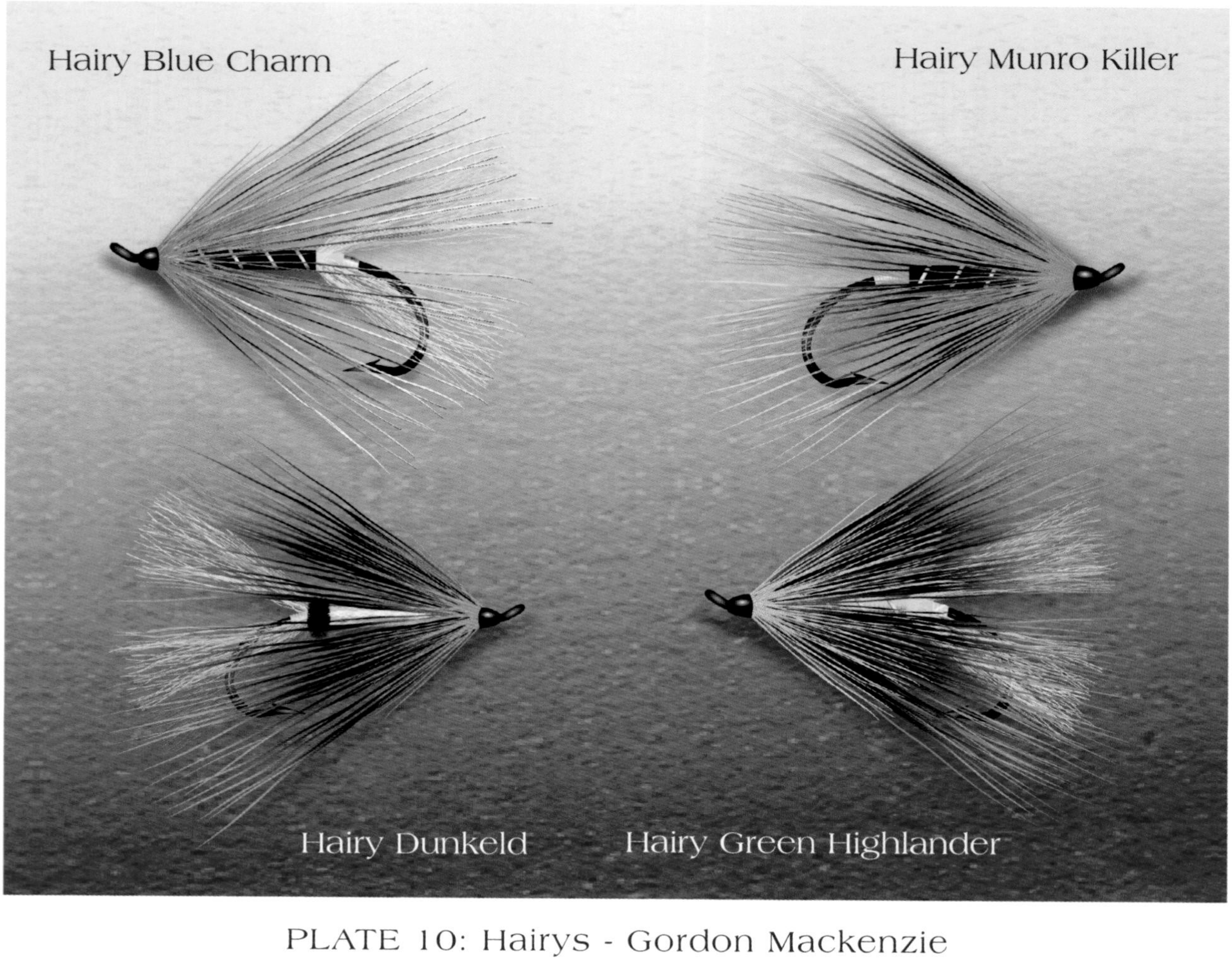

Hairy Blue Charm

Hairy Munro Killer

Hairy Dunkeld

Hairy Green Highlander

PLATE 10: Hairys - Gordon Mackenzie

Jamie's Fancy - Mathieson

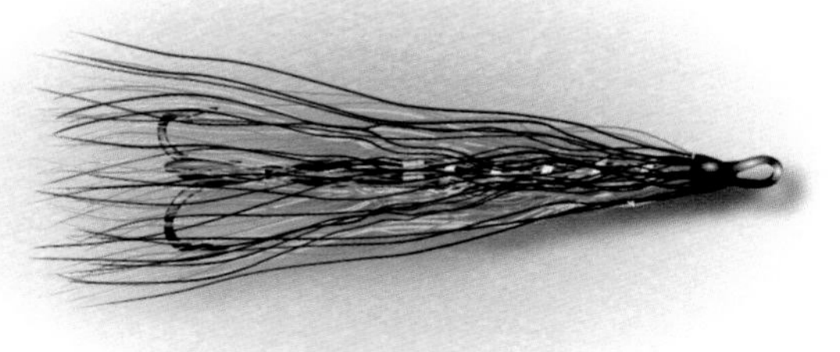

We have previously seen that badger-winged flies are extremely popular in Ireland (see page 43) but the next fly originates from Derek Knowles in the UK. The Yellow Badger is dressed extremely sparsely and has a very simple construction – a tinsel body and a long, sparse wing. It seems that this is all the salmon require. This fly was taken to the Miramichi in Canada in 1985 and proved to be very successful even though it is completely unlike the style of fly normally used there.

Yellow Badger - Knowles

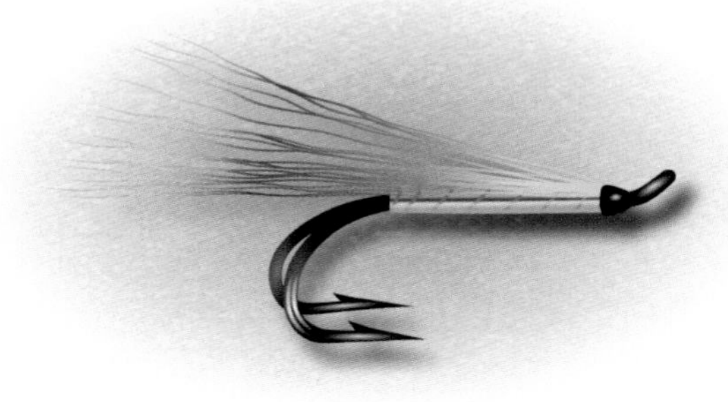

In *Shrimp & Spey Flies for Salmon*, Robert Gillespie and I described a range of hairwing shrimp and Spey patterns from Gordon Mackenzie of Redcastle. Known as Hairys, these flies incorporate hackles which are composed of hair wound in a dubbing loop rather than feather. Since the publication of *Shrimp & Spey Flies for Salmon*, Gordon has published his own book giving full details and tying instructions for this style of tying as applied to a wide range of fly types for trout, salmon and steelhead. *Hair-Hackle Tying – Techniques & Fly Patterns* is published by Frank Amato in the USA and is available in the UK from Merlin Unwin Books. I can highly recommend his book if you wish to tie these patterns for yourself. A range of Gordon's Hairy salmon flies is illustrated in plate 10. They have a unique look to them and offer the ultimate in mobility and translucence. The flies illustrated are shown on single hooks but the Hairy technique can also be applied to tube flies. A range of Matuka style flies tied in this fashion and which are intended for steelhead is illustrated on page 131 in the chapter on North America.

We have already seen a range of fatback tubes from Davie McPhail and Magnus Angus. To illustrate further just how popular this style of fly is becoming in Scotland, here is another from Davie. It is a fatback version of the phenomenally successful Ally's Shrimp, from Alastair Gowans. The fat back tube retains all the essential elements of the original fly but the ultra long tail has been replaced by a long overwing.

Ally's Shrimp Fatback
McPhail

The Akroyd is a fly that has been around for a very long time. It started life in the last quarter of the 19th century and is one of the classic strip wing Dee flies. Having gone through many reincarnations, it is still in use today. The Akroyd has been tied as a hairwing, more recently as a shrimp fly and, as shown above, a tube or Waddington. The rear part of the body can be either yellow or light orange. Some versions of this fly have the black hairwing tied all around the body but in the version shown below it is restricted to two bunches, above and below the shank. I prefer this configuration as it allows more of the yellow hackled rear body to be seen.

Akroyd Tube

The next fly is also an adaptation of an old classic, the Mar Lodge. The hairwing version illustrated uses Arctic fox hair for the winging but still retains the overall look of the original. The fly was tied by Mark Purvis who recommends it for spring fishing in clear water conditions using a sink tip or sinking line. The original fly had a golden pheasant topping over the wing. Gold Crystal Hair could be used instead. A simplified featherwing version of the Mar Lodge is still used in Ireland for spring fishing and is listed by Peter O'Reilly in *Trout & Salmon Flies of Ireland*. The hairwing would be a good alternative for those who would like to try this venerable but effective fly without meeting the complexities of feather winging.

Mar Lodge - Hairwing

The Haslam, devised by Sam Haslam of Rutland Water fame, is a fly that has been around for some time and is known in two reincarnations. Firstly, as a trout fly which has associations with Loch Lomond and, secondly, as a seatrout and salmon fly in Wales, particularly on the river Dovey. The following hairwing pattern is from John Buchanan. It is regularly used for salmon on the river Eden, in Cumbria, where some anglers use little else. In this version, natural brown squirrel tail replaces the hen pheasant tail winging of the original dressing. The pattern as given by both Moc Morgan and Stan Headley, together with the variant shown below, all retain the horns which on the original fly were of blue macaw. These horns are normally regarded by modern tyers as an unnecessary affectation of the Victorian fly dressers and it must be nearly unique for a modern pattern to retain them.

Haslam - Hairwing

A classic fly with a silver body and subdued tones is the Silver Grey. Peter O'Reilly notes that it is a good spring pattern for salmon on Lough Beltra. Peter has also used it on rivers further south in Connemarra and would also fish it on a bright

Silver Grey - Fatback Tube

day when the water has cleared from a flood. The version shown above is a fatback tube hairwing conversion that retains all the essence of the original but uses fox hair winging.

I pondered long and hard before putting the next fly in this section. On the face of it there was no doubt where Sweep should go, the fly after all originates in the UK. In all my research, however, I could find no mention whatsoever of this fly being used in the UK in modern times. Buckland & Oglesby have the featherwing version in their book under Icelandic flies. The following tying is from Mark Purvis and has been used with success in Labrador, with and without a riffling hitch.

Sweep - Hairwing

The Jeannie (see page 22) is a very old classic strip wing salmon fly, always considered a reliable summer fly for the river Dee. The following derivative, first tied by Jeannie MacKay, sister of Donnie MacKay, gillie at Achnabourin on the Naver and known as the Naver Jeannie is a very successful fly for peaty water conditions in the spring. Personally, I don't think that it looks much like a Jeannie at all, but it is still an effective fly for all that.

Naver Jeannie

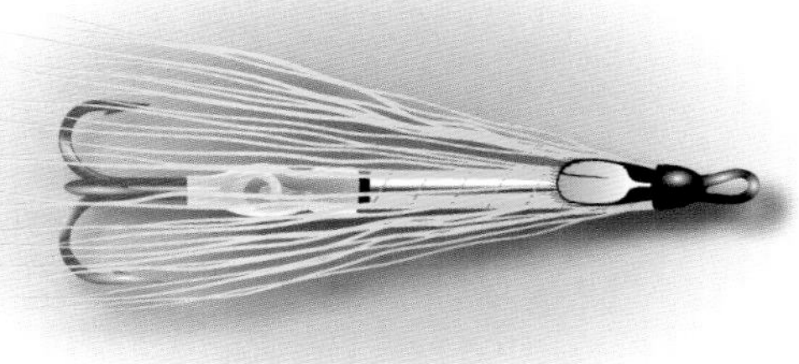

The Red Butt is one of the most popular flies used on the River Umba on the southern Kola Peninsular. The Red Butt, in slightly different form, is one of the standard Butt series of flies from the east coast of Canada and it is, therefore, most likely that it was brought to the Kola by North American anglers. In its Umba form, the wing material is of black Arctic fox and it has gained a pronounced tail of fluorescent red floss. Added impact is provided by jungle cock cheeks and the optional addition of a few strands of red or silver glitter material to the wing. A bit of red in a fly is always useful towards the season's end and the Red Butt is no exception.

Red Butt

Kola Bottle Tube #1 - Fairgrieve

Kola Bottle Tube #2 - Fairgrieve

The Kola Bottle tube is a variant of the Red Butt by Eoin Fairgrieve and is tied on a Loop Bottle Tube. The pattern is the same as the normal fly, but the body dressing is omitted and two or three stripped hackle stalks are tied to the hook to represent feelers, giving the fly a shrimpy appearance.

In an article in the November 2002 edition of *Trout & Salmon* Eoin also noted that turning the double hook into the wing – together with the feelers – produced a highly effective leaf guard. This is no small advantage when fallen leaves can turn an autumn day's fishing into a nightmare of hang-ups. The Kola Bottle has since been tested on the River Tweed and has proved to be highly effective when fished deep on a high density sinking line.

The wing of the Kola Bottle tube stands off the fly body much more than is normally the case with a tube fly due to the shouldered form of the Loop Bottle Tube and follows the trend which began with the Templedog. Other manufacturers have adopted this form and some interesting new variants from Juri Shumakov are shown on pages 77 and 78.

Apart from the Collie Dog, long streamer flies have been unfashionable for many years but this may be about to change. In an article in the August 2002 edition of *Trout & Salmon*, John Buckland wrote about experiments with long streamer patterns tied to imitate sandeels. Buckland suggests that these baitfish may be the last food source for migratory fish as they pass the coastal sandbanks to the river mouth.

The patterns that he uses are large – up to 150mm (6") long. The fly is cast square across the river and fished fast near the surface, either by hand lining or by sweeping the rod tip around.

This tactic has been so successful that there is obviously something about a long, sinuous fly moving fast that attracts fish. Somewhat heretically, Buckland suggests that if refusals are experienced, the fly size should be *increased* rather than reduced. When fishing the Findhorn in August, flies of 40mm (1.5") were found to be too small and 75mm (3") flies were needed before rises were converted into takes. Remember that this was at a time of year when conventional flies are usually fished in sizes 8 and 10.

Generally, these flies are tied on short shank trebles or doubles (sometimes tubes), some with a detached Mylar tube body, some with no body at all. The principal construction of the fly consists of Krystal Hair and other fluorescent and luminous materials; generally in the order, white at the bottom, silver and pearl in the middle and blue, green, peacock and black on top. The barred effect is obtained by a long genetic grizzle hackle tied in last of all. Large eyes of various types are a feature of all these flies, as shown below.

In an article in the February 2003 issue of *Trout & Salmon*, Mick Williams wrote about three flies that have been consistently successful for him over the last few seasons. The first is the Eternal Optimist (see page 31). Richard Vipond's Ice Maiden is a pattern which was tied for some terrible late November conditions on the Tweed when there was grue in the water and the air temperature was -8°C. The only fish taken that day fell to the Ice Maiden. Since that time it has been a cold water favourite, not just in winter but also in snow-melt conditions in spring. It has proved to be effective in Scandinavia and Iceland as well as Scotland tied in sizes ranging from tiny trebles to large tubes.

Sandeel Streamer - Buckland

The Cascade Shrimp is an Ally Gowans fly from the Ally's Shrimp series. Mick Williams ties a variant of this as a tube (shown below) and also as doubles or trebles. This fly has been so good over the last few seasons, especially in Scotland and Russia, that Mick rates it as even better than the original Ally's Shrimp.

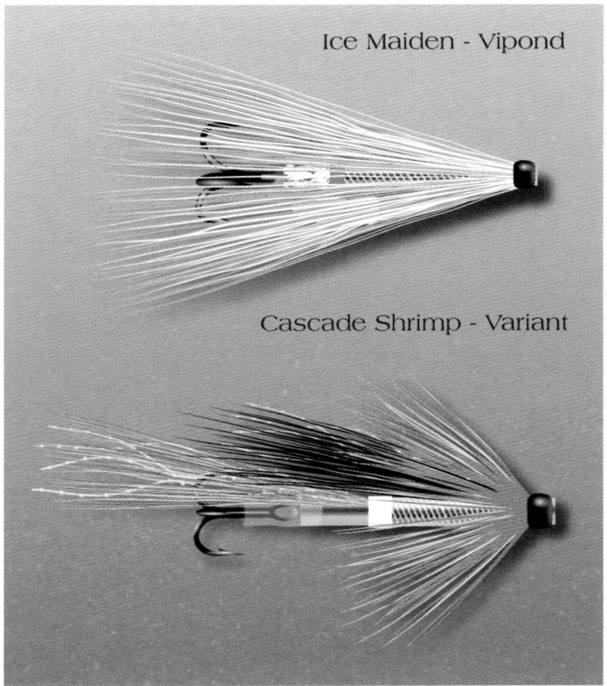
Ice Maiden - Vipond

Cascade Shrimp - Variant

The Thurso Dog is another of the new green flies, this time from Kenny McDonald which he published in the March 2004 issue of *Trout & Salmon*. Originally just called the Dog, I have taken the liberty of changing it to Thurso Dog (to avoid confusion with other Dogs – Garry, Northern etc.). Tied for spring fishing on the River Thurso, home of the Fast Eddie, this fly was designed to combine the best elements of that fly, together with the Willie Gunn and the Garry Dog. The fly was almost immediately sucessful and since then has proved to be effective in both peat stained water and in faster, clearer conditions. In Waddington form the fly is altered slightly: the rib is of flat gold Mylar rather than oval tinsel, the tag is of oval silver tinsel rather than silver wire and the tail is of two GP toppings mounted splayed into a 'V'.

The next fly, devised by Ronald Sutherland

Thurso Dog - McDonald

and called the Mosquito, is more of a style of dressing rather than a particular pattern. The details of the fly were given in the April 2004 issue of *Trout & Salmon*. The special feature of these flies is the use of the metallised foil from a crisp (potato chip) packet to form two aerofoil-like fins which give the fly its unique action. This construction is unusual but produces a fly which swims and hovers in the current in an exceedingly attractive manner, reminiscent of that of a lightweight Devon minnow. The foil at the rear of the tube forms a single, upward pointing fin rather like the dorsal fin of a fish. The foil at the front is divided forming downward sloping fins on either side of the tube.

The fly illustrated below is called the Black Mosquito and has proved to be deadly in very coloured water, taking fish from deep and also from near the surface. Other colours are effective as well: black and yellow, orange and red and orange and black are all recommended, but the technique may be adapted to your own favourite tube fly.

Black Mosquito - Sutherland

The next three flies are all basically orange and red and all were designed for use on the river Findhorn by local fishermen. They were described in an article by Andrew Graham Stewart in the July 2003 issue of *Trout & Salmon*. All of them are effective in peat stained water.

The Lilley Killer was designed by George Lilley in 1976 and since then has been consistently successful, particularly when the water is dark and peaty.

Lilley Killer - Lilley

Katie's Killer is a fly from Campbell Ross and got its name because the colours and materials were selected by Campbell's daughter Katie. The fly took a 16lb. salmon on its first outing.

Katie's Killer - Ross

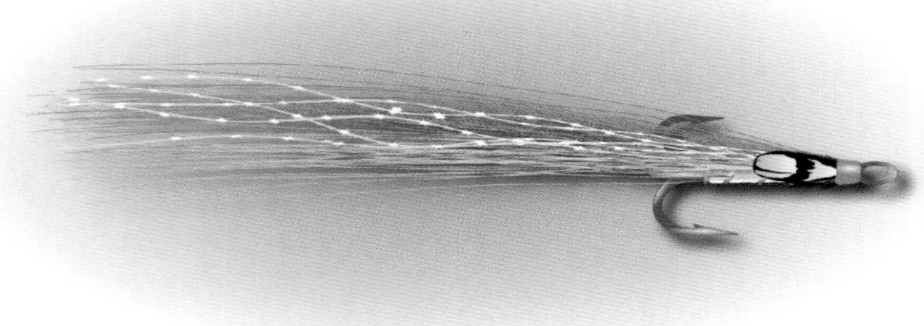

Jake's Shrimp was devised by Jake Fraser and is also a fly for peat stained water although it has also been used with success on other rivers. Although it is called a shrimp, the design is that of a fairly standard hairwing, albeit with an extra long wing and tail.

Jake's Shrimp - Fraser

ICELAND & SCANDINAVIA

The first British fisherman to rent fishing in Iceland appears to be Charles Akroyd, who visited in June 1877 and recorded his visit in *A Veteran Sportsman's Diary*, published in 1926. Ernest Crosfield and his brother also took fishing on the river Ellidaár at around the turn of the 19th century. The flies used for these early encounters with Icelandic salmon were mainly the classic British featherwing flies of the period, together with flies such as the Crosfield, which maintained their popularity until the 1930s when visiting North American anglers began to bring their hairwing patterns with them. It was around this time that specific patterns began to appear that could be called Icelandic in their own right.

The Crosfield – almost certainly devised by Ernest Crosfield – was originally a featherwing fly. Buckland and Oglesby give a wing of grey feather but the illustration in their book shows a wing of grey barred mallard or teal. This fly is also shown with a sparse hackle tied as a collar in front of the wing. Bates also records the Crosfield but with an underwing of brown mallard or turkey, veiled with an overwing of teal. The hairwing version illustrated below, taken from *Hairwing Atlantic Salmon Flies,* by Fulsher & Krom, has a wing of grey squirrel.

Crosfield

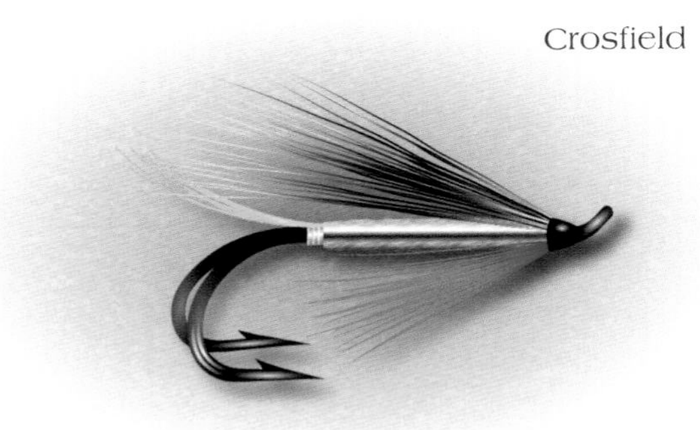

Somewhere about the 1930s, a strong belief took hold that flies for Icelandic waters must contain blue if they were to be successful. Many of the flies used by visiting anglers met this requirement and they were certainly effective. This may have been because the season in Iceland is very short, during which the rivers contain large numbers of extremely fresh fish. Many of these flies are silver as well as blue and this combination has a long history of success for fresh run fish.

Iceland has also become well known for its association with shrimp patterns, particularly the Francis, the Krafla and the Raeken. The Francis was devised by Peter Deane in the UK around 1965 but the other two flies are the products of Kristjan Gistlason, an Icelandic flytyer. Details of these flies may be found in *Shrimp & Spey Flies for Salmon*.

In *The Art of the Atlantic Salmon Fly*, Bates notes a fly which he calls the Irish Hairy Mary. This is similar to the standard Hairy Mary but with a butt of fluorescent orange floss and a wing of badger hair. Bates considered this pattern his all time favourite for Iceland. Apart it having an orange butt rather than yellow, he may well have been describing the Ballynahinch Badger (see page 43).

Irish Hairy Mary

The Blue Sapphire is an Icelandic fly that seems to have been around for some time. Bates describes the original featherwing version in *Atlantic Salmon Flies & Fishing*. The hairwing version we show here has been slightly simplified. The tail originally consisted of golden pheasant topping with red, blue and Guinea fowl hackle fibres over. The wing was of brown turkey or mallard with an outer wing of married strips of blue swan, mottled turkey and brown mallard and finished with a golden pheasant topping. In the hairwing version, the tail has been reduced to topping alone and the wing is of dark brown hair with a few strands of blue either side.

Blue Sapphire

As previously discussed, the golden pheasant topping is a feature that may well be worth retaining. This fly contrasts with other blue Icelandic flies in presenting a generally much darker image.

One of the most popular flies in Iceland is the Blue Rat, devised by Poul Jorgensen specifically for Joe Bates and first used by him on a trip to the Laxa i Kjos. Jorgensen includes this pattern in *Salmon Flies*, published in 1978, but does not give a date for it. It is not included in the first edition of Bates's *Atlantic Salmon Flies & Fishing*, first published in 1970, so might have originated sometime between these years.

Blue Rat - Jorgensen

The Thvera Blue is mentioned by Thomas Clegg in *Hair & Fur in Fly Dressing*, published in 1969, and also by Buckland & Oglesby. Stan Headley gives a variant of this fly in *Trout & Salmon Flies of Scotland* with the note that it has been used to good effect on the Dee in small sizes. I can well understand that this fly would be extremely useful for fresh run fish and, although Stan doesn't mention it, it would probably be at its best in clear water in the spring or early summer.

Thvera Blue

Thvera Blue - Variant

The Laxa Blue is listed by Randle Stetzer in *Flies, the Best One Thousand*, published in 1992. It is another typical Icelandic fly, repeating yet again the silver/blue theme. A tag of fluorescent orange floss adds an 'aiming point' at the rear of the fly. No history is given for this fly, but I think that it is obviously a variant of the Silver Blue or a simplified version of the Silver Doctor. An alternative dressing from a Canadian source has a body of ice blue floss rather than tinsel and has the hackle tied as a collar in front of the wing (see page 94).

Laxa Blue

It should be said that while the Silver Blue originated in the UK, it is seldom used there anymore (at least not for salmon). Tied short and slim for low water use, it still finds its place in the fly box for Iceland. The original fly had a wing of barred teal feather but the modern versions normally use grey squirrel hair instead.

Silver Blue

Not all Icelandic flies are blue based! The next fly employs that other effective colour combination of gold-black-orange. The Dentist – no doubt so-called because it is good at 'extractions' – is extremely popular amongst many of the guides in Iceland who regard it as indispensable. Adrian Latimer, who fishes all over the world as a sideline of his work in the oil industry, wrote about the Dentist, the Veidlist and the Sunray Shadow when describing a visit to the Ranga in the May 1997 issue of *Fly-Fishing & Fly-Tying*.

The Veidlist is a bright, yellow-winged fly which, with its red ostrich herl butts at each end of a silver tinsel body, is very much reminiscent of the Doctor series. Adrian noted that both the Veidlist and the Dentist had also proved effective on small rivers in Sutherland, such as the Kirkaig, Inver and Dionard.

The Dentist

Veidlist

The Sunray Shadow is a pattern that has gained a wide reputation since its inception and it is also used in Iceland. The version that Adrian Latimer gave in the aforementioned article is a variant with a yellow underwing. This has proved to be particularly effective on the long, flat gliding pools when moved smartly across the current with the help of some handlining. Pearl Crystal Hair can replace the peacock herl strands to give a more durable fly.

Sunray Shadow - Variant

The Black Sheep, from Joe Hubert, dates from about 1977 and is generally held to be an elver imitation. Whether elvers (immature eels) form a significant part of the marine diet of Atlantic salmon remains open to question but there is no doubt that this type of long winged fly can be very effective in the right conditions. Incidentally, there is nothing sheep-like in the construction of this pattern: the name derives from its looking so out of place amongst the other standard flies in the fly box. The Black Sheep is one of those flies – like the Francis – which has become firmly established as an Icelandic pattern, although it actually originated elsewhere. It is interesting to note that the black and yellow colours of the Black Sheep are also preferred for the Icelandic variant of the Sunray Shadow, shown above.

Black Sheep - Hubert

The Black Bear, Green Butt, also known as simply the Green Butt, has been popular in Iceland for many years, having first been introduced by fishermen from North America where it is used for Atlantic salmon and steelhead from east to west. Not surprisingly there is an Icelandic variant that incorporates blue hair in its makeup.

Green Butt - Variant

The earliest flies in use on the rivers of Sweden and Norway were imported British classics brought over by the Victorian sportsmen who had discovered the enormous runs and huge fish to be found in Scandinavia. Jones's *Guide to Norway & Salmon Fisher's Pocket Companion*, published in London in 1848, gives a flavour of the flies that were in use at the time.

This list includes such standards as the Popham, the Colonel, Childers, Assassin, the Doctors and a fly called the Namsen, after the Norwegian river of that name. By the end of the 19th century this list had changed to embrace the Jock Scott, the Durham Ranger, the Bulldog and a fly called the Gula. This last was probably the pattern we now know as the Gaula. By the 1930s, the flies in use were of the simplified types that had become popular in Britain, together with North American hairwings that had been brought over by visiting anglers. North American flies, which have retained their popularity to the present day, include members of the Rat family as well as the Cossebooms.

In due course, indigenous Scandinavian patterns also developed. At first these were no more than local variants of the British standards but, gradually, Scandinavian flies began to take on a distinctive character of their own. A list of these flies would include the Namsen, the Gaula, Peer Gynt, the Sheriff, Ola, Ottesen, Pålsbu, Laerdal, Tana, Valdum and Vi Menn Flua. All these flies were originally featherwings, but hairwing versions of many of them were subsequently brought into use.

The latter of the above-mentioned flies were devised well into the 1980s so it is clear that hairwings had by no means replaced featherwings at that time and, in fact, featherwing flies still find use in Scandinavia. Fulsher and Krom, in *Hair Wing Atlantic Salmon Flies*, published in 1981, mention correspondence with Ole Mosesen from Alta in Norway in which he lists the flies that he commonly used in 1974. These included the Hairy Mary, Red Abbey and Grey Rat, together with hairwing conversions of flies such as the Black Dose, Green Highlander and Thunder & Lightning. These flies were tied on double hooks from size 1/0 to 3/0 – big flies for big rivers and big fish!

As early as the late 1970s, however, a new movement was under way. Fishermen such as

Hakan Norling, Mikael Frodin and Roger Ahlfors were developing fly patterns with much more mobility than that offered by either the old featherwings or even the standard hairwing patterns that had begun to replace them. This movement culminated in the fox winged tube flies and the Templedog or fatback style of tying which has now become a trademark of Scandinavian flies and has spread to salmon rivers all over the globe.

The Namsen is one of the earliest flies that is specific to Norway, the original dressing dating back to 1848. Since then it has varied a lot and in *Atlantic Salmon Flies & Fishing*, Bates gives three different versions of patterns called Namsen. The following illustration is a hairwing conversion of the pattern that Bates notes as the most popular.

Namsen Hairwing

John Veniard, in *A Further Guide to Fly Dressing*, first published in 1964, gives a completely different version of the Namsen. In his version, the body is of brown seal's fur and the wing is of white goose with strips of barred teal each side and golden pheasant crest over the top. This is so different from any of the dressings given by Bates that one wonders if it is the same fly at all.

Incidentally, nearly all the salmon flies that Veniard listed for Scandinavia are featherwings. The only hairwing mentioned is a fly called the Em-Te Flugor, from Sweden, which features a wing of cinnamon dyed Polar bear hair with a furnace hackle each side. The body is of mixed red-brown and green wool, with flat gold ribbing. The fly gives a very sombre impression, quite unlike most other Scandinavian salmon flies.

Em-Te Flugor

The Valdum is a fly from Børre Pettersen, dating from 1974, which was first tied for the river Gaula. It has since been used on many other rivers and has been successful for both salmon and seatrout. It is very much like a salmon version of the old Scottish trout fly, the Butcher, but the body is unusual in having a ribbing of black floss over silver tinsel.

Valdum - Pettersen

The following fly originates from the river Tana – the largest river in Norway. It is located in the far north and forms part of the boundary with Finland (where it is known as the Teno). This river is fished in the high summer when there is no night at all and the recommended patterns are light and bright. The original fly had a wing of Amherst pheasant tail strips. The hairwing version uses natural white-tipped, brown hair. In *Trout & Salmon Flies of Scotland*, Stan Headley gives a tube or Waddington variant of this fly, which was devised by Alan Donaldson for spring fishing in Scotland and which is also illustrated below. The wing colours of this fly have been amended to yellow bucktail, with white over, but the essential look of the fly has been maintained.

The Laerdal is a fly from the famous Norwegian flytyer and gillie, Olaf Olsen, who died in 1984. The fly is named for the river Laerdal and proved to be very effective on days of changing cloud and sun and also again in the fading light of evening. This is another of those flies whose generally subdued colouring fail to make any obvious visual impact, but which nevertheless seem to find approval with the salmon.

Originally winged with white-tipped turkey feather, the hairwing version uses dark, white-tipped hair to achieve the same effect.

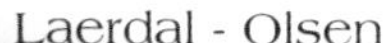
Laerdal - Olsen

The Pålsbu is a very old Norwegian pattern. Originally tied for trout, it has been successfully adapted as a salmon fly. It seems to be particularly effective for cock fish when the rivers are low and warm in summer. The body should be bulky, using at least five strands of bronze peacock herl. The wing was originally bronze mallard. Dark brown hair is substituted in this hairwing version.

Most of these flies were finished off with golden pheasant topping and – for reasons already explained – it may well be worth the extra effort of retaining this feature. Strands of gold Crystal Hair or Krystalflash may serve the same purpose in a more modern idiom and are easier materials to tie with.

Pålsbu

The Børre Flua is another fly from Børre Pettersen. This fly presents a generally dark image, relieved by a splash of yellow and red at the tail.

Børre Flua - Pettersen

The Gullnøkk was devised by Torgeir Steen and has a reputation of being extremely effective when the water is carrying some colour. The original fly was winged with mottled turkey with a topping over. The hairwing conversion shown below uses brown hair with strands of gold Crystal Hair to replace the topping.

Gullnøkk - Steen

The Peer Gynt is a fly developed by John Sand, one of the most famous of Norwegian flytyers, in 1963. The original wing was of brown turkey with brown mallard over. The hairwing version has brown hair with gold Crystal Hair replacing the topping.

Peer Gynt - Sand

In the July 1995 issue of *Trout & Salmon*, Par Jansson described the Janssons, a Swedish fly that was created in 1989 as a variation of the Rat series from the USA. It was intended primarily for use in the early hours of the morning, just before sunrise, when the green fluorescent Antron gives off a lovely sheen in the pale light. Janssons has proved to be a really deadly fly for the early hours. With this kind of colouring and given the proven effectiveness of the Rat flies, this fly should be of interest to the salmon fishers of the east coast of Canada. Reed's Green Rat, from New Brunswick, described on page 86 is also very much in this vein.

Janssons

The Fireball is a fly devised in 1973 by a Swede, Mikael Ingvarsson, for use in Norway. Since its inception it has proved to be universally effective and is now used all over Scandinavia. Its form, with a collar hackle at the front, is very much in the Cosseboom style.

Fireball - Ingvarsson

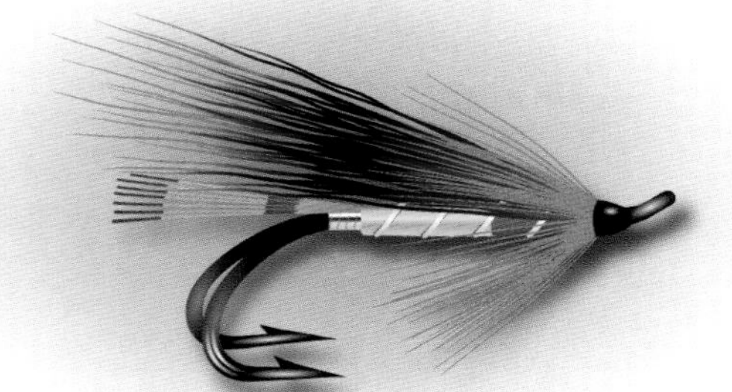

We have already looked at the development of the fatback or Templedog style of tube fly from Hakan Norling in the History chapter. The following flies are further examples of this type, some with modifications.

The Green-Black Highlander is clearly a Green Highlander derivative. It got its name when Jonas Hammarstedt, a fellow guide with Norling was asked to identify a fly shown to him by a visiting American angler. Having heard a

Green-Black Highlander

Red Templedog

Black Templedog

Silver Grey Epoxy Head

PLATE 11: Templedogs - Hakan Norling

discussion at breakfast about flies such as the Green Highlander and the Black Doctor and being confronted with a totally unfamiliar pattern with both black and green in its makeup, he confirmed to his client with total confidence that the fly in question was in fact a Green-Black Highlander. Trust me, I'm a gillie!

The Red Templedog is a variant of the Red Sandy, an old British classic whole featherwing which dates back to the 1880s. The Red Sandy was popular in Norway and was also one of the most highly regarded flies for Iceland. This modern version is extremely effective in the early season when seeking fresh fish in water that is carrying some colour.

The Black Templedog is slightly different in its treatment, as the original tying included a red tag and butt and a silver body dressed on the hook. The illustration shows a more normal approach with all the dressing confined to the tube. The eyes on this fly are of jungle cock, dyed fluorescent orange but more recent versions have used cheeks of orange Spectratape cut to shape and finished off with yellow/black or pearl/black adhesive eyes.

The Silver Grey Epoxy Head is self-explanatory. The tube is tied in conventional Templedog style, but is completed with a large head of clear epoxy glue on which 3D eyes are mounted. With the extra weight at the front of the fly it is not necessary to tie this fly on heavy metal tubes to get it down in the water. The swimming motion is also very different and, I think, more enticing.

Black & Silver Egghead Zonker - Norling

Zonker - Jansson

The name Zonker denotes a fly which has a 'wing' made from a narrow strip of fur still on the skin. The Zonker strip is tied along the back of the fly in the same way that feathers are used on a Matuka-style fly. The free end of the strip can extend well past the body of the fly, producing a sinuous motion that is highly attractive to all kinds of predatory fish. The Zonker style comes from North America where it was first used on the west coast as a steelhead attractor. It gained prominence in Europe when Zonkers became popular in England as stillwater lures for rainbow trout. It took some time before modern lures of this sort became acceptable to salmon anglers, but they have proved to be extremely effective due to their mobility and unique action in the water.

The Black & Silver Egghead Zonker is another Hakan Norling pattern which combines the Zonker style of fly with a head, in this case formed of 'egg yarn'. Egg yarn or Glo-Bug yarn is a crinkly synthetic tow which was first developed for the Pacific salmon and steelhead fishermen of the west coast of North America for tying imitations of salmon eggs. The yarn is tied in and then cut to size: as soon as the tension is released the yarn flares to form a fuzzy ball. The eye effect on this pattern is obtained by using yarn of three different colours.

The second Zonker is a pattern given by Par Jansson in the April 1996 issue of *Trout & Salmon*.

The Swedish Killer is another fly given by Par Jansson in the article mentioned above. It was originally used as a night-time seatrout pattern for the Aurland river in Norway. Its use quickly spread and it has been successful for both seatrout and salmon in both Sweden and Norway.

Swedish Killer

Muddler type flies are quite popular in Scandinavia, together with other types of surface effect or wake flies. The same applies in North

America where buoyant wake flies with deer hair heads or bodies, such as Bombers, are very widely used for salmon and steelhead. This type of fly has never become popular in Britain for reasons that are not immediately clear.

There has been a long-held belief amongst British anglers that the salmon of Scotland are much less likely to rise to the surface to take a 'wake fly' than are those of North America and Scandinavia. This theory is, however, contradicted by the many cases where fish, particularly grilse, have been shown to be susceptible to a fly fished fast on the surface, whether the wake effect was intended or not. It should also be said that experienced Scottish gillies of a younger generation, such as Davie McPhail, firmly believe that the riffle hitched fly has an important role in the armoury of the modern salmon fisherman in Scotland.

The Mörrum is one of the major rivers of Sweden and is home to both salmon and seatrout of tremendous size. In 1997, the average weight of the nearly 800 salmon taken from the Crown Fishery was over 9.14kg (just over 20lb). A 20lb fish won't raise many eyebrows in Mörrum, though a 20kg fish (44lb) might. Seatrout of over 18kg (39.5lb) have also been taken on the Mörrum – these are big fish by anybody's standards! The following flies are all recommended for the Mörrum and were described by Mark Bowler, editor of *Fly-Fishing & Fly Tying*, in an article in the April 1999 issue of that magazine.

Spey Gillie

The Spey Gillie is another Arctic fox winged fly but this time the colour combination is black and yellow, with a touch of orange. Yellow and black is a combination that was out of favour for many years but has made a big come back in recent times. The revival seems to have been led by the widespread use and success of the Tosh and its variants (see page 35).

The Lawson, created by Mikael Frödin in 1984, is a mix of black, gold and orange: a combination that has proved its worth over the years. For maximum mobility, the wing is of Arctic fox, typical of so many modern Swedish flies. Originally designed for seatrout on the river Em in southern Sweden, the fly has proved equally good for salmon and is now used all over Scandinavia in a variety of forms, ranging from tiny doubles for low water summer fishing, up to large tubes for heavy water. Zonker versions, where wing is a black Zonker strip, are also regularly used. The second version illustrated, from Nestor Dupo, varies in so far as the red tag has been replaced by

Lawson - Frödin
Lawson Variant - Dupo
Lawson Zonker

an undertail of red floss and the body and throat hackles are of orange-dyed badger, rather than black with an orange throat hackle. Jungle cock cheeks finish the fly.

Glödhäck

The Glödäck is a black fly, the dark image of which is relieved only by the flash of fluorescent red floss used as a tag. Apart from the wing material – which is again Arctic fox instead of bucktail or bear – this fly is almost identical to the Black Bear, Red Butt fly from the eastern seaboard of Canada. Small dark flies, such as this, with a splash of colour as an aiming point for the fish are universally successful, particularly in clear, low water conditions, and are used all over the world.

Ismo Saastamoinen is a professional flytyer from Sweden whose flies are sold all over Europe and North America. All Ismo's flies are hallmarked by the care he takes to make them both beautiful and durable. This includes underwinding all body parts with white thread, applying multiple coats of lacquer to the tags and to lacquering all the wing elements at their tying in point. It takes time but he considers it worth the effort.

Green Dawn

Black Dawn

Yellow Dawn

Blue Dawn

Red Dawn

Thunder Dawn

PLATE 12: Dawn Series - Ismo Saastamoinen

The Dawn series was first created for a friend who wanted flies to take to the Russian rivers such as the Pana and Umba. There are seven flies in this beautifully elegant series to cover a wide range of water colour conditions. All of these flies have an underwing consisting of two hackles set back to back, with a fox hair overwing. This combination of hair and feather is not all that common, although the Em-Te Flugor from Sweden, shown on page 69, is one example. Further examples can be found amongst the steelhead flies of north-western USA The idea of underwinging with hackle tips actually has much to recommend it: it provides a veil of colour with almost no bulk, it keeps the head small and in no way reduces the mobility of the fly. Indeed, it may well enhance it.

Dawn - Saastamoinen

Dream - Saastamoinen

The Dream is another fly from Ismo Saastamoinen and very much in the same vein as the Dawn series, which it pre-dates. Hackle tip underwinging is again a feature of this fly, which has certainly proved to be effective, having taken fish in Norway, Finland and Scotland, as well as Sweden. Paul Marriner liked the look of this pattern and included it in *Modern Atlantic Salmon Flies*. Ismo obviously has a liking for golden brown fox hair because it is featured in the wing of this fly as well as in all of the Dawn series.

The Beaivvas was devised by Jan Gunnar Furuly, a Norwegian journalist who lives just outside Oslo. In July 1996, this fly hooked his largest ever salmon – a fish of 14kg (nearly 31lb) – on the Karasjohka. It is no surprise that it is now his favourite pattern for sunny days. The name of the fly is the Lapp word for the sun and the fly is at its best on sunny days.

Beaivvas - Furuly

Karasjohka Special - Furuly

Jan Furuly also devised the Karasjohka Special in the winter of 1995/96. During the hot, sunny and mosquito buzzing month of July 1996

the still unnamed fly proved itself to be a winner on the river Karasjohka: the upper part of Tana river system, in Norway's Finnmark region. It produced a salmon of 9kg on the 3rd July and a salmon of 8kg on the 5th July. After this success, the fly was then named the Karasjohka Special.

Spring Tube

The next fly has a black and yellow theme, this time in tube format. The Spring Tube is a fly which, as the name suggests, is used for early season fishing. It is much like a combination of a Tosh with a Hairy Mary, but is tied in the Scandinavian style of dressing tube flies, with a floss tag and tail, with the wing above and the hackle beneath the shank in the conventional single hook configuration.

The Heggeli is one of the most famous Norwegian flies with salmon, seatrout and brown trout to its credit. It was originally devised in the 1960s by Bernhard Caspari for use on the Heggeli lakes and river in the Nordmark, north of Oslo. It has since caught many thousands of fish all over Norway. The original fly had a wing of bronze mallard but Jan Furuly's hairwing version, shown below, replaces this with brown polar fox hair. The wing in this variant is dressed very sparsely for use in the clear rivers of Finnmark. If more impact is needed for coloured water, the wing can be dressed more fully.

Heggeli Hairwing

The Skaidi is a predominantly green Norwegian pattern that is locally popular on the Borselv river in the Finnmark and which has a great reputation for taking fish when the conditions are difficult.

The Reippu was first devised by a Finn, Matti Huitila, for use on the Reppar-fjord river in Finnmark. The fly is tied short and sparse on a low water double hook in sizes 8 to 12 and has proved to be effective in warm, low water conditions. It is recommended for other rivers in these conditions, particularly if there is a greenish-brown tinge to the water.

Skaidi

Reippu - Huitila

The Kotkan Kerttu is a famous Finnish salmon fly created by Hannu Kopra which has been one of the most reliable salmon catchers on the river Kymi. This version, from Mikko Stenberg, varies a little from the original, in as much as the amount of red in the fly has been reduced somewhat in order to give it a more universal appeal.

Kotkan Kerttu - Kopra

The Frafjordselva has a good reputation in Norway for taking both salmon and seatrout. The fly illustrated was tied by Jan Hansen. The squirrel hair wing is tied in in two separate bunches, the second shorter than the first in order to obtain the white-black-white banding effect. The head is of long-fibred seals fur wound in a dubbing loop to produce a collar and then clipped into a sort of Muddler head.

Frafjordselva

The next two flies were documented by Alastair Gowans in an article in the June 2002 issue of *Fly-Fishing & Fly-Tying*. Both of these flies have Arctic fox wings combined with fluorescent materials, a combination that is fast becoming a standard for all Scandinavian waters. Both are illustrated tied on the new Salar double hooks from Partridge which have a curved body and are available in gold as well as black.

The Norway #1 is unusual in that it has cheeks of goose biots dyed fluorescent yellow.

Norway #1

Norway #2 has a wing of fluorescent orange Arctic fox combined with a body of fluorescent green floss and a tail of fluorescent green multi-yarn. The combination of green and orange may not look particularly appetising to our eyes but salmon seem to think otherwise.

Norway #2

The next group of flies are all designed by a Russian fisherman. They are intended for use on

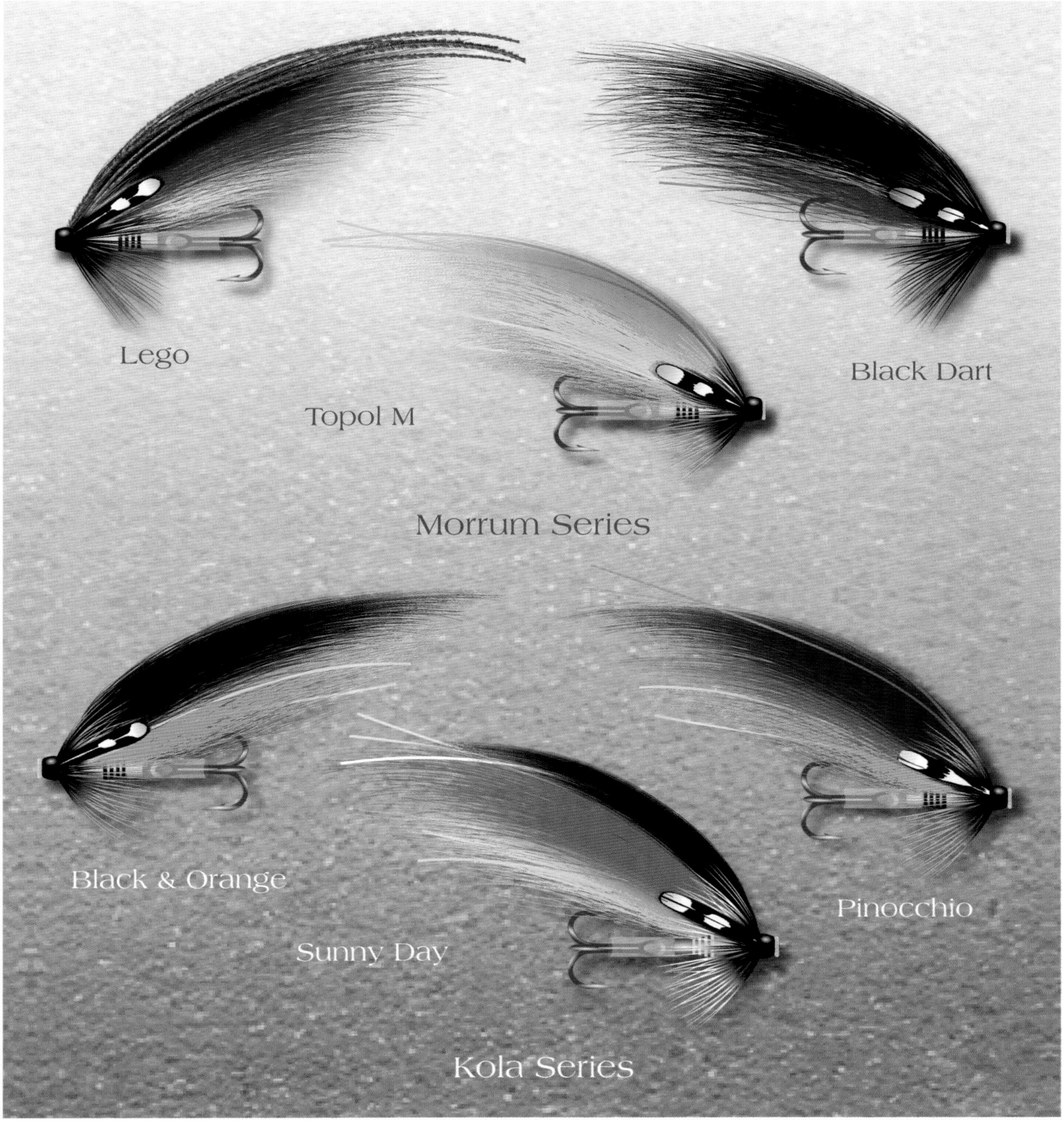

Lego

Black Dart

Topol M

Morrum Series

Black & Orange

Pinocchio

Sunny Day

Kola Series

PLATE 13: Shumakov Special Tube Flies

the rivers of northern Russia as well as Scandinavia.

The flies shown are taken from two series, the Mörrum series and the Kola series. In the article that I read, which featured these patterns, they were shown tied on tubes which utlised three coneheads, strung on to a plastic tube insert, over which the winging was tied in separate bunches between the coneheads. This was intended to counteract the fact that a conehead mounted conventionally – at the head of the tube – destroyed the classic Scandinavian profile. The dressings shown here have been slightly adapted so that they are tied in a more conventional manner: with the winging being made in a series of layers at the front of a specially shaped small tube, as detailed below. Strictly speaking, the illustrations should therefore be called variants, although the essence of the look and design has been retained. The front wing on all of these flies is tied in the typical Templedog style, i.e., first tied in with the fibres facing forwards and then folded back and retained in position with turns of thread in front of the wing.

One of the problems with tube flies (especially those tied on brass or copper tubes intended to sink deep) is the strong tendency for the fly to adopt a tail down attitude in the water. This is all the more pronounced in the newer types of bottle-shaped tubes, which are unavoidably tail-heavy. The creator of these flies, Juri Shumakov, originally tried to overcome this tendency by tying an extra hackle right at the rear of the tube, often on the plastic insert. He eventually came to the conclusion that the only real answer was to design a series of specially shaped tubes in which the weight was concentrated at the front. The grooves in the rear of the body of the Skittle tube and the Long Range tube are intended to further reduce the weight at the rear. Details of these tubes, which are all 13mm (0.5") long, with a diameter of either 4mm or 5mm, can be found on the excellent *Rackelhanen on-line Flyfishing Magazine* web site (www.rackelhanen.com), which deals with all aspects of Scandinavian fly fishing.

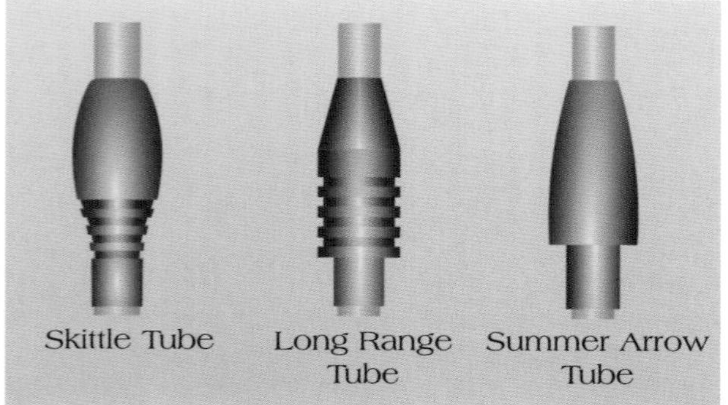

Shumakov's Special Fly Tubes

As mentioned, Juri Shumakov is Russian, his family coming from the Caucasus region of

northern Russia. During a recent visit he came across a new material in a local market. The item in question was a silver white fleece which had a long, soft, transparent hair with a shine that looked almost synthetic. A hair that has the structure of Arctic fox combined with the translucency of Polar bear is a marvellous find and the following flies utilise this superb material. It comes from the Caucasian Silver Goat: at least that is how he translated the local name 'Serebrjanka'. Apparently, the hair from the adult animals grows as long as 23cm (9")! Don't ask how you can lay your hands on this wonder hair. I haven't a clue! The Caucasus is politically unstable, subject to ethnic tensions and is not the easiest place in the world to visit. Before you think about raising some of these animals in your back yard, Juri says that only the hair from animals that graze the highest mountain pastures produce the highest quality hair, with the almost unnatural transparency and shine. Animals from the lowlands just don't give the same quality. It sounds to me like a quest for Frodo Baggins and company (with quite a lot of help from Gandalf!) but for the adventuresome it is out there!

The Purple & Copper is a tube fly from Stig Larsen, of Denmark, which has been used with success on the Orkla. Purple is rarely used in Scandinavia, but this fly shows that it may well be worthwhile. The wing is in three layers, the bottom layer is Arctic fox fur, the middle layer is of polar bear and the top layer is of Icelandic sheep hair. The differing materials not only provide a full wing, but the different textures are important as well. The unribbed body is of braided copper Mylar tubing. The fluorescent red tubing used to hold the hook in alignment gives added impact.

Purple & Copper - Larsen

The next pattern may be seen a bit old fashioned as it retains the standard construction which has been used for years. Not only that, the colour is subdued as well: burnt orange rather than hot or fluorescent orange. This has, however, not made it any the less effective in both clear and coloured waters. The Marius was devised by Stig Larsen and named after the seven-year-old son of Jan Gunnar Furuly who caught two grilse with this fly on the river Anarjohka within fifteen minutes. Since then it has also taken fish on the Karasjohka and Steindalselva.

Marius - Larsen

We described earlier how blue flies have been very popular in Iceland for many years, but so far we have seen comparatively few blue flies for use in Norway or Sweden. The next pattern is a blue Templedog from Sweden's Thomas Urbig. The fly was first tied on a short 12mm (0.5") brass tube so that it sank quickly in high spring water conditions. Since then it has also been tied on aluminium and plastic tubes for use in more moderate flows. For low water summer fishing, the wing is also tied shorter.

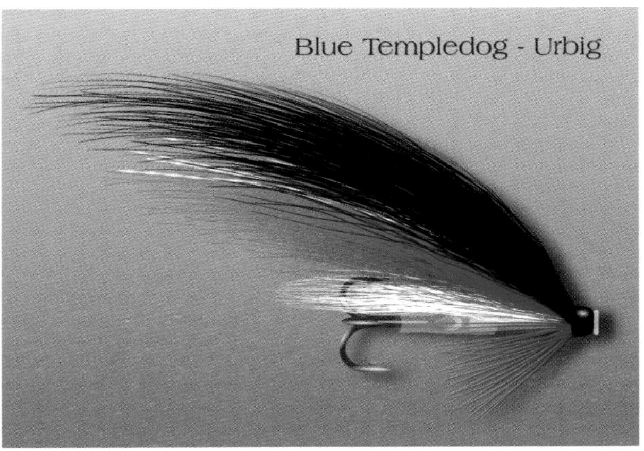

Blue Templedog - Urbig

The next fly is also tied in the Templedog style, this time from Martin Jorgensen. The body is a 38mm (1.5") tube wound with silver tinsel over which is tied an underwing of white Polar bear hair. This stiffer hair is used to give support to the sparsely tied overwings of yellow under orange Icelandic sheep hair. Six strands of peacock herl are tied over the wing to give a strong, dark line at the back of the fly.

Yellow & Orange Templedog - Jorgensen

The Aurora Borealis Blue is an unusual fly from Petru Dima. The body consists of eight strands of blue floss woven together with eight strands of white floss. This technique produces a body which is not only beautiful to look at but which is also very durable because the strands cannot unravel if they are cut by a fish.

Aurora Borealis Blue - Dima

The Green Erling, shown below, also uses the same braiding technique, in this case with eight yellow and eight olive strands of floss. The weaving process is time consuming and some may wonder if it really makes a difference to the fish. It is, however, hard to be critical of what is obviously a labour of love. If a flytyer wishes to lavish time and attention on a special fly for a special fish, then who would disagree with that?

Green Erling - Dima

Nestor Dupo is a professional fly tyer from Sweden who specialises in tube flies, which are sold to customers all over the world.

The first pattern shown below is called the Gold Sheep because of the fluorescent yellow overwing of sheep's hair. The throat hackle is of Marabou and, as can be seen, it is tied very full, approaching a secondary wing, to give maximum mobility in the water. Because of the masking effect of this hackle, the body is tied very simply with gold Mylar tinsel although a few turns of oval gold tinsel may be used simply to add some strength.

Gold Sheep
- Dupo

The Durham Ranger Tube is a fatback version of the famous classic salmon fly of that name. The wing combines orange and black Arctic fox with strands of peacock herl over to give a strong back line. The body elements are those of the traditional dressing.

Durham Ranger
- Dupo

North American Hairwings

If Europe and Great Britain in particular was the home of the classic built wing salmon fly, then North America can rightly be considered to be the home of the hairwing fly. This is not a view based on any claim that the very first use of hair for winging salmon flies was made in North America, but rather on the assertion that it was in North America that hairwings were developed into the effective and widely used patterns that dominate the world game angling scene today.

As we have seen in the chapter on the history of the hairwing fly, the earliest North American patterns were largely hairwing adaptations of the classic British featherwings. It was not long, however, before indigenous patterns began to appear. Details of many of these early patterns such as the Night Hawk, Red Abbey, the Rat and Cosseboom series, together with a wide range of early west coast steelhead patterns can be found in the history chapter, starting on page 5.

The widespread use of hairwing patterns seems to date from the 1930s. It was during this decade that the major innovations and setting of styles seem to have taken place. A notable exception is the Rat series of patterns, the first of which were devised as early as 1911. It seems odd that writers such as Bates appear to have rather ignored the historical precedence of the Rats in the modern history of the hairwing fly and concentrated on the two decades before the Second World War. It is, perhaps, all the more surprising as the Rat series has enjoyed continued popularity and employment to the present day. They must be considered to be amongst the great salmon flies in the history of the sport. Any fly that has been in continuous use for nearly a century and with no sign of imminent retirement, must be something quite special. It should also be noted that new variants of the Rat continue to appear each year.

ATLANTIC SALMON FLIES

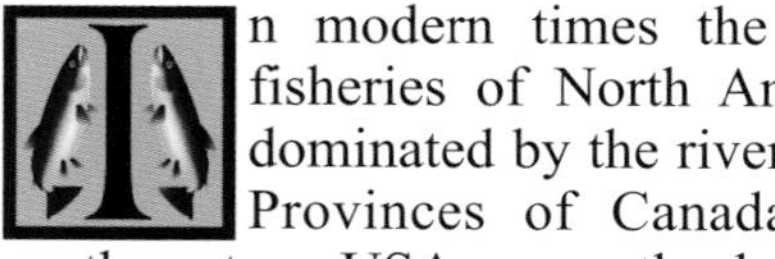

In modern times the Atlantic salmon fisheries of North America have been dominated by the rivers of the Maritime Provinces of Canada. The rivers of north-eastern USA, once the home of enormous runs of fish on rivers such as the Hudson and the vast Penobscot system, remain a shadow of their former selves. On most of them, the Atlantic salmon is still classed as an endangered species. Writing in *Atlantic Salmon Flies & Fishing* (1970), Bates noted that the rivers of Maine were part of an ongoing restoration program which was starting to shown results (the program began in 1948). He expressed the hope that they would soon be returned to the angler with at least some of their former glory. Unfortunately, over thirty years latter, the struggle still continues and if the story shows anything, it shows just how difficult (and expensive) it can be to restore salmon runs to rivers once they have disappeared!

In terms fly patterns, therefore, the emphasis in this section is very much on the rivers of Quebec, New Brunswick, Nova Scotia, Newfoundland and Labrador. Rivers such as the Restigouche, Matepedia, Margaree and Miramichi are familiar to salmon anglers throughout the world and have played a pivotal role in the development of the hairwing salmon fly.

As we have seen in the History chapter (see page 10), the Rat series of flies have become modern hairwing classics, despite the fact that they were first devised as early as 1911. These flies were first used on the rivers of New Brunswick and were immediately successful. Bates gives some details of catches for the Restigouche, in Quebec. In the summer of 1965, of 221 fish caught, 159 were taken on flies from the Rat series. The Rusty Rat accounted for 64, the Silver Rat for 56 and the Black Rat for 34 – testimony enough to their effectiveness. Curiously enough, Bates, writing in 1970, noted that although the patterns were first developed in New Brunswick, they were much more popular on the rivers of Quebec, such as the Restigouche, and were rarely used on the Miramichi.

The first four flies in the series are shown on page 10. The flies here are later developments in the same series. Firstly we have five patterns as given by Bates in 1970 in *Atlantic Salmon Flies & Fishing*. Amongst these is the Rusty Rat. According to Bates, the Rusty Rat was devised by Dr. Orrin Summers. It is probably the best known of the whole series and is still widely used today in almost every salmon angling country. Writing in *The Atlantic Salmon Fly – The Tyers and Their Art*, by Judith Dunham, Warren Duncan tells a very different story to Bates and credits its invention to an angler named Joe Pulitzer and a flytyer, one Clovie Arsenault, who worked in the Restigouche area from the early 1920s. Duncan also mentions Arsenault's contribution to the invention of other flies in the Rat series, mentioned in an article in the winter 1965 *Atlantic Salmon Journal*. It is possible that Bates omitted to mention the part played by Arsenault after getting a very dusty reception once when visiting Arsenault's shop to obtain fly patterns for *Atlantic Salmon Flies & Fishing*. Apparently, Arsenault was very gruff and not the easiest person to get along with! Be that as it may, it is a pity that almost nothing has been recorded about Arsenault's life as a flytyer throughout one of the most interesting periods of development on one Canada's leading salmon rivers.

On of the earliest patterns in the series is the Copper Rat, devised by Herbert L. Howard in November 1911. The body is of flat copper tinsel, a material that is not often used – primarily, I believe, because it is not always easy to obtain.

The Black, Red and Brown Rats are the simplest patterns in the series and are all very similar with a one-piece body of dubbed seal's fur of the appropriate colour. The split body – with a front section of peacock herl – is missing on all three of these flies. It is, however, a feature which has become very much associated with the Rat series.

The King Rat is not found in Bates but is given by Fulsher & Krom in *Hairwing Atlantic Salmon Flies*, published in 1981. The King Rat is a combination pattern containing elements of the Rusty and Silver Rats.

The Blue Rat was devised by Poul Jorgensen for Bates to use in Iceland and is shown on page 66. Although this fly is primarily known for its use in Iceland, Keith Fulsher has commented on his own partiality to a bit of blue in salmon flies and stated that the Blue Rat has proved very effective for him in Newfoundland.

PLATE 14: Rat Series Variants

The style of the Rat series with the sloping hairwing and a collar hackle wound in front of the wing remains very influential and has become one of the distinguishing features of east coast hairwings. Rat variants continue to be devised and the following group of flies fall into this category.

Reed's Green and Orange Rats are variants of the Rusty Rat, created by John Reed of New Brunswick. They have been reliable flies on the Matepedia for many years.

Another green Rat variant is the Fluorescent Green Rat from Rob Solo. First devised as an evolution of a pattern called the Fluorescent Green Stonefly, it has proved to be extremely successful on the west coast rivers of Newfoundland, the Gaspé rivers and is a favourite on the Jupiter river.

Reed's Green Rat

Reed's Orange Rat

Fluorescent Green Rat - Solo

The Black Krystal Rat is one of a series devised in 1993 by Eric Baylis of Dartmouth, Nova Scotia. The other flies in the series include orange, chartreuse and red variants. I like the look of the black version very much. It has a dark silhouette relieved by a small touch of sparkle and should be an ideal pattern for clear water conditions.

Black Krystal Rat - Baylis

The Purple Rat is a fly from Brian Sturrock. It has to be said that it doesn't have all that much in common with the other members of the Rat family. Purple is fairly uncommon among Atlantic salmon flies, although it is much used by the west coast steelheaders. It could be considered a very useful alternative when a dark fly is required and black doesn't seem to be having the desired effect. Theoretically, flies like this should be at their best when there is a degree of back-lighting. They will then produce the required dense silhouette, but with a halo of colour around it to interest the fish.

Purple Rat - Sturrock

The Claret Killer was devised by Bill Baker of Biscay Bay, Newfoundland. It is reckoned to be deadly on the rivers of the southern Avalon Peninsular. From its form and construction it could fairly be classified as a Rat derivative.

Claret Killer - Baker

Probably the second most influential hairwing flies to come out of Canada are the Cosseboom, originally devised by John Cosseboom in 1923. In the History chapter (see page 11), I illustrated the first six of the Cosseboom series. Here are a few more of the great many Cosseboom variants that have been developed since and which are still being widely used.

It's difficult to know when a Cosseboom variant is no longer a Cosseboom. In *Modern Atlantic Salmon Flies*, Paul Marriner inclines to the view that the minimum requirement for a Cosseboom is a wing of grey squirrel and a yellow collar hackle. Unfortunately, under these criteria, at least five of the original six Cossebooms must be disqualified! I take a more relaxed view: it is a Cosseboom variant if the tyer thinks it is or, alternatively, if the fly otherwise has all the elements of a Cosseboom.

Peacock Cosseboom

The Peacock Cosseboom was one of the earliest in the series and the dressing is given both by Bates and Fulsher & Krom. Peacock herl and sword fibres have been very popular over the years. They have such an attractive iridescent sheen that many flytyers and anglers are convinced that salmon and steelhead must also find the material attractive. Whether or not this is true is probably a moot point. If an angler has confidence in a pattern he will fish it with confidence and it will most likely be effective. It should be noted that the Peacock Cosseboom is atypical – most obviously in its lack of a proper collar hackle.

The Miramichi Cosseboom is a stylistic variation of the original Cosseboom that has a body of fluoresent green floss rather than the light olive of the original. Paul Marriner rates this fly very highly and says it's one pattern he'd never want to be without.

Cosseboom - Miramichi Style

The Silver Cosseboom is another popular variant, which is extremely effective on the rivers of the Bay St. George area. Paul Marriner lists a very similar fly called the Capelin Body Cosseboom, which is basically the same fly but with a deeper body of silver Mylar tubing, giving a baitfish like appearance.

Silver Cosseboom

Winston's Green Cosseboom

Green Butt, Black Cosseboom

Krystal Cosseboom

Fluorescent Green Cosseboom

Hair Hackle Black Cosseboom

PLATE 15: Modern Cosseboom Variants

The next five flies, shown in Plate 15, are all to be found in Paul Marriner's *Modern Atlantic Salmon Flies*. They are all comparatively recent inventions and show an interesting range of variations for different uses.

The Fluorescent Green Cosseboom is a variant from Earl Roberts, of Newfoundland, recommended as extremely effective for all western Newfoundland rivers. A very similar fly, from Marc Madore, is regarded as being more effective than the standard Cosseboom for the Miramichi when it becomes coloured after rain. Considering the general popularity of fluoresent green flies on many of the Canadian rivers, it is not surprising that a Cosseboom is one of the best.

The Black Bear, Green Butt is one of the signature patterns of the Canadian east coast and has proved to be consistently successful over the years. It was only a matter of time, therefore, before some enterprising flytyer came up with the idea of tying a Cosseboom with the same colour scheme. The Green Butt, Black Cosseboom, devised by Daryl Burry, has been used with success on rivers all over Newfoundland and Labrador.

Another green Cosseboom variant is named Winston's Green Cosseboom, after Winston Farthing who devised it in 1988. Regularly used throughout Newfoundland, it is a steady producer throughout the season and is particularly well regarded for the lower Humber. The body is of light green Phentex yarn which has a blueish tinge to it and which is noticeably different in colour from the fluorescent green used on other similar flies.

The Hair Hackle Black Cosseboom is a fly devised by Rob Solo in 1985. It has a hackle of spun deer hair at the front, rather than feather. By varying the amount of deer hair used, the depth at which the fly fishes can be regulated. The deer hair does not darken when wet like a feather hackle, so it retains its brightness and makes the fly particularly effective in low-light conditions. Any fly that can take a thirty-eight pounder from the Humber must be taken seriously. It has also been used with great success on many other rivers in Newfoundland, Labrador and Nova Scotia as well, taking fish on both the Miramichi and Restigouche. Definitely one to have in your fly box.

Another Rob Solo fly, the Krystal Cosseboom, is a green-based fly which was devised for the Bay St. George rivers in the early season. The front collar is of hen rather than cock hackle and is well swept back. This, together with the sparse wing, provides minimum water resistance and a pulsating action.

Warren Duncan is one of the best known of the modern generation of Canadian flytyers and is highly regarded throughout the world for his hairwing flies. I have had the pleasure of seeing him work on one of his visits to the UK for a Partridge fly tying day. He is a magician with hair and ties incredibly quickly. He says that he ties flies for durability and use, not as perfect flies to be photographed. They still look incredibly good to me! The following Cosseboom is tied in typical Duncan style, with a short body. The head is of fluorescent red head cement and the body and tail are of dark green floss.

Cosseboom - Duncan

In the History chapter we have already noted the widespread use of the Butt family of flies, the most famous of which is the Black Bear, Green Butt. The fly illustrated was tied by Gerry Doak, the son of Wally Doak. Their flytying business in Doaktown, near the Miramichi, has been an institution among anglers for many years and thus the style of this fly is absolutely typical of that used by hundreds of anglers on the Miramichi today.

Black Bear, Green Butt - Doak

The next fly is the same pattern as tied by Warren Duncan. Apart from it lacking a tail, the tying recipe is identical, which just goes to show how personal style can make a major difference to a standard pattern.

Black Bear, Green Butt - Duncan

The close, tight turns of tinsel and tapered cigar shaped bodies are typical of both these flies and seem to be the standard on many flies from Canada.

The standard variants of this fly are the Red, Orange, Blue and Yellow Butts. In each case the butt is replaced by floss of the appropriate colour (usually fluorescent) – the tying otherwise remains identical. Fulsher & Krom give the ribbing for all these flies as gold rather than silver tinsel. All the modern tyings that I have seen have silver. If Paul Marriner is correct and the Black Bomber or Black Spider are the antecedents, then a silver rib is correct. The Conrad series of flies, which are almost identical, do indeed have a tag and rib of silver tinsel. This series of flies, more of a marketing exercise than a real development of a fly pattern, have, in the meantime, been subsumed into the Butt series anyway.

One of the most highly regarded variants of the Black Bear, is the Black Bear, Brown Hackle. This fly has been around since the 1960s, but news of its effectiveness was kept quiet for a long time by those in the know. Tied in size six or smaller, it is extremely effective in low, clear water conditions. This is another of those flies that seem to crop up all over the world that look pretty non-descript in the hand but are real killers in the water.

Black Bear, Brown Hackle

If the black wing hair of the Butt series of flies is replaced with red squirrel tail hair, the flies become the Squirrel Tail, Red Butt, etc. The original fly in the Squirrel series – known simply as the Squirrel Tail, or Red Squirrel – lacked the butt of fluorescent floss and had a tail of red dyed hackle fibres. The original tying is shown below.

Squirrel Tail

A modern version of the Squirrel Tail, from Warren Duncan, is shown below. The tail of red hackle fibres has been replaced by a butt of fluorescent red floss. The wing is of pine squirrel tail and the throat hackle is fiery brown. For other flies in the series, the butt is simply made of fluorescent floss in the appropriate colour.

Squirrel Tail - Duncan

The Fulkro is a fly developed jointly by Keith Fulsher and Charlie Krom (hence the name) for use on the Miramichi. It combines elements of both of the above flies. Tied very sparsely, on a size 8 low-water hook or smaller, this is an extremely effective low-water fly. Charlie Krom has commented that he and Keith Fulsher, when fishing the Miramichi at Doaktown, would often catch their limit on this fly, in the morning just before the sun came up. Although it is no longer commonly used, it shows very clearly that a fly does not have to be large and heavily dressed to be effective.

Fulkro - Fulsher & Krom

Another fly, closely related to the Squirrel Tail series, is the Mill Pool Special. This fly is of interest because it has both a tag and butt of fluorescent floss, in this case green and red respectively.

Mill Pool Special

The Undertaker is a fly that Warren Duncan devised in 1979. In general terms it is very similar to the Mill Pool Special in that it also uses green and red fluorescent floss, in this case as a double tag. The body of peacock herl is different, but the overall effect is not dissimilar. The Undertaker is shown in *Hair-Wing Atlantic Salmon Flies*, by Fulsher & Krom, but in the example they show the double tag is tied very small compared to the bulky body and does not a have great visual impact. The example illustrated here is as tied by Warren Duncan himself and shows the style in which he ties it today. The Undertaker remains extremely popular and has become one of the standard patterns for the Miramichi.

Undertaker - Duncan

The use of a two-coloured butt would seem to have a lot to recommend it. It certainly makes the choice of fly much easier if one is not certain whether it is going to be a 'green' day or a 'red' one.

In the introduction to this section I mentioned the ongoing struggle to restore salmon runs to the rivers of the north-eastern USA. There is no great tradition of salmon fly patterns from this area if one disregards the streamer flies developed for the land-locked salmon of Maine. Nevertheless, there are some patterns that are worth mentioning for historical reasons if for no other. The next two patterns are listed by Bates in *The Art of the Atlantic Salmon Fly* and also by Fulsher & Krom.

The Wringer is a pattern that originated on the Penobscot river in the 1960s. The yellow tag, black body and blue throat hackle are found on many of other salmon flies. Less usual is the wing of yellow dyed squirrel hair over red dyed squirrel hair.

Wringer

I have looked through my pattern lists and, to my surprise, have not found this combination of colours elsewhere. Be that as it may, there is no doubt that this fly has all the ingredients to be successful on a wide range of rivers.

The Coburn or Colburn (Bates disagrees with Fulsher & Krom on the spelling) also originates from the Penobscot and forms one of a series of flies. The one illustrated is the original Colburn or Colburn Special.

Colburn Special

The other three flies in the series are the Blue, Claret (or Red) and Orange Colburns. In each case, the body colour, tail and winging are of the nominated colour. In the tying recipe for the Colburn, Bates gives the wing as green dyed grey squirrel under an equal amount of red dyed grey squirrel, Fulsher & Krom give black over green.

Allen's L.T. - Budgell

Allen's L.T. is a comparatively new pattern from the USA which was first publicized in 1998. It was devised by Lester Budgell and has had success on several rivers in Burlington and, tied in small sizes has also been effective on the Penobscot River in Maine, USA. The winging is of moose hair which is certainly not common for a normal hairwing fly, although very sparsely winged, low-water style flies using this material are to be found in Newfoundland.

Lady Amherst - Hairwing

The Lady Amherst is of great interest because it is a rarity – an original North American classical featherwing, very much in line with the Ranger series of flies, but which uses Amherst pheasant tippets instead of those from the golden pheasant. Originally designed by George Bonbright, in 1925, it is now rarely used in its original form. The fly shown below is a hairwing conversion, as given by Buckland & Oglesby. The hairwing version retains the overall colour scheme of the original, but the high, flat wing structure of the featherwing is completely lost.

The Grizzly King has been around since the 1930s and has appeared in several forms over the years. It is one of the few North American patterns that has a long history both on the east coast, for salmon, and on the west coast, for steelhead. The original wing of grey mallard slips has been replaced by grey squirrel tail and the dark green wool body is often replaced by fluorescent green wool or floss in modern versions. The tail can vary from red-dyed hackle fibres, red fox squirrel fibres to red-dyed topping, as in the second version shown below. Bates notes that this pattern is particularly popular in the Restigouche area.

Grizzly King - Original

Grizzly King - Modern variant

PLATE 16: Butterfly Variants

We have elsewhere noted that claret is a colour that is not often used for salmon flies, but one which is very much underrated. Although never as popular as the bright reds and oranges there has, nevertheless, been a steady trickle of claret coloured flies over the years. Many of these claret coloured flies seem to have been deadly effective for their inventors, but for some reason have never gained widespread acclaim.

Claret & Grizzly

The Irish seem to have cottoned on to just how effective claret can be, particularly late in the season, and they also have a great predilection for grizzly or badger hackles. The Claret & Grizzly, shown above, combines both. It could easily be an Irish fly, although in fact it originates from the Matepedia river. For details of other claret flies, see page 49 in the European chapter and also the Claret Killer on page 87.

A more unusual type of fly is the Butterfly, devised by Maurice Ingalls in 1956. The trademark of this fly is the set of the two wings, which are divided and set slightly upwards but spread outwards, at an angle of about 45º. The Butterfly is popular on all the eastern Canadian rivers, but is particularly favoured on the Miramichi. The spread of the wings, in conjunction with movement imparted by action of the rod tip, make this fly swim in an unusual manner: the wings pulsating or breathing as it is fished. The original tying is still often used but, as with all successful flies, a number of variants have developed. One of the most common variations of all flies in eastern Canada is the addition of the ubiquitous fluorescent green or yellow butt. The Butterfly has not escaped this treatment and the fly shown on the right of plate 16 above was featured in the summer 1995 issue of *Fly Tyer* magazine, tied by Warren Duncan.

The Butterfly Green Machine, pictured in the centre of the plate, is a combination of the Butterfly with the colours of the Green Machine, which was devised by Frank Somer. Combinations of two successful flies are not always guaranteed to work but this one certainly does. It is considered by many anglers to be absolutely deadly on the Miramichi.

The Silver Down-Easter is another early hairwing fly, which is attributed to Bert Miner of Doaktown. Bates holds that this fly is a derivative of Miner's earlier Blackville featherwing fly, which dates back to before 1950. Despite its long history, the fly is still in use today and is effective on the Margaree, LaHave and St. Mary's rivers, in Nova Scotia, as well as being used successfully for steelhead in British Columbia.

Silver Down-Easter - Miner

The Orange Blossom is another fly that has been around for a long time but is still used today. The fly originated with Carmelle Bigaoutte who had a fly dressing shop next to the Restigouche Hotel in Matepedia, Quebec. It has a reputation for being at its best in spring when the rivers are running high and dirty and in such circumstances can be tied as large as size 1. With a wing of woodchuck guard hairs, the Orange Blossom is also used on the west coast for steelhead fishing, especially in early spring and winter.

Orange Blossom - Bigaoutte

The Golden Fox is a pattern recommended by guide Bryant Freeman as being particularly useful when the water is tannin coloured, or cloudy with suspended silt after heavy rain. This fly is not particularly gaudy like some patterns used in these conditions. Nevertheless, the combination of gold and golden olive presents a shining image, heightened by the tail of barred wood duck.

Golden Fox

The following fly is a variant of the Icelandic Laxa Blue. The fly has been changed with the addition of a red butt to the rear of a body made of ice blue floss, instead of silver tinsel. In keeping with the Canadian style, the throat hackle has been moved in front of the wing and tied as a full collar. There aren't that many light blue flies around, but this pretty little example has the looks to suggest that it would be a good fly for fresh run grilse in the summer, much in the same vein as the Bourrach is used on the River Spey in Scotland.

Laxa Blue - Variant

Although blue has never been the most common colour for salmon flies there has,

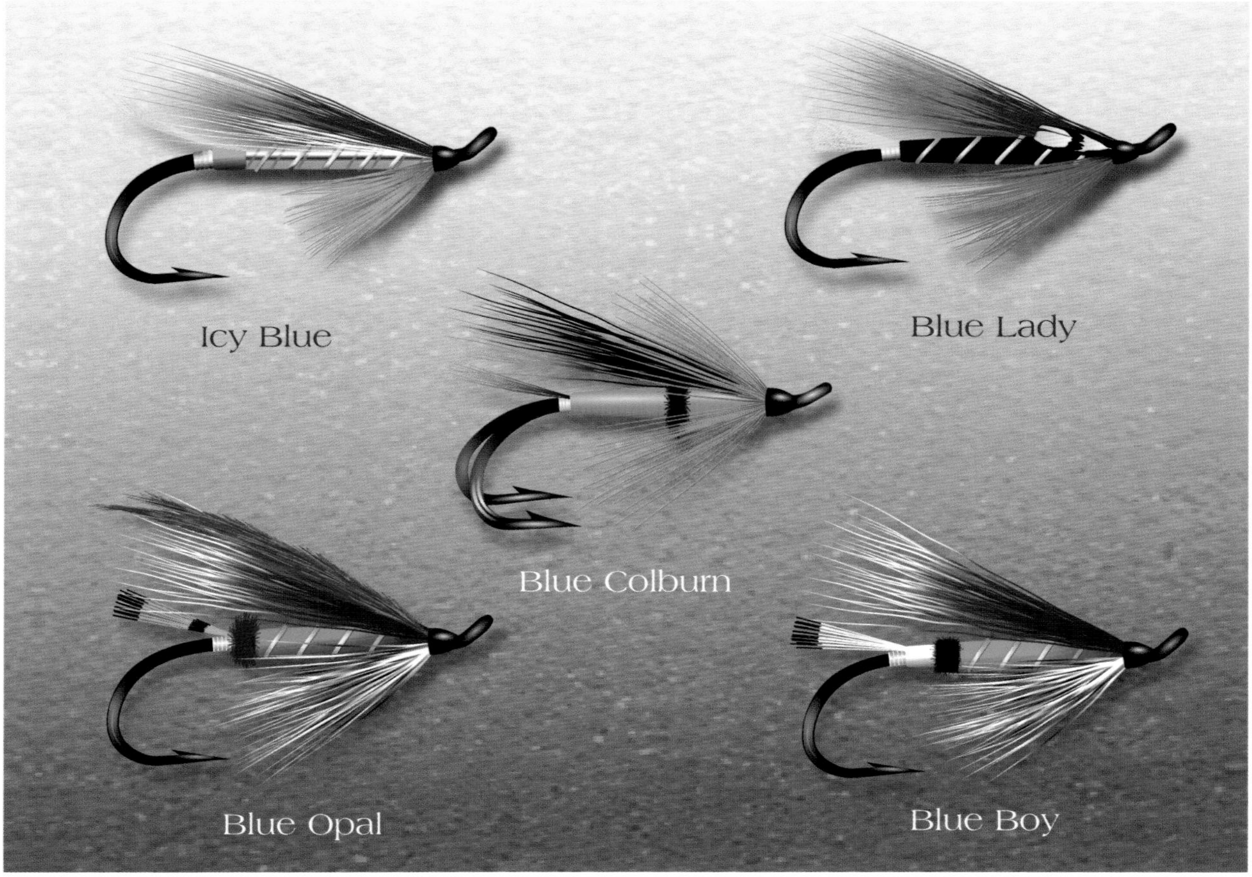

Icy Blue

Blue Lady

Blue Colburn

Blue Opal

Blue Boy

PLATE 17: Variations On a Blue Theme

nevertheless, been a steady trickle of blue flies over the years which have held their own under the right conditions. Blue flies always seem to have had a reputation as good takers of fresh run fish and are also highly rated for summer conditions with blue skies and low water. The classic example of the breed is the Blue Doctor which, in its hairwing form, continues to be widely used.

One reason that blue may be so effective in clear water conditions is the fact that although it is bright and has sparkle, particularly when combined with silver, it does not have the garish impact of hot or fluorescent orange. These colours are possibly just too much in clear water and may frighten fish away rather than attract them. Blue, on the other hand, blends in with the sky and water colours that fish are accustomed to seeing in the marine environment.

The following flies are older patterns which are no longer commonly used, perhaps because modern anglers are no longer aware of them, rather than that they are not effective. It is a great mistake to believe that because a fly pattern is no longer used it no longer works. The Icy Blue, Blue Lady, Blue Opal, Blue Colburn and Blue Boy all belong to this category, most of them dating back to the 1950s. I can see no reason why they should not be used today. With these flies available, there would seem little purpose in devising new blue patterns. There are variations for all tastes here: one fly has a silver tinsel body, three have blue floss bodies and one has black.

Other blue flies of interest include the Blue Rat (see page 66), the Blue Reynard (see page 98), the Blue Charm and Blue Doctor (see page 19) and the Laxa Blue, Silver Blue and Thvera Blue from Iceland (see page 66).

PLATE 18: Copper Killers

Copper is another colour which is not used on many flies, despite the fact that several of the most successful patterns used over the last thirty or forty years are predominantly copper. The Copper Rat is a good example. Dating back to 1911, it was one of the earliest Rats. It is still very effective and still in use (see page 85). As mentioned before, I believe that the reason that copper has not been more often used has been to do with availability of material, rather than choice. In the past, copper tinsels have always been much harder to obtain than either silver or gold. The naming of the Pot Scrubber, shown opposite, illustrates the point. It has a body of copper tinsel that came from a kitchen pot scrubber, bought from a hardware store. Even with the advent of modern synthetic materials, the difficulty continues. Most fly-tying catalogues list a wide range of round, oval and flat tinsels in silver and gold, but only a few will offer copper, and then in a greatly reduced range of sizes and types (normally only flat Mylar and copper wire).

Copper may have advantages over gold and silver-bodied flies in clear water conditions, probably for the same reasons that blue does. It has a more subdued, subtle gleam than either silver of gold and thus presents a less threatening image to the fish whilst still maintaining enough flash to attract attention.

A long-standing favourite in eastern Canada is the Copper Killer, which was devised in the Cains River area of New Brunswick. The fly dates back to perhaps the 1940s. Despite its long history, it is still used regularly and features on the current pattern lists of such tyers as Warren Duncan, Jerry Doak and Charlie Krom. I have illustrated examples of this fly tied by each of the above tyers, as well as the version which, according to Bates, was the original one, given to him by Bert Miner. They all retain the same basic appearance, but there are differences in the materials used.

The Cains Copper is another fly that originated on the Cains River. It was originally dressed as a long-winged 'bucktail'. It has a black collar hackle, in the classic eastern style, and is a good darker alternative to the Copper Killer, to which it is most probably related. This is a handsome looking fly and, although it has rather fallen out of fashion in recent years, it has all the attributes to make it a successful fly under a wide range of conditions.

Cains Copper

The Pot Scrubber is copper-bodied pattern that originated in Scotland in 1961. Bates names the originator as John McKenzie, a gillie on the River Conon. The pattern is also listed by Fulsher & Krom. A slightly unusual feature is the combination of silver tinsel with the copper body.

Pot Scrubber - McKenzie

The Tarnished Silver has a combination body of both copper and silver tinsel, which is ribbed with oval gold tinsel. The throat hackle is black and the wing is of red squirrel. This combination would seem to cover all possibilities for those who like to hedge their bets. In fairness, the combination of tinsel colours produces a very attractive pattern that has been around for a long time and continues to be effective.

Tarnished Silver

Many of the foregoing flies are listed in *A Guide to Salmon Flies*, by Buckland & Oglesby where, without exception, the illustrations show flies that are very sparsely winged and hackled. The illustrations shown here have been taken from current tyings and are much more fully dressed. In *Modern Atlantic Salmon Flies*, Paul Marriner also notes a recent trend for much more fully dressed collar and throat hackles with the avowed intent of producing an intense colour signature at the head of the fly.

The next three flies are more recent inventions on the copper-bodied theme. The Moose Bogan is an André Belaïeff pattern, named after the pool on the Dartmouth River where it has had considerable success. The fly is very simple in construction: there is no tail or hackle, just a ribbed copper body; a wing of green dyed squirrel tail and a collar of fluorescent green chenille. Its creator says that the fly works in all kinds of water and as it has taken fish up to 28lb. It certainly seems to have something going for it.

Moose Bogan - Belaïeff

The River Philip Copper is a pattern of uncertain origin, which is named after the River Philip where it is very productive. Although it is

Blue Reynard

Yellow Reynard

Black Reynard

Green Reynard

Orange Reynard

PLATE 19: Reynard Series - Keith Fulsher

not widely known outside the Philip River area, its combination of red, orange and copper gives it the look of an effective end-of-season pattern. The tying is again very simple: a body of copper Diamond Braid; throat of red calf tail and a wing of orange bucktail over copper Krystal Flash.

River Philip Copper

L.T. Special - Tracy

The LT Special is named after its creator, Larry Tracy, of Saint John, New Brunswick, who guides on the Miramichi. This fly has been consistently successful since its introduction, particularly in autumn and is now widely carried by fly shops. The colour combination of a copper body, with orange and green wing, together with red and yellow hackling is not one that would immediately spring to mind when designing a new pattern. Perhaps this unusual combination helps explain its success?

Keith Fulsher is very partial to flies with a strong blue content. Jorgensen's Blue Rat is one of his favourite flies for Newfoundland. When Fulsher himself devised a new series of hairwing flies in the late 1980s, it was not surprising that he started with a blue-hackled variant. The Reynard series (shown in Plate 19) uses the guard hair from the back of the red fox. This hair is rather unusual in having dark roots that shade to a cream coloured centre and finish with fiery brown tips. It was while working on the pattern index for *Hairwing Atlantic Salmon Flies* that Fulsher noticed a dearth of patterns winged with red fox and prompted him to look further. It seems very odd that this material is so rarely used as it is not hard to come by and one only has to look at the flies to see the brilliant effect which the winging produces. Following the success of the Blue Reynard, the series was expanded to take in black, green, yellow and orange versions. Fulsher prefers flies with tinsel or black bodies. All the flies in the series have bodies of gold or silver tinsel except the black variant.

The following gold-bodied fly, the Gold Fever, is illustrated from an example tied by Charlie Krom, co-author of *Hairwing Atlantic Salmon Flies*. Strictly speaking, it could be called a variant as the body consists of gold Mylar tubing rather than the embossed gold tinsel specified in the original. Several flies tied by Charlie Krom are illustrated in *The Atlantic Salmon Fly, The Tyers and Their Art*, by Judith Dunham and all of them

Gold Fever Variant - Krom

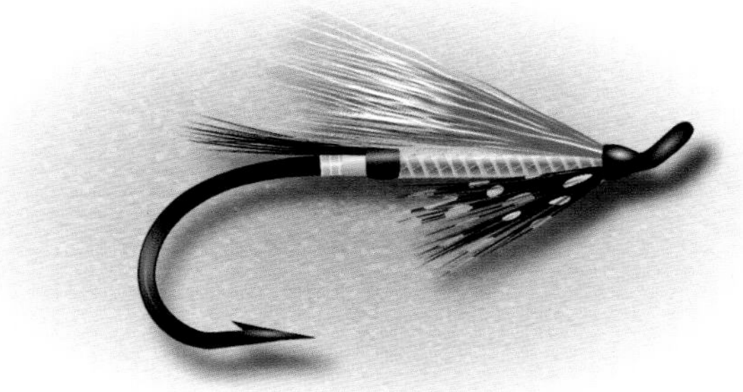

feature unribbed bodies of braided Mylar tubing, rather than tinsel. It has to be said that they look very good in this guise (see also Copper Killer, page 96). Charlie Krom is a great admirer of the work of Charlie DeFeo, who preferred sparsely dressed flies. As can be seen, the Gold Fever illustrated is tied short and sparse in typical low water fashion.

Another feature of many of Krom's flies is his use of teased out strands of fluorescent floss as an underwing, which he believes produces a glittering iridescence most attractive to salmon. The Silver Monkey is an example of a DeFeo fly tied in this fashion. Krom has modified the pattern by again using a braided Mylar tube body and by adding a fluorescent red tip. The end effect is a sleek, streamlined fly, which has a subdued glitter and a bright target spot.

Silver Monkey Variant - Krom

Following the trend towards full collars noted by Paul Marriner (see page 97), the Hairwing Neptune, which is listed in *Modern Atlantic Salmon Flies*, has a very full and long collar of Guinea fowl. This is a feature that has also been adopted with success for steelhead flies by many of the west coast flytyers. The original pattern came from Yvon Gendon of Neptune Flies and had a wing of black turkey feathers. According to Peter Farago, who devised this variant, the hairwing version is one of the best flies that he has ever fished and was responsible for a catch of 110 salmon in six days on the Moisie River. Any fly that can produce a catch like that, whatever the circumstances, deserves to be taken very seriously indeed. Black and silver has always been an effective combination, but the Guinea fowl hackle seems to make all the difference here.

Hairwing Neptune - Farago

Nipisiguit Grey

Grey-bodied flies have always been rare, even from the earliest days, but the few that do exist have stood the test of time. The classic grey bodied fly is the Lemon & Grey (or Lemon Grey) which seems to have originated in Ireland around 1830 (a hairwing version is shown on page 43). The Lemon Yellow seems to be no more than a variant of the Lemon Grey and differs only in small details. The Lemon Grey was generally considered to be one of the very best flies for use on Irish rivers and was also recommended for use in Scotland. It is listed in books by Kelson, Hale, Hardy, Maxwell, Hodgson and Pryce-Tannatt. With such a general endorsement, it is surprising that there is not a whole family of grey-bodied flies. Whatever the reason, the number of grey-bodied flies has always been limited. The few that do exist, however, have proved their worth over the years. Most commentators seem to agree that these grey-bodied patterns are at their best on overcast days.

The following fly is a hairwing version of the Lemon Grey as given by Fulsher & Krom.

Lemon Grey Hairwing

The Nipisiguit Grey in its original featherwing form dates back to 1927 and was for many years the most popular fly on the Nipisiguit River. The hairwing version, shown below, uses brown hair to replace the mallard wings of the original. Fulsher & Krom quote black hair winging rather than brown and replace the silver tinsel with gold. They also note that the grizzle throat hackle may be replaced with black. If both the wing and throat are made black, then the fly produced looks so different to the original that it can hardly be called by the same name.

Down East

Downeaster

The Down East and Downeaster are two patterns which are also closely connected with the

Silver Down-Easter, devised by Bert Miner (see page 94). According to Bates, these three, plus the Orange Blossom and the Cains River are all related to and derived from an earlier Miner pattern – the Blackville.

Texas Jack is another grey-bodied pattern from Fulsher & Krom. This is a much more subdued pattern, with a body of well picked out seal's fur and a throat hackle of natural Guinea fowl. The only bright spot is provided by a tip of fluorescent red floss. If the old saying of 'dull day – dull fly' has any truth, then this is surely a fly for overcast days.

Texas Jack

The Whalin Galen is also listed by Fulsher & Krom and is a much brighter affair altogether. The silver ribbed body of grey rabbit's fur is combined with a blue throat hackle, a grey squirrel tail wing and, most unusually, a yellow head. This has much more the look of a summer fly than any of the previous offerings and could possibly be a good, less flashy alternative to flies such as the Silver Blue or Icy Blue. The curious name probably arose from a rather forced effort at alliteration!

Whalin Galen

The next three flies are both classic and current: old patterns that remain effective and which are still widely used. All of these patterns are to be found in *Modern Atlantic Salmon Flies*, by Paul Marriner, an excellent book which concentrates on the salmon flies of the eastern provinces of Canada.

The Royal Charm was devised by Peter Farago in 1979 and is a variant of the Blue Charm. Although it is not widely known, it has proved to be consistently successful since its inception. The body colour has been changed to royal blue; a fluorescent green tip has been added, and also an underwing of golden pheasant tippet. None of these changes are dramatic, but the overall effect has been to give new life to a good old standard.

Royal Charm - Farago

Knowing the predilection of fishermen in Canada's Maritime Provinces for patterns featuring yellow and green, it comes as no surprise to see many variants of that famous old classic, the Green Highlander. Of the many Green Highlander variants that have appeared, the two flies shown below are in regular current use.

Ed's Highlander was devised by Ed Myers who owns, appropriately enough, the Green Highlander Fly Shop in Dartmouth, Nova Scotia. Its colours, particularly in the winging, have been slightly revised to make it more appealing to autumn salmon and it has been effective on many east coast rivers. The combination of yellow and red with green is similar to the LT Special (see page 98), which is also very effective in the autumn.

Ed's Highlander - Myers

The next version is a fairly standard conversion from the featherwing original. The fly, as shown by Paul Marriner, has summer duck added to the tail, an ostrich herl butt, a body hackle over the green part of the body, jungle cock sides and Indian crow cheeks. It is suggested that the rarer feathers are optional on flies that are actually used for fishing. I have, therefore, shown the fly in this more practical form: omitting the summer duck, butt, body hackle and Indian crow. The underwing of golden pheasant tippets and the jungle cock cheeks, whilst certainly not compulsory, seem worth retaining.

Green Highlander Hairwing

Following on with the yellow and green theme, this next fly incorporates a black body. The Influence was devised in the late 1980s by Richard Lauzon, a professional guide and flytyer from Pincourt, Quebec. It has proved to be very effective on the Ste. Marguerite, York, Dartmouth and other Quebec rivers, particularly when fished in the early morning or evening.

Influence - Lauzon

The name of Lee Wulff is synonymous with hairwing flies for salmon and in particular with dry flies. Wulff did not always fish dry flies, however, and wet versions of the Black and Grey Wulffs were quite commonly used.

Tied as a wet fly, the Black Wulff has been used with considerable success in Newfoundland.

Black Wulff Wet - Wulff

The Haggis was devised by Wulff in 1962 for use on the river Dee in Scotland and later became one of his favourite dark flies. The Haggis is tied both with and without an underwing of a few strands of extra long black bucktail. These strands are intended to provide extra flotation when the fly is fished with a riffling hitch. The throat hackle consists of the fluffy fibres found at the base of the feather. Fulsher & Krom also list this pattern, but without the golden pheasant topping.

A golden pheasant topping over a hairwing is something that is rarely used by modern tyers. The fact that one of the great proponents of hairwings felt it worthwhile to retain this feature on many of his own salmon flies should give cause for thought. Perhaps not all of the adornments of yesteryear were excessive? The GP topping may actually serve a real purpose other than mere decoration.

Haggis - Wulff

The Lady Joan was derived by Wulff from the Orange Fish Hawk trout fly. The fly has a burnt orange body, which is very tightly ribbed – one of Wulff's trademarks. Note again the inclusion of the topping over the wing.

Lady Joan - Wulff

Cullman's Choice - Wulff

Cullman's Choice was originally called the Silver Birch but was later renamed after a friend of Wulff. The body is of apple green floss but the throat hackle is white rather than the ubiquitous yellow.

The next flies are some of the very few white patterns around. There has always been a minority of anglers who consider white flies to be effective, particularly in fading light in the evening. In Scotland, the river Tweed has had a long history of flies that have a substantial white component (see Whitewing, page 32). White flies, nevertheless, remain a minority interest.

The Torrent River Special was derived from Lee Wulff's White Wulff and invented by Len Rich. It is named after the river in Newfoundland where it gained its first success. It is effective throughout the season and seems to be particularly good in bright, sunny conditions.

Torrent River Special - Rich

The Priest has been around for much longer and was devised by the Rev. Elmer Smith of Doaktown, New Brunswick. He found that it was a killing pattern for cold water pools and was also effective in slow water if extra movement was imparted. Rev. Smith also recommended it as a good autumn pattern.

Priest - Smith

Although less popular than they once were, streamer patterns are still highly regarded by a minority of anglers, particularly in the larger sizes for spring fishing. Bernie's Comet was devised by Danny Ripley in 1997 and was listed by Paul Marriner in *Modern Atlantic Salmon Flies*. A combination of white, blue and silver is not uncommon for salt water baitfish patterns, such as the Coho Blue used on the west coast for Pacific salmon, but the use of such a fly on the east coast for Atlantic salmon is much less common. This pattern has proved to be extremely effective and took five salmon on its first outing.

Bernie's Comet - Ripley

One of the objections to streamers has always been that – when tied on large, long shank hooks – they are susceptible to a great deal of leverage which may in turn lead to the loss of fish. Long shank hooks are by no means compulsory for streamer type flies. John Buckland has gone the other way and ties extremely long flies on short doubles and trebles to produce his Sandeel imitations (see page 62).

Roger's Fancy was designed in the early 1970s by Shirley Woods, author of *Angling for Atlantic Salmon*. It was named for his fishing companion Major-General Roger Rowley. Although it is not new it is still regularly used, not only in Canada but also in Iceland. Many experienced anglers believe that certain colours of fly are particularly suited to certain rivers. Woods's view was that the Sainte Anne was very much a 'green' river. Poul Jorgensen considered it worthwhile to include it in his list of hairwing patterns in *Salmon Flies, Their Character, Style and Dressing*. Jungle cock or barred wood duck cheeks are specified as optional.

Roger's Fancy - Woods

The Green Thing could be referred to as a poor man's Green Highlander. Although the origin of the fly is not certain, it seems that it came from the Gaspe coast of Quebec in the late 1980s. The front body of the fly is often tied with a green body hackle over the green dubbing. Pat Orpen, who tied the fly illustrated, prefers instead to pick out the dubbing because he feels that it gives a more 'buggy' look to the fly. The Green Thing has performed well on the Matepedia, Bonaventure and Matane rivers and has also been effective in waters that are stained the colour of tea.

Green Thing

The Phantom is an Eric Baylis pattern, devised in 1992. It has been extremely effective on bright autumn mornings. The front body is of chartreuse Krystal Flash, which is wound like floss. The holographic green tinsel that is now available may be good alternative. Plenty of target points for the fish are provided by the fluorescent orange tag, butt and head. Tied short on a curved shank hook, this is an elegant looking fly.

Phantom - Baylis

In the History section on page 6, mention was made of the early multi-winged flies from Ireland known as 'maned' flies. Flies in which the winging consists of several discrete hair bunches tied along the shank have several advantages over the conventional tying, with just one wing at the front. The multiple wing can consist of a prismatic range of colours which can interact dynamically as the fly moves in the water and which may be more effective in a wider range of water conditions than a single wing. Additionally, the fly has a Matuka-like keel structure which helps maintain shape and stability in the water. Lastly, the head can be kept extremely small as only the final bunch of hair needs to be covered. It should be obvious that, with minor adaptations, this construction could be applied to almost any hairwing fly if so desired. The following flies are patterns devised by Albert Charest, of Quebec, which use this idea. Others may be found on page 42 and page 117.

Charest Special - Charest

The Charest Special is recommended as an all-season, all round pattern. The Yo-Yo is at its best in early season, high water conditions.

Yo-Yo - Charest

The Garry Dog is a Scottish pattern with a long history. It is used all over the world and Canada is no exception. The next two flies are Garry Dog variants. The first uses the multiple winging technique, just described. In this case, the wing is divided into three bunches of hair: red followed by orange, followed by yellow. The first wing is placed approximately in the middle of the body. The second fly is a variant popular on the Miramichi. In this case, the wing is of mixed red and yellow hair, and the fly has a blue collar hackle, very much in the classic Canadian manner.

Garry Dog - Multi-Wing Variant

Garry Dog - Miramichi Style

The Barnes Special is another typical Canadian fly with predominantly green colouring. It is recommended for clear water conditions and is at its most effective for fresh-run fish.

Barnes Special

John Johnston of Newfoundland developed the next fly, called the Bo Diddley after the great rhythm and blues man. This a bright pattern which would certainly be seen in off-colour water ...perhaps for when your mojo just ain't working with other flies?

Bo Diddley - Johnston

STEELHEAD FLIES

There has been surprisingly little exchange of fly patterns between the West Coast steelhead fisheries of North America and the Atlantic salmon fisheries of Europe and the North American East Coast. This is all the more surprising when one considers that the first flies used for steelhead fishing were largely patterns devised for Atlantic salmon. In the early days, the flow of information was understandably, therefore, very much east to west. What is less understandable is that this bias seems to have continued to the present day. Steelhead flyfishers still pick up and use good ideas and new developments that originate with the salmon fishermen, but salmon fishermen rarely seem to cast their eyes to the west, perhaps to their cost. Whilst I cannot be certain why this is so, I think that there is a basic misunderstanding among salmon fishermen about what steelhead flyfishing involves. There seems to be a perception, certainly among European fishermen, that all steelhead flies are pink and orange monstrosities consisting largely of marabou and epoxy resin. Nothing could be further from the truth. Some of the most beautiful, elegant and, dare I say, classic flies in use anywhere in the world are used for steelhead. In recent years, however, there seems to have been a considerable change in attitudes. Atlantic salmon fishermen are beginning to be much more catholic in their tastes, using flies and lures made of flashy new materials. Steelhead flyfishermen, for their part, have rediscovered the effectiveness of old types of fly such as the Spey and Dee flies, albeit using modern materials and modified tying methods. Whilst comparisons may be invidious, based on the sample flies that I have received during the preparation of this book, I believe that there are now probably more world class flytyers on the west coast of North America than anywhere else in the world.

We have seen in the History section a range of the early hairwing steelhead flies. What is perhaps surprising is that many of these early flies are still in regular use. Flies such as the Polar Shrimp, Thor, Skykomish Sunrise and the Purple Peril continue to appear on the recommended fly lists of even the most recently published books. To these can be added a second list of near classics, which would include flies such as the Del Cooper, Mack's Canyon, Skunk, Green Butt Skunk, Brad's Brat, Patriot, Rick's Revenge, Fall Favourite, Coal Car and Freight Train. Most of these patterns are now twenty or thirty years old, but have lost none of their effectiveness and are still widely used on rivers all over the North West. The dressings for all these flies have been widely published elsewhere. I have included them here not only to avoid readers having to refer to other publications, but because they have spawned a huge range of variants and derivatives and are thus well worth looking at.

Trey Combs listed the Del Cooper, a Mike Kennedy pattern, in *Steelhead Fly Fishing and Flies*, in 1976. Combs noted that it was a little known pattern that was certain to gain a wider following. He was right. In *Steelhead Fly Fishing* (1991), Combs had promoted it to the list of traditional steelhead flies and it has appeared in just about every other book on steelhead published since. Incidentally, in his earlier book, Trey Combs also commented that, in his opinion, purple was one of the least appreciated colours for steelhead flies. How that has changed over the last twenty-five years!

Del Cooper - Kennedy

The Surgeon General is very similar to the Del Cooper. Trey Combs gives the same basic construction, but with all the colours being fluorescent and with the addition of a throat hackle of natural Guinea fowl. Just to confuse things further, *Flies of the Northwest*, published in 1998, gives the fly as illustrated above but names it as the Surgeon General, originated by Del Cooper. Whatever the truth, it was and remains a very effective fly.

Mack's Canyon, from Doug Stewart, is a pattern that has also been around for a long time. The earliest dressing that I have found gives the wing as white bucktail, with orange bucktail over the top. More recently, many dressings reverse this and place the orange underneath and the white above. The jungle cock cheeks are optional.

Mack's Canyon - Stewart

The following flies are two variants of Mack's Canyon that have been devised over the years. The Blue Mack's Canyon was developed by Mark Melody for use on the Deschutes River. Tied sparsely, it has proved to be well suited to clear water conditions. The blue hackle provides a bit of colour but not too much flash. The Dark Mack's Canyon is a good, dark fly with just a flash of colour. Not too flashy for clear water, it nevertheless shows a strong silhouette in stained water.

Blue Mack's Canyon - Melody

Dark Mack's Canyon

Brad's Brat was devised in 1937 by Enos Bradner, long-time outdoor editor of the Seattle Times. It has become a steelhead classic in a number of guises. Originally designed for summer-run fish on the Stillaguamish River, it has now become an all season fly which is tied in a myriad of styles and which has inspired many variants.

Brad's Brat - Bradner

One of the most useful and effective variants of Brad's Brat is the Purple Brat, from Dave McNeese. This fly is an all year round pattern that has proved successful on rivers from British Columbia to California. McNeese believes that purple is one of the most effective colours for steelhead at any time of year and many of his flies such as the Pale Peril, Pale Pearl, Purple Polar Bear Matuka, McNeese Madness and Deschutes Madness feature this colour.

Purple Brat - McNeese

PLATE 20: Skunk & Variants

The Skunk is another pattern with a venerable history. It originated in the 1930s but surprisingly, little is known about its origins. Trey Combs suggests that its beginnings were on the North Umpqua and that it may have been devised simultaneously by both Mildred Krogel and Wes Drain but no absolutely concrete evidence is available. The fly has stood the test of time and is still in widespread use. As late as 1998 it was still reckoned to be the most popular steelhead pattern in the North West. Inevitably, there are many variants, including ones with the addition of a green or red butt. The green butt version is probably the most generally used today. This fly can be seen as the steelhead equivalent of the Green Butt series, which are so popular in the eastern provinces of Canada for Atlantic salmon. Another variant, from Clarence Gordon, has a yellow butt and a wing of black hair over the white, the red tail being dropped completely. Alec Jackson also ties variants in which the body is of home-made chenille consisting of peacock and/or ostrich herl, twisted into a rope with silver ribbing tinsel. The slim bodied versions have been christened the Coastal Skunks, while the versions with a bulkier body are known as Inland Skunks.

The theory behind this is that steelhead lose their visual acuity the longer that they are away from the sea, thus necessitating a more bulky fly for inland waters. Both these flies are winged with polar bear hair rather than bucktail because of its translucence.

The Purple Skunk is another variant: a combination of the Green Butt Skunk with a Purple Peril (see page 17). It was devised by Keith Stonebreaker for use on the Clearwater, in Idaho.

The Purple Skunk quickly became popular and was one of the first steelhead flies with Idaho origins to become widely known.

Purple Skunk - Stonebreaker

One of the most widely used steelhead flies is the Spade, a hackle fly with no wing, devised by Bob Arnold. The Skpade, from Joe Butorac, is a combination of a Spade with a Skunk. A second version is nearly identical, but with the addition of a palmered black body hackle and is known as the Hairy Skpade. This fly has a larger silhouette and is intended for use in low light or coloured water.

Skpade - Butorac

The Deschutes Skunk, from Forrest Maxwell, is a modified Spey style variant of the Skunk. The red tail fibres and black body are retained, but the fly is completed by a collar hackle of long Chinese pheasant rump with teal in front. The wing was originally bronze mallard but the fly illustrated uses brown bucktail.

Just to avoid confusion, I should mention that, in Steelhead Fly Fishing and Flies, Trey Combs lists an earlier fly from Don McClain which is also called the Deschutes Skunk. This is a floating pattern which retains the red tail, black body and black hackle of the original Skunk but which has a wing of white bucktail over brown deer body hair.

Deschutes Skunk - Maxwell

The Fall Favourite is another pattern that has been around for a long time but which is still in regular use. It was first introduced in 1946 by Lloyd Silvius for use on the Eel River's autumn run steelhead and was often tied in the Optic style with a large, eyed head. The Optic version quickly fell from favour and it is the version shown below that has endured. Deceptively simple, this fly can be dressed in several styles and in modern times is commonly tied with fluorescent materials. The wing is usually of polar bear or bucktail.

Fall Favourite - Silvius

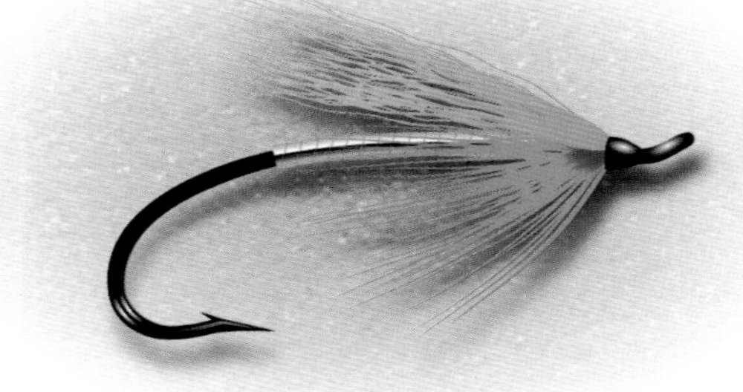

Yellow-bodied patterns were extremely popular in the early days of steelheading. Although yellow has lost popularity and has largely been superseded by flies with orange, purple and black bodies, a few yellow-bodied flies such as the Skykomish Yellow, Patriot and Kalama Special still remain effective. The Kalama Special was devised by Mooch Abrams of Oregon but became so intimately connected with Mike Kennedy that it is very often credited to him. In 1998 this pattern was still included in the list of recommended flies for the North West by the Inland Empire Fly Fishing Club in its book *Flies of the Northwest.*

Kalama Special - Abrams

The next two patterns are hairwing derivatives of classic, old strip wing Dee flies, from Harry Lemire. They may not be commonly used but I have included them because they are both beautiful and practical. With flies such as these the steelhead angler can feel part of the great tradition of angling whilst at the same time presenting a fly which will certainly catch fish.

Gardener

Tartan

The original Gardener was devised by a Mr. W. Garden on the River Dee in the middle of the 19th century. The Tartan is credited to a Mr. Brown, also for use on the River Dee, and dates back even further to the middle of the 18th century. Anyone catching a fish on either of these patterns can truly feel that they are sharing part of angling history.

The squirrel tail winging on these flies is tied in low and divided to simulate the feather strip wings of the original patterns. The jungle cock cheeks of the Gardener are tied in a low, drooping position below the line of the body: a feature shared by other Dee flies. I believe this was done so as to avoid masking the action of the strip wings which were intended to open and close in a scissors-like manner as the fly was worked in the current.

The next few flies are also the work of Harry Lemire and join a select group of flies that have become inextricably interwoven with the history of steelhead flyfishing.

The Grease Liner has the distinction of being the very first 'waking' fly designed specifically for steelhead fishing. Designed back in 1962, it is still as popular as ever and would certainly appear on almost everybody's 'Best Ten Flies' list. The original body was black dubbing and this is the best choice if the river has some colour. For clear water conditions, a burnt orange body is a good alternative but other shades of brown or olive may be used to match the colour of local caddis.

Grease Liner - Lemire

The Harry Kari Bucktail was devised in 1957. It was originally a wingless nymph pattern but later a black bear wing was added and the fly used for trout fishing on Canadian lakes. The pattern was subsequently found to be very effective for steelhead in Washington and British Columbia and has remained a favourite to the present day.

Harry Kari Bucktail - Lemire

Randle Stetzer thought it worthwhile to include both these flies in his book *Flies: The Best One Thousand*, published in 1992.

First devised in 1963, the Black Diamond is a dark fly named after the town in Washington in which Lemire lived. It was intended as a small black, buggy kind of fly for greased line fishing in the summer and autumn. Trey Combs rates it for fishing shallow tailouts, particularly in low light. The jungle cock cheek is optional and if it is not used the hackle is tied as a complete collar rather than a beard. This is an elegant little pattern and one that will always take fish in the right conditions. The wing is of squirrel tail with combed out guinea fowl fibres over the top. The combination of hair with feather fibres for the winging is a trademark of Lemire's patterns and used on many of his flies.

Black Diamond - Lemire

As can be seen in the foregoing flies, most of the patterns that Lemire uses are small and fairly subdued in colour. There is, however, one exception which is primarily used for winter conditions, particularly when the water is off-colour. This is Lemire's Winter Fly, which is his single concession to bright colours. Even here, though, he uses subtle shades of salmon combined with white and red, rather than fluorescent oranges and pinks. Tied in sizes from 2/0 to 4, it is often fished deeply sunk in a very slow, dead drift.

Lemire's Winter Fly

Bill McMillan is one of the great names of steelhead fishing and the small but select group of fly patterns that he has developed, such as the Paintbrush, Winter's Hope, Steelhead Caddis and the Washougal Olive, are of enduring quality and popularity.

The Washougal Olive was developed in 1968 as a pattern for use on the Washougal river in the heavy flows of winter and early spring. The conventional wet flies of the time were normally tied with chenille bodies and wings of bucktail and whilst these were satisfactory in the lower flows of summer, they had a marked tendency to skate to the surface in the stronger currents of winter. The tinsel body of the Washougal Olive enables the fly to sink quickly and the wing, tail and hackle of calf tail are also low in natural buoyancy. The colour was chosen because, at the time, there were no steelhead patterns around which were predominantly green. McMillan found this unsatisfactory, particularly as the dominant coloration of the river in spring was of various shades of green. His choice of colour was also influenced by the Green Highlander and Cosseboom Atlantic salmon flies, both of which have a good reputation for fresh run spring fish. For low clear flows, the fly may be tied on an Alec Jackson Spey hook. It is, however, usually tied on stout 5x heavy hooks, such as the Mustad 7970: getting the fly down to the correct depth deemed more important than any perceived lack of elegance.

Washougal Olive - McMillan

The Washougal Olive is yet another example of a fly which, in the hand, seems to have no particular allure, but which is transformed when in the water. A flash of the gold body, a flicker of green and white produces a fleeting illusion of life which has accounted for many steelhead.

There is no doubt that green and yellow flies are consistently productive for fresh run fish, whether Atlantic salmon or steelhead.

Apart from the Green Highlander and Cosseboom, already mentioned, there are a whole raft of flies from the east coast of Canada and a lot more from Ireland which share this coloration – almost all of them being recommended as early season flies.

The Springer Green is a fly from Walt Johnson, which was devised in the 1970s for the early summer run steelhead of the Columbia system. I doubt very much that this fly has ever been tried on Atlantic salmon but, considering its colours in combination with the flowing hackles which give lots of action in the water, I am certain that it would be extremely effective for spring fishing.

Springer Green - Johnson

We have already seen that comparatively few yellow-bodied flies remain in general use. The Patriot was developed by Frank Amato as the lighter of a pair of flies of similar construction; the darker of the two patterns being the Night Dancer. In *Steelhead Fly Fishing* Trey Combs recounts taking a steelhead in almost complete darkness with this fly and, although he does not use yellow flies with any frequency, considers this pattern to be the best yellow fly around.

Patriot - Amato

The Night Dancer (originally named Queenie), with its combination of black and purple, is one of the quintessential, dark steelhead flies and, since its inception, has been tied in many variations. The top fly in the illustration is the original pattern as tied by Frank Amato. The lower one is a variant in which the wing of black calf tail or bucktail has been replaced by Arctic fox hair, dyed black. The body is of dubbed black seal's fur, the throat hackle has been moved to the front and tied as long, flowing collar. An underwing of purple Krystal Flash is optional.

The use of claret as an alternative to the ubiquitous purple has been touched upon several times in this book. I believe that claret is very much underrated and underused, not only for steelhead but also for Atlantic salmon. Randle Stetzer (author of *Flies: The Best One Thousand*) shares this view and his pattern, Patricia, shown below, is one of the few claret steelhead flies around. Tied originally for use on the Deschutes River, it has since proved its worth on many other rivers as well. The second fly below is a dark-winged variant which should perform well in a wide range of water conditions. It has been called the St. Estephe because, whilst I was playing around with this fly on my bench, I happened to be drinking a fine glass of wine from the Médoc town of that name. The colour of the fly matched that of the wine exactly! The wing is of Arctic fox dyed black. I like this material a lot: it has the mobility of marabou but is much more durable.

The name Randall Kaufmann is familiar to all steelhead fishermen for two reasons. Firstly, he is a widely respected steelhead angler and author of several books including *The American Nymph Fly Tying Manual*. Secondly, he is the man behind the Kaufmann's Streamborn fly-fishing stores and mail order business. The flies described below were all born out of his own fly fishing experience and through his business have been marketed to a wide audience.

The Freight Train had its origins on the Deschutes River but has since proved its worth on rivers throughout the North West. The top illustration shows the fly in its original form, while the lower one is a variant with pearl over blue Krystal Flash for the wing. The iridescent effect of this version attracts fish from greater distances, so it is ideally suited to off-colour conditions, such as occurs when the White River deposits a heavy load of glacial silt into the main Deschutes river during exceptionally hot periods, causing it to run a milky white colour.

Freight Train - Kaufmann

Krystal Flash Freight Train

The Coal Car is basically a black-winged version of the Freight Train intended for use in the fading light of evening. Added sparkle is given by the addition of an underwing of Black Krystal Flash. The original wing specifies black squirrel tail but the version shown uses Arctic fox.

Coal Car - Kaufmann

The Signal Light was so named because the colours were reminiscent of the signal lights on the railroad alongside the Deschutes River. The overwing in the fly illustrated is of Arctic fox, the original was of marabou. Trey Combs notes that he often replaces the marabou with black squirrel tail, which is more durable, but I prefer Arctic fox which retains much more mobility. The Signal Light is one of Kaufmann's favourite patterns and is used from Oregon to British Columbia for all water conditions. Sizes can vary from small to large and the dressing style from weighted for subsurface fishing to very sparse for greased-line presentation.

Signal Light - Kaufmann

Purple Flash - Kaufmann

Purple Flash is a combination of the Purple Marabou and Street Walker patterns. The overwing in the example illustrated is again fox rather than marabou as originally specified. This is quite a flashy pattern but the Krystal Flash and hair in the wing combine nicely and the fly has a great deal of mobility. The same fly with the addition of a fluorescent fire orange butt is named the Ferry Canyon after an area on the Deschutes River.

The last fly is the Flat Car. This has a butt of fluorescent green wool and is basically a black-winged version of the Green Butt Skunk. Apart from the winging material, this is the same as a Black Bear Green Butt as used in the Maritime Provinces of Canada for Atlantic salmon.

Deschutes Madness - McNeese

Flat Car - Kaufmann

McNeese Madness - McNeese

Dave McNeese is a phenomenon. Apart from being a steelhead flyfisher of the highest order, a flytyer of great skill and a designer of flies that incorporate modern materials and colours with the elegance of the classics, he also runs a fly shop, collects rare books on Atlantic salmon flies, custom builds fly rods and organises fly fishing classes. The following group is typical of the flies he produces. They are all tied to the highest standards and are marked by an inbuilt elegance and grace. Not only that, they catch fish. Each of these patterns has accounted for at least 150 steelhead.

The Deschutes Madness dates back to about 1978 and is near to being the perfect all round steelhead dressing. The wing is of polar bear but a more mobile hair such as Arctic fox mixed with pearl Krystal Flash would be a good alternative. The cheeks of jungle cock are optional but undoubtedly add to the appeal of the fly.

The McNeese Madness is another pattern that had its origins on the Deschutes and which has grown more popular as time as gone by. The body construction is unusual, being fluorescent orange floss, ribbed with four turns of purple sparkle chenille. Just to emphasise the interchangeable application of many steelhead and salmon flies, Trey Combs noted that this fly has also been used with success for Atlantic salmon in Norway, Iceland and Canada. It also confirms that purple can be just as effective for salmon as it is for steelhead and suggests that many other steelhead flies would be equally effective were they to be given a try. It is something that salmon anglers might bear in mind when searching for a fly to show to fish that have 'seen it all'.

The Pale Peril is a variant of the Purple Peril which is primarily used for summer fishing. The Pale Pearl was first introduced in 1976 and has been successful on rivers from British Columbia to California. It has been McNeese's top producing fly on the North Santiam and seems to be at its best in the morning.

The Purple Polar Bear Matuka is a fly tied in the Matuka style but where the conventional feather hackle has been replaced by bunches of polar bear hair tied in along the top of the body. This wing construction helps the fly maintain an even keel when it comes under tension, making it a very good fly for fast water. The multi-layer wing also provides a substantial colour signature without too much bulk. The Purple Polar Bear Matuka is one of McNeese's most popular patterns, so much so that he has problems fulfilling customer demand even when charging over three dollars a fly. In *Steelhead Fly Fishing*, Trey Combs also notes that a very effective winter pattern substitutes hot orange for the purple in the above tie. McNeese also uses this style of construction for several other flies such as the Polar Shrimp, Thor and Brad's Brat. The wing is highly visible and extremely mobile, giving tremendous movement in the water.

The Bi-Color Polar Bear Matuka has the same construction as the previous fly but in this case the polar bear wing is dyed in two colours – purple on the top and hot orange beneath.

The Stratman Fancy was named after a fishing colleague. It is a flashy pattern that has all the right colours and also long, mobile hackles.

Stratman Fancy - McNeese

The Spawning Purple has been around since 1977 and was first tied for winter steelhead in clear water conditions. The unribbed body is of hot orange seal's fur spun in a dubbing loop to produce a rounded form. The winging may be of purple

Flashabou, hot purple hackle tips or, as shown, of Arctic fox hair. John Shewey also ties a variant of this fly with a flame orange floss body and the wing consisting of four or five separate bunches of hair, tied Matuka fashion.

Spawning Purple - McNeese

Spawning Purple Variant - Shewey

Rick's Revenge is also a John Shewey pattern. This is a very bright fly with an unusual double tail construction of fluorescent red floss. The fly certainly has impact and is intended for use in coloured water conditions.

Rick's Revenge - Shewey

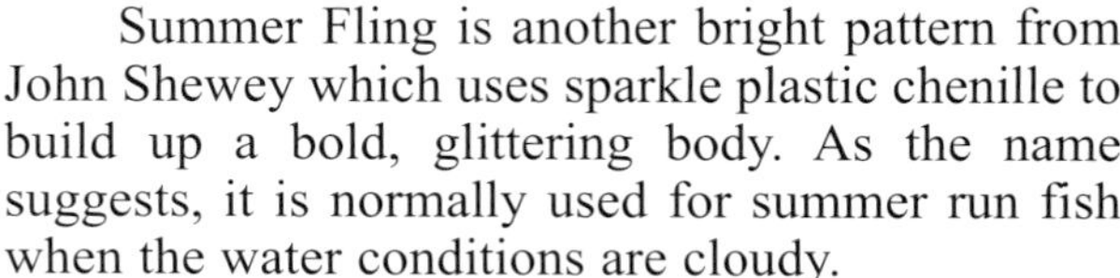

Summer Fling is another bright pattern from John Shewey which uses sparkle plastic chenille to build up a bold, glittering body. As the name suggests, it is normally used for summer run fish when the water conditions are cloudy.

Summer Fling - Shewey

As the name implies, Marabou Madness was originally tied with marabou as the wing material, in two bunches. The following version uses fine, mobile Arctic fox hair instead. This is in line with the general trend in Europe where fox hair has supplanted marabou to a great extent because of its greater durability whilst still providing the desired mobility. The front body of the fly is of glitter plastic chenille, which is one of Shewey's favourite materials and is used on many of his flies, usually tied over an underbody of floss or tinsel.

Marabou Madness - Shewey

Just for a change from the plethora of purple flies, the following pattern is one of the few blue steelhead flies. Devised by Tom Darling, it was named in honour of the late Wes Drain. The fly was designed for spring, summer and winter-run steelhead on the western rivers draining into Puget Sound. With this coloration I would expect it to be at its best in clear water conditions for fresh-run fish. Other colour combinations are also effective: simply replace the blue with red, orange or purple.

Blue Drain - Darling

We continue the blue theme with the following group of flies, all of which have important blue elements. The inventors of all these patterns seem to agree that blue flies are at their best in clear and cold water conditions, they also seem to be effective when used in pools that have been heavily fished. This might be as much to do with simply showing the fish something different as with any inherent allure of blue as a colour. The combination of blue, white and silver gives a very different image underwater to the blacks, oranges and purples of the majority of flies. Blue, silver and white are typical baitfish prey colours and this may explain why they are effective, particularly for fresh fish that are not long separated from their marine experience.

The Ice Blue is a fly from Thomas Duncan and should not be confused with a pattern of the same name from Gerald Bartsch (see *Shrimp & Spey Flies for Salmon and Steelhead*). It is also recommended for clear water. The rear body of white floss is wound over an underbody of silver tinsel so that the colour is not lost when the fly is wet.

The Peacock Undertaker is a pattern from John Arnold that shares the same body construction as the Undertaker Atlantic salmon fly from the east coast of Canada (see page 91). Arnold notes that finding peacock swords for flies larger than size 2 is a problem. Firefox Peacock Lite-Brite or Peacock Krystal Flash may be good substitutes.

The Kaleidoscope, from Walt Balek, has a body of pearl Flashabou wound over an underbody of purple floss. This unusual combination gives the body a luminous appearance on overcast days or in dark water.

Ice Blue - Duncan

Peacock Undertaker - Arnold

Kaleidoscope - Balek

Steve Gobin is one of the best flytyers in Washington State and has created a series of extremely beautiful and effective Spey flies (see *Shrimp & Spey Flies for Salmon and Steelhead*). The Rose Petal is a hairwing Spey fly with a pretty name. It is not just good to look at, but is a very good fly for clear water conditions. The body colour is a combination of fluorescent pink floss and light claret seal's fur dubbing that is seldom seen.

Rose Petal - Gobin

The Witch series was devised for use on the Snoqualmie River by Steve Brocco, one of the best known tyers in the North West. There are three Witch patterns which, while fairly simple and straightforward, have an elegant appearance. All three share a collar hackle of golden pheasant rump, but followed by a flowing collar hackle of teal flank for the Black Witch and bronze mallard for the other two. This gives the flies a Spey-like look and lots of action in the water, without any of the complications of palmering a long hackle.

It is difficult for anglers from the USA, and even more so for European anglers, to appreciate just how little was known about the rivers of the west coast of Canada as recently as the 1980s. Trey Combs relates a typical tale in *Steelhead Fly Fishing*. In 1982, Gary Miltenberger and Rai Thomas started a float trip from Bear Creek on the river Sustut with the intention of exploring the Sustut down to its confluence with the Skeena River and then continuing down the Skeena, past its confluences with the Babine and Kispiox Rivers, until it met the Bulkley River at Hazelton. The aim of the trip was to find a suitable site for a steelhead fishing lodge. Even in 1982 this area was still true wilderness and almost nothing was known about the Skeena between the Sustut and the Babine. Drifting down the Skeena they entered an area of inaccessible canyon waters which overturned their raft. They were separated and both men believed that the other had perished. After spending five desperate days in the wilderness and suffering from frostbite, both were rescued. In the meantime, Miltenberger had found his site on the Sustut for the lodge which became known as the Steelhead Valhalla.

The river system, which includes the Skeena, Sustut, Bella Coola, Kispiox, Babine and Bulkley rivers, provides the stuff of legends as far as steelhead fishing is concerned. All of these rivers can produce massive fish of over 20lb and on some, such as the Kispiox, fish well in excess of 30lb have been recorded, if not often landed. There are also believable tales of fish even bigger than this. Fish of over forty pounds have been mentioned in hushed tones and these are probably

PLATE 21: Witch Series - Steve Brocco

not fairy tales, coming as they do from some of the most experienced and skilful flyfishers in the world.

The following flies were developed by Miltenberger for use on the Bella Coola, Sustut and Dean Rivers but have also proved to be very effective on both the Kispiox and Babine.

The Purple Ugly is typical of many of the large, gaudy flies used on the Sustut. It is not the most elegant of patterns but it certainly works. Bead chain eyes provide weight to get the fly down in the water. Unusually, both the tail and wing are of calf tail dyed claret, a much-underrated colour for steelhead.

Purple Ugly - Miltenberger

Sustut Boss - Miltenberger

The Sustut Boss is a derivative of the well-known Boss pattern and was devised in 1984. In October of that year, Keld Olsson from Denmark took a 28lb buck steelhead on this pattern: a lodge record that stood for several years. Bead chain eyes seem to have become popular with the Boss and Comet series of flies and date back to around 1949 on the Russian River, although there is some evidence that they may have been used on conventional bucktail flies even earlier than that. The Boss and Comet flies have never lost their popularity and continue to be used in many different variants (see page 132). This pattern may not look elegant but I think I could learn to love almost any fly capable of taking a 28lb fish.

The Sustut Sunrise is a bright pattern that Miltenberger first tied in the late 1980s in order to offer a contrast to the darker, black and purple patterns that were so widespread. Named in deference to Ken and George McLeod, inventors of the Skykomish Sunrise, the Sustut Sunrise took a buck fish of 27lb in 1987 for Dr. Fred Miller.

Sustut Sunrise - Miltenberger

Purple Jesus - Miltenberger

The Purple Jesus was so named after one of the guests at the Valhalla Lodge walked over to the tying vice where Miltenberger was working one evening, looked at the fly being tied, and remarked "Jesus, look at that purple thing." Trey Combs notes that if the fly is dressed down a bit, it can look pretty, but then they do say that beauty is in the eye of the beholder.

The Kispiox Bright and the Kispiox Dark are two flies from Bob York, designed for differing water conditions on the Kispiox River. When the water is high but not too discoloured, the Kispiox Bright is a good choice. With a colour scheme which includes red, purple, hot orange, white and yellow, fish should find something they like.

The Kispiox Dark is favoured for off-coloured conditions, even if the river is brown. York also believes that green is a good colour for the Kispiox whatever the water conditions. If necessary, the Kispiox dark can be tied with small lead eyes at the head to take the fly down in the water.

Kispiox Bright - York

Kispiox Dark - York

The Low Water Green reflects York's predilection for green flies on the Kispiox and is intended for use only in low water conditions when it is fished in size 4 or smaller.

Low Water Green - York

The Spring Favourite is a pattern for the late winter-run steelhead on the Skagit, Sauk and Bella Coola rivers. The colour combination of red and orange with a fluorescent green butt is unusual but has the advantage of appealing at both ends of the colour spectrum.

Spring Favourite - York

The Thomson River has an awesome reputation for producing huge steelhead. The average weight of the male fish is over 16lb and that of the females around 13lb. Fish of over 30lb are taken regularly. The Thomson Special is York's favourite pattern for the river's late arriving summer-run fish. Thomson River steelhead have a reputation for being 'trouty' in their behaviour and this fly presents a buggy, slender look which York believes is especially effective.

Thompson Special - York

Mike Brooks has strong feelings about steelhead flies and takes Atlantic salmon flies as his yardstick. He feels, with some justification, that the most effective Atlantic salmon flies are much subtler than their steelhead counterparts. He points to the use of dubbed hair bodies rather than wound chenille and the use of soft winging materials such as fox and black bear rather than the comparatively stiff bucktail and polar bear used on many steelhead flies. It is no surprise, therefore, that all of his patterns reflect these ideas and that classic old salmon flies such as the Beauly Snow Fly and the Orange Blossom, from Canada's east coast, find a place in his armoury.

The Steelhead Rats comprise a series of five flies with a body construction very similar to the Rusty Rat Atlantic salmon fly that is extremely popular on the east coast of Canada. In *Steelhead Fly Fishing*, Trey Combs notes that the derivation comes from the Pack Rat salmon fly, but this is itself also a derivation from the Rusty Rat. Whichever ancestor is correct, all five of the flies in this series share a body in which the rear third is of floss in various colours, with peacock herl for the front two-thirds. The wing is of black and white barred hair (Brooks uses woodchuck guard hairs) and the fly is finished off with a backward sloping collar hackle. These are all typical Rat features.

PLATE 22: Steelhead Rats - Mike Brooks

The two flies in the McKenzie Sapphire series are closely related to classic salmon patterns, albeit in slightly simplified form. The dark winged Sapphire #2 is a direct descendant of the Black Doctor and Blue Charm: all share a yellow tag, black body ribbed with silver tinsel and a blue throat hackle. Jungle cock cheeks are optional on both of these flies.

McKenzie Sapphire #1 - Brooks

McKenzie Sapphire #2 - Brooks

The Fiery Brown is quite nondescript in its construction. The colour is what makes this fly special. Fiery brown has a distinguished history in Ireland where it has been a long-standing, open secret. The famous flytyer, Michael Rogan of Ballyshannon, was renowned for being able to produce a fiery brown which other flytyers were unable to duplicate. It is said that one of the secrets of his dyeing process involved the use of donkey's urine. Brooks's Fiery Brown is a direct descendant of Rogan's Irish Fiery Brown which dates back to about 1850. Real pedigree!

The body of Brooks's Fiery Brown is made from hare's mask dyed hot orange rather than the traditional fiery brown seal's fur. The natural barring and shading of the hare's mask means that the dye takes unevenly, producing a superb rich colour. Other alternatives are now once more available in ready blended form, noteworthy amongst these is the new range of Irish dubbings from Frankie McPhillips which includes three wonderful shades of fiery brown. Brooks fishes the Fiery Brown in extremely low water conditions when fish are cheek by jowl and are very wary of anything that is too extreme.

Fiery Brown - Brooks

Fly tyers who are interested in following up on the traditional Irish fiery brown flies should refer to *Irish Trout & Salmon Flies* by E.J. Malone where various patterns are listed. The re-print of this book by Coch-Y-Bonddu Books also has some wonderful examples of the flies tied by Frankie McPhillips.

Jim Garrett lives and works on the Olympic Peninsular at the Beaver Springs salmon hatchery on the Sol Duc river. A fisherman of great skill and a fly dresser of the highest order, he is probably best known for the Olympic Stonefly series of dressings and a whole range of elegant feather wing flies which are amongst the most beautiful in steelhead fishing. Details and illustrations of these flies may be found in *Steelhead Fly Fishing*, by Trey Combs. The following flies are however, more in the traditional steelhead hairwing mould.

The Orange Trinity, shown in Plate 23, was the first of the Trinity series of flies and devised in 1968 for pink salmon fishing on the Dungeness river. It was so effective that it was soon used for chum and chinook salmon, as well as for steelhead. Since then it has become one of Garrett's most reliable patterns for winter steelhead. The Hot

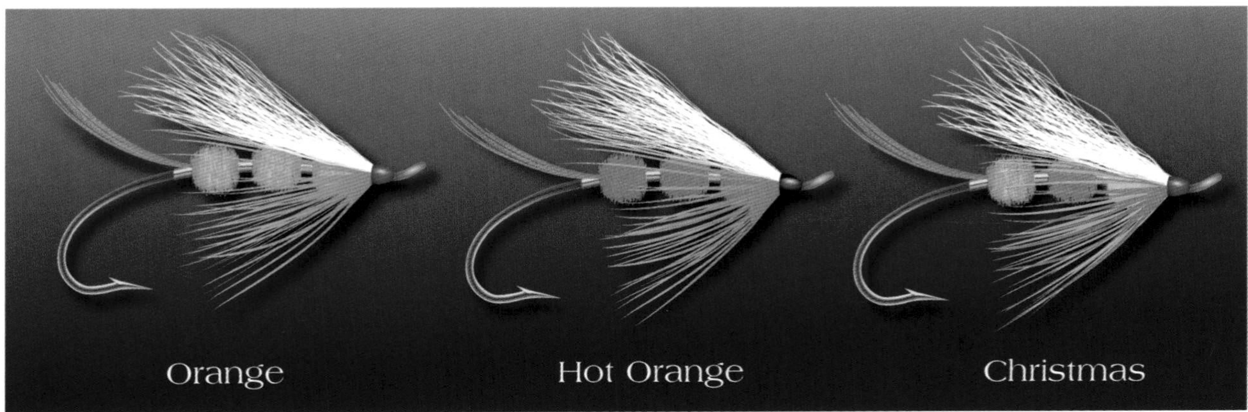

PLATE 23: Trinity Series Flies - Jim Garrett

Orange and Christmas variants were added later and give a range of bright colours for various conditions. The name Trinity derives from the unusual body construction, which consists of three ball-shaped chenille segments separated by gold tinsel.

Garrett's Shrimp, although called a shrimp, is a straightforward hairwing design. The name probably has more to do with the colour – typical of many shrimp patterns world-wide – than any particular feature of the construction. The general effectiveness of wine red (claret) as a steelhead colour has been discussed earlier and this fly is another prime example of just how good it can be.

Garrett's Shrimp - Garrett

Trey Combs came up with an almost identical dressing which uses golden pheasant flank feathers for the winging instead of bucktail and considers that the blend of colours make this fly a superb overall winter pattern for use on many different waters.

The next two groups of flies, shown in Plate 24, share a special body construction, which consists of a strip of Edge Bright wrapped over an underbody of silver tinsel.

Edge Bright is a plastic material which has the property of collecting light and transmitting it from its edges giving an intense glow (in a similar way to fibre optic filaments).

The Dean River Lanterns were first developed by Dr. Art Cohen, of San Francisco. Cohen discovered that if Edge Bright is wound over silver tinsel the effect is amplified and it emits an almost lantern-like glow, thus giving the name to this series of flies. Although he didn't invent them, the Dean River Lanterns have become closely associated with Bob Wagoner who has popularised them through his flytying business.

The Steelhead Charlies were developed by Bob Wagoner and are steelhead versions of Bob Nauheim's Crazy Charlie saltwater bonefish patterns. Tied specifically for cold water fishing, the Steelhead Charlies incorporate silver bead chain eyes. With their sparse dressings they sink like a stone and fish deep with an upside down attitude that avoids bottom hang-ups.

Dean River Lanterns

Steelhead Charlies

PLATE 24: Dean River Lanterns & Steelhead Charlies

Plate 25 shows two hairwinged Spey flies from Joe Howell, founder of the Blue Heron Fly Shop in Oregon. These flies are possibly pushing the limits of what could legitimately be regarded as hairwing flies, but they are so elegant that I couldn't resist including them. A further variant, the Purple Phase Spey simply replaces the red elements of the Red Phase Spey with purple. The extremely long Spey hackle in the original tying is of black heron. Substitutes could be used, even if they are not so long in the fibre. Although the wing is of hair rather than the traditional bronze mallard, these flies encapsulate all the features and attributes that give Spey flies such a wide appeal to anglers and, fortunately, to steelhead as well.

We have already discussed the relative merits of purple and claret for steelhead flies so the next pattern should offer the best of both worlds by combining a purple body with a claret shoulder hackle. Called the Tranquilizer, this is an old pattern which was first devised by Mike Kennedy for use on the Rogue River. It was originally fished in small sizes (8-10), but was later popularised in larger sizes by Ed Harzel on the North Umpqua. Dick Stewart and Farrow Allen, in *Flies for Steelhead*, give it with a purple collar hackle which is incorrect.

Tranquiliser - Kennedy

The following series of flies are all taken from *Fly Patterns of British Columbia* (1996), by Arthur Lingren. This book's section on steelhead fly patterns gives quite a different perspective on the history of steelhead fly fishing to that given by authors from the USA. Lingren's book mentions names like General Noel Money, Roderick Haig-Brown, Tom Brayshaw, Bill Cunliffe, Denny

PLATE 25: Hairwing Speys - Joe Howell

Boulton, Cliff Welch and others. Some of these names are well known to American steelhead fishermen, but others are less so. Among the rivers mentioned are the Coquihalla, Capilano, Cowichan, Stamp and Campbell. Most of these are less well-known than the Rogue, Deschutes, Skykomish and Stillguamish rivers that have been so widely written about by anglers from the USA. British Columbia has, nevertheless, been very important in the history of fly fishing for steelhead and the fly patterns that were developed on its rivers have had a seminal influence on the flies of today, even though modern day anglers may not realise it.

The Claret and Black is one of Arthur Lingren's own patterns It is a sparsely dressed fly which echoes the low-water style pioneered by A. H. Wood on the Scottish Dee and is intended for floating line, summer fishing. Although first tied in 1983 and therefore a comparatively new fly, it retains many of the features of the old classics such as full tag and butt. The tail is of orange-red dyed hen neck feather, reminiscent of the Indian crow specified in many classic salmon patterns. The fly has a good, dark silhouette when viewed from below against the sky.

Claret & Black - Lingren

The Black Butt Black was devised as a combination of features from the Doc Sprately together with the British Stoat's Tail (see page 44) and was intended to be used where a dark silhouette was required. A further version has a fluorescent green butt rather than black, but from Lingren's experience is actually no more effective than the black pattern. Apart from the use of Guinea fowl feather for the throat, the green butt version is almost identical to the Black Bear Green Butt so beloved and so effective in the eastern provinces of Canada for Atlantic salmon.

Black Butt Black - Lingren

As Specified #2 is the hairwing version of a classically styled Spey fly from Arthur Lingren which was devised in 1982 and had a wing of bronze mallard. This is also a slimly dressed fly for the floating line and has been used with success on the Morice, Dean, Campbell and Thomson rivers.

As Specified #2 - Lingren

As can be seen, Lingren's flies retain all the elegance of the Spey fly combined with elements such as the tip, tag and butt of the classic, fully dressed Atlantic salmon fly. Lingren himself admits that some of the fine details probably don't make any difference to the fish. He feels, nevertheless, that an opponent like the steelhead deserves a fly of the highest quality: to harp back to the introduction to this book, a treasure to catch a treasure!

The Black and Blue, from Van Egan, is another fly with a fine pedigree. It was first devised in the 1970s following some advice from Frederick

Hill in his book *Salmon Fishing: The Grease Line on Don, Dee and Earn* about flies that were dark but with a touch of blue. The original fly was tied with a wing of married strips of blue, yellow and red goose with an overwing of bronze mallard and golden pheasant topping. This fly was designed for sunk line fishing on the Campbell River and in its winter version, illustrated below, has a body of black seal's fur and a wing of brown bucktail with small bunches of blue, yellow and red polar bear hair as an underwing. Following the lead given by Lee Wulff, I think I might be inclined to retain the golden pheasant topping, even on the hairwing version. Since its inception it has not only been effective on the Campbell river but also on the Gold, Nimpkish and Dean rivers. A variant with a blue tag, rather than yellow, has also been found to be effective on occasions, particularly on the Gold River.

I have to say that I rather like the look of the blue tagged version as a spring or cold water pattern for Atlantic salmon. It seems to have all the right ingredients.

The Stewart was devised by Marty Sherman,

Black & Blue - Van Egan

editor of *Flyfishing* magazine. It is a pattern of classic simplicity using classic colours. The black of the body, wing and hackle is relieved by a flash of gold tinsel and an orange overwing, producing a dark pattern that has just the necessary amount of flash. The Thunder Stoat, from Scotland, uses the same combination of colours, the only difference being that the orange element here is a throat hackle rather than an overwing. Black and orange remains an outstanding combination with proven general appeal. Trey Combs rates the Stewart highly as an all round silhouette pattern for both clear and coloured water conditions and it has proved to be effective in both bright and dull conditions.

The next two flies are a bit of pure speculation

Stewart - Sherman

on my part, but I hope you will forgive the presumption because it is in the good cause of keeping alive two of the most influential patterns in the development of British Columbian steelhead flies. The General Money No.1 and No.2 were both developed in the 1930s and remained popular for decades. They were the two most commonly sold steelhead flies from Harkley & Heywood until the 1970s.

The No.1's unique colour combination of silver, black, orange and claret seems to me to be well worth preserving because I am certain that it would be effective for summer run fish throughout the North West. A claret hackle is palmered over the black front body and a claret collar hackle is tied at the front. The wing has been changed to hot orange hair and the tail is of orange-red dyed hackle fibres.

General Money #1 Spey

The No.2 is a classic mix of black, yellow and red and there is no doubt that it would still take fish at least as well as many of those flies of the same coloration that have "replaced" it over the years.

General Money #2 Spey

The following two flies are from Bob Arnold, inventor of the Spade and a regular for many years on the Stillaguamish and Wenatchee rivers. Both are intended for winter fishing and have impact without being too overwhelming. Both share the same simple construction in which a double wing is tied in both above and below the body, thus allowing the body itself to be visible to the fish. In the original flies, the winging is of marabou but in the examples illustrated I have used Arctic fox. These flies are fished on a sinking line, which is quartered downstream and slack line mended into the drift until they are touching bottom. Many other colour combinations are possible and Arnold recommends black body/orange wing; yellow body/orange wing; red body/black wing and purple body/cerise wing. Most of these patterns have remain unnamed but the two illustrated have proved to be very effective over the years and because of their enduring success deserve to be named.

Bob Arnold is also the author of books on steelhead fly fishing and I can recommend *Steelhead Waters* and *Steelhead & the Floating Line*, both from Frank Amato Publications. Not instructional in the conventional sense, these books are more personal reflections based on many years' experience and observation of steelhead fishing and are quite fascinating as well as being a very good read. I like these books. Arnold has a nice line in self-deprecating humour and comes across as a thoughtful man who doesn't take himself too seriously and who has a great regard for the rivers that he fishes and the fish that they hold.

Deer Creek - Arnold

Royal Flush - Arnold

We have already seen some examples of Gordon Mackenzie's hairwing flies in the chapter on European flies (see page 58). The next group of Matuka flies, shown in Plate 26, have been included in the steelhead section because, although they are tied by a British tyer, they are primarily intended for use on steelhead in the USA and Canada. All these flies are tied using a hair loop technique that creates a fly with a good image but one which is not too bulky. All the Hairy flies are extremely mobile and have a great action in the water but this is especially true of the Matukas. The keel-like structure gives added stability and keeps them swimming correctly even in heavy, fast water conditions. The hair hackle is pre-prepared and then tied in along the back of the fly and secured with the ribbing in the same way as a featherwinged Matuka is tied. The flies shown include dark patterns as well as some lighter ones which use pearl Lite-Brite to give added sparkle. The colour schemes can be altered to any that the tyer desires: black and purple spring readily to mind. All the techniques for tying Hairys, including the Matukas, are clearly explained in Gordon's book, *Hair Hackle Tying – Techniques and Fly Patterns*, published in the USA by Frank Amato Publications and available in Great Britain from Merlin Unwin.

One of the most enduring steelhead patterns of all is the Comet, first developed in 1940 for the steelhead in California's Russian river. Since then, many versions have been devised but the basic construction remains the same: a long tail, normally of bucktail, at least as long as the hook shank; a body of tinsel, floss or chenille and a collar hackle at the front.

Plate 27 shows a range of the most popular Comet variants.

Pearl & Black Matuka
Olive Matuka
Black & Red Matuka
Black Matuka
Ross Matuka
Pearl & Blue Matuka

PLATE 26: Hairy Matukas - Gordon Mackenzie

Note that the large collar hackle is tied substantially at right angles to the body and not swept back. This protruding collar may cause turbulence that gives added movement to the tail fibres. Bead chain eyes were originally optional, but they must now be regarded as a distinguishing feature of these patterns. Trey Combs believes that the Boss may have been the first of these flies, followed by the Howard Norton Special and the Orange, Black, Yellow, Brown, Gold and Silver Comets (see also the Purple Ugly and Sustut Boss on page 121). Of all these variants, the Boss and Orange Comets remain popular, not surprisingly because they have a lot going for them. They sink quickly and have flash and colour, as well as the mobility and action provided by the long tail. They are also cheap and easy to tie.

Boss

Howard Norton Special

Black Comet

Orange Comet

Salmon Fly

Gold Comet

PLATE 27: Comet Series

The flies developed over the years for the Great Lakes steelhead fisheries have differed significantly from the flies of the west. There has been a much greater emphasis on the use of realistic nymph patterns and thousands of these have been devised. The effectiveness of these flies has largely to do with the nature of the steelhead which run the rivers decanting into the Great Lakes. The fish do not undergo the complex metabolic transformation from true salt sea to fresh water which is normal for the anadromous steelhead of the west and this seems to affect their feeding habits significantly (the term potamodromous describes their fresh water to fresh water spawning cycle). River feeding, particularly in the early part of their spawning runs has been documented on many occasions and explains why nymph and egg patterns (which also abound) are so effective. To this must also be added the fact that because the Great Lakes steelhead are planted, artificially maintained populations, catch-and-release has never had the impetus that it has had on the west coast where environmentally aware anglers have made a sustained effort to maintain wild populations. Much of the steelhead fishing on the Great Lakes has been done with spinning tackle and even when flies are used they are very often fished on weighted set-ups that could not be cast with fly rods in the conventional manner. The classic wet fly down-and-across swing is used far less often here and, consequently, there has been far less emphasis on the elegant hairwing and Spey patterns so common in the fisheries of the North West. Until recent years, a look through a fly pattern book for the Great Lakes would show you pages of naturalistic nymph flies; pages of glowing fluorescent egg flies; a few baitfish imitating streamer flies; a mixed bag of leeches and bunnies and lastly, a few standard hairwings and Spey style patterns. Things are now changing and a growing number of Great Lakes steelhead fishermen are less interested in the numbers game or catching fish by any legal method. They are beginning to discover the delights of fishing for steelhead using beautifully tied flies, fished using conventional fly tackle and techniques. There have, however, been a few notable bastions of classic flyfishing in the Great Lakes. Flytyers such as Steve Schweitzer, Bob Blumreich and others have tied and fished lovingly crafted Spey and Dee flies for many years (see *Shrimp & Spey Flies for Salmon & Steelhead* for examples of their work) and their example is now gaining momentum.

The next flies are typical examples of the work of Great Lakes flytyers such as Larry Halyk, John Valk, Mike Yarnot and Rick Kustich.

The fly illustrated below is the Purple Bunny Spey from Rick Kustich, owner of the Oak Orchard Fly Shop, near Niagara and co-author with his brother Jerry of *Flyfishing for Great Lakes Steelhead*.

This pattern is tied in the Zonker style with a strip of rabbit fastened along the back of the fly Matuka fashion. Although it is called a 'Spey', the Purple Bunny isn't a Spey fly in any conventional sense. The name probably comes about because of the long collar hackles tied at the front. Rabbit strip flies of this type are extremely effective in fast, heavy water because the fur strip retains its mobility and action. It is no coincidence that they are also very popular in Norway where the large, brawling rivers with steep gradients have a lot on common with many of the rivers in the Great Lakes area.

Purple Bunny Spey - Kustich

The Purple October is another Kustich fly. It has the purple and orange colour combination that is so widespread amongst steelhead flies. The wing is of purple Arctic fox and the purple body hackle is of burnt goose feather. For flytyers unfamiliar with this expression, the word 'burnt' describes a hackle that has been immersed in a corrosive medium (normally household bleach) with the object of removing most of the flue from the fibres. This is done in order to make a slimmer hackle for use as a heron substitute for Spey style flies. Ready treated feathers (usually of goose and other wildfowl) are also available commercially under the designation of burnt Spey hackle.

Purple October - Kustich

The Catnip is a bright little fly with an orange body, a soft orange throat hackle and a wing of yellow calf tail. It presents a sparkling dot of colour in the water which has the necessary impact but, being small, does not overwhelm and frighten the fish with an image that is too garish.

Catnip - Kustich

The October Spey, from Halyk, is another fly that combines dark and light tones: this time orange and dark brown relieved by a flash of gold tinsel. As the name suggests, this is primarily an autumn fly but, because of its comparatively subdued colouring, would probably be effective in clear water conditions at any time of the year.

October Spey - Halyk

The Akroyd is a strip wing Dee fly which dates back to 1878 and which is still used in many guises (see also page 60). The following version was tied by Larry Halyk, of Ontario, and retains all the essential elements and elegance of the original fly although the feather wing has been replaced by deer hair.

Akroyd Variant - Halyk

Mike Yarnot of Wisconsin has a reputation as one of the premier Spey flytyers in the Great Lakes area and has become one of the best exponents of classic swing fishing using hairwing wets and elegant featherwing Spey flies. The two flies illustrated below are hairwings which are simple in their construction but elegant in looks. Both have thoraces of well picked out seal's fur, giving the flies a purposeful, hunched shoulder appearance which displays the slim rear body to maximum advantage. The wing is of mobile Arctic fox hair.

John Valk, owner of Grindstone Angling Outfitters of Watertown, Ontario, is a great supporter of steelhead fly fishing using wet flies. As the waters of the Great Lakes clear dramatically due to the filtering effects of zebra mussels, small flies are bound to becoming increasingly important. The Steelhead Petite series is John Valk's answer to this growing challenge and are tied in a series of effective colours in sizes 6 to 12. Although designed for the Great Lakes, these pretty little patterns are sure to be effective for low and clear water conditions anywhere. For slower flowing but clear water conditions, as well as for drought conditions, I would think that the Irish style of shrimp fly could be extremely effective. Perhaps some Great Lakes steelheaders might think of giving them a try (details can be found in *Shrimp & Spey Flies for Salmon & Steelhead*).

Beadhead flies have become very popular for rainbow trout fishing for the simple reason that they are extremely effective! It is, therefore, surprising that bead-headed steelhead flies are extremely uncommon. Valk's Beadhead Squirrels have all the attributes that make this style of fly so effective. They are small and buggy looking with a mobile wing and hackle and have just a touch of colour and sparkle about them to attract attention without being too extreme. The beadhead provides some weight that takes the fly down well in the water. You could almost guarantee that these flies would be sure-fire patterns on any water containing rainbow trout anywhere in the world, so it is hardly surprising that they are also effective for steelhead. Beadheads are not an attempt to look like anything specific, but they are a pretty good impressionistic imitation of a stonefly and just about any other bug that is good to eat.

PLATE 28: Steelhead Petite Series - John Valk

PLATE 29: Beadhead Squirrels - John Valk

The next two patterns are low water hairwing versions of two old standard flies, one from Europe and one from the west coast of the USA.

Winter's Hope, from Bill McMillan, is one of the classic winter steelhead flies. The colour combination of orange and yellow hackle tip winging, together with an electric blue and purple throat hackle gives the fly a glow in the water unsurpassed by any other fly. The hairwing version, shown below, lacks the subtlety of the featherwing original but is nevertheless a very effective low water fly.

The Blue Charm has a long history, dating back to the middle of the 19th century. It is one of those patterns which, despite the fact that it isn't startling to look at, has always been effective wherever anglers fish for Atlantic salmon or steelhead. For anglers devoted to the greased line method, invented by A. H. Wood, this is a very appropriate pattern to use. The Blue Charm was Wood's favourite fly and accounted for the majority of the more than 3,500 salmon that he caught on the Cairnton stretch of the river Dee between 1913 and 1934. The low water, hairwing version shown below has a more colourful wing than the original, which was of bronze mallard with strips of barred teal.

Catalogue of Dressings

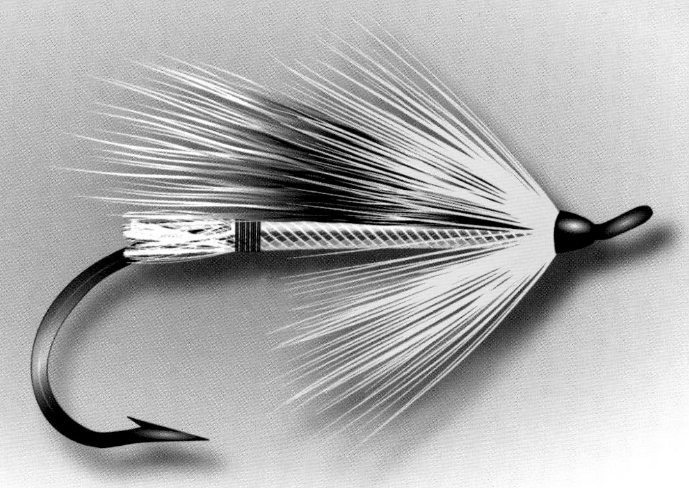

The following pages contain a full catalogue of all the flies which are illustrated within the main text. Dressing details for each fly are given, together with an illustration. The flies are organised in alphabetical order and are split into two groups - salmon flies and steelhead flies. In order to keep certain groups of related flies together we have generally used the generic part of the name within the alphabetical sorting - i.e. Tosh, Gold Tosh and Silver Tosh will be found under Tosh, Tosh Gold, Tosh Silver etc. Both forms of the name are cross-referenced in the index.

We have not given hook details for these dressings: this is not an oversight but simply because hook types vary so widely and the rules governing what is and is not allowable in each area and country vary equally as much. The typical hook sizes also vary according to the geographical area and the type of fish. For example, grilse flies in the west of Ireland may be tied as small as a size 14 or as large as size 4, steelhead flies for winter fishing may be as large as a size 5/0. Dressings have also been shown on a variety of hook types - singles, doubles, trebles, Waddington shanks and tubes. Most of the dressings given here will translate quite easily from one type of hook to another with only minor alterations, Templedog tubes are perhaps the exception..

Be aware that the stiffness of the material, particularly for the wings, is critical to the performance of the fly. Small flies need flexible fibres so that a fly normally tied as a size 4 may need a different winging material when tied as small as a size 14.

Some of the dressings given in the following pages may mention feathers from birds such as macaws, toucans etc. in order to maintain historical accuracy. On no account do we wish to encourage the illegal use of plumage from protected species, particularly when perfectly acceptable substitutes are readily available. Even if the use of such plumage is not illegal we can see no reason why rare species should be further endangered by flytyers. The fish certainly can't tell the difference when a substitute is used!

AKROYD TUBE

TAG: Oval silver tinsel
TAIL: Hot orange marabou plus orange flash
RIB: Oval silver tinsel
BODY: Rear 2/3rds. orange floss, front 1/3rd. black floss
BODY HACKLE: Yellow over orange floss
WING: Black bucktail tied above and below body
COLLAR HACKLE: Natural Guinea fowl
HEAD: Black

ALISTAIR

TAG: Oval gold tinsel
RIB: Oval gold tinsel
BODY: Flat gold tinsel
WING: Dirty yellow bucktail tied all round for tubes and Waddingtons, top and bottom for single, double and treble hooks
HEAD: Black

ALLEN'S L. T.

TAG: Oval gold tinsel and scarlet floss
TAIL: Purple hackle fibres
RIB: Oval gold tinsel
BODY: Black floss
THROAT: Black cock hackle
WING: Dark moose hair
HEAD: Black

ALLY'S SHRIMP - Gowans

TAIL: Hot orange bucktail with four strands of pearl Crystal Hair optional
RIB: Oval gold
BODY: Rear half red floss, front half black floss
UNDERWING: Top & bottom, natural grey squirrel, tied flat extending to bend of hook
WING: Golden pheasant tippets, extending to hook barb
HACKLE: Hot orange, tied as collar and dressed back, length to match tippets
HEAD: Red

ALLY'S SHRIMP FATBACK - McPhail

RIB: Oval silver
BODY: Rear half red floss, front half black floss
UNDERWING: Top & bottom, natural grey squirrel, tied flat to slightly beyond end of tube
COLLAR HACKLE: Red cock
WING: G. P tippet feather, length of body. First layer, orange Arctic fox tied fatback fashion. Second layer, orange Arctic fox, longer than first, fatback style. Third layer, orange Arctic fox, longer, tied in normal style. Fourth layer, orange goat hair, very long, tied in normal style. A few strands orange Crystal Flash over.
HEAD: Red

AURORA BOREALIS BLUE - Dima

TAG: Oval silver tinsel & sky blue floss
TAIL: G.P. topping
BUTT: Black ostrich herl
BODY: Eight strands of sky blue and eight strands of white floss interwoven together.
WING: White and sky blue Arctic fox mixed. Black arctic fox with strands of blue and silver Angel Hair as overwing
HACKLE: One turn widgeon and one turn blue cock. Black dyed G.P. body feather tied collar fashion over.
HEAD: Black

BALLYNAHINCH BADGER

TAG: Fine round silver tinsel and yellow floss
TAIL: G.P. topping
RIB: Oval silver tinsel
BODY: Black floss
THROAT: Kingfisher blue cock
WING: Badger hair
HEAD: Black

BARNES SPECIAL

TAG: Flat silver Mylar and pale yellow floss
TAIL: G.P. topping
BUTT: Black ostrich herl
RIB: Oval silver tinsel
BODY: Rear third, pale yellow floss, front 2/3rds. green floss
WING: Grey fox hair
CHEEKS: Jungle cock
COLLAR HACKLE: Chartreuse tied as a collar Cosseboom style
HEAD: Black

BEAIVVAS - Furuly

TAG: Oval silver tinsel and yellow floss
TAIL: Mixed fibres red, black and orange fox hair
BUTT: Black ostrich herl
RIB: Embossed silver tinsel
BODY: Rear half, yellow Antron, front half, black Antron
THROAT: Natural Guinea fowl
WING: Green fox hair under black fox hair with yellow fox hair as topping over all
HEAD: Black

BELTRA BADGER

TAG: Fine round silver tinsel and yellow floss
TAIL: G.P. topping
BUTT: Black ostrich herl
RIB: Oval silver tinsel
BODY: Flat silver tinsel
BODY HACKLE: Lemon yellow from second turn of tinsel
THROAT: Kingfisher blue cock
WING: Few fibres of red bucktail with badger hair over. Topping over all.l
HEAD: Black

BERNIES COMET - Ripley

TAG: Medium flat silver tinsel
TAIL: White polar bear under fur and four strands silver Krystal Flash
RIB: Oval silver
BODY: Fluorescent white Antron body wool
WING: White polar bear with strands of silver Krystal Flash over, fluorescent blue polar bear over all
HEAD: White thread with pearl nail varnish over

BERTHDEE MUNRO

TAG: Fine oval gold
BUTT: Yellow floss
TAIL: Orange cock fibres or squirrel hair
BODY: Unribbed black floss
THROAT: Black cock
WING: Yellow dyed squirrel hair with a few of the throat fibres over
HEAD: Black

AKROYD TUBE | ALISTAIR | ALLEN'S L. T.

ALLY'S SHRIMP - Gowans | ALLY'S SHRIMP FATBACK -McPhail | AURORA BOREALIS BLUE - Dima

BALLYNAHINCH BADGER | BARNES SPECIAL | BEAIVVAS - Furuly

BELTRA BADGER | BERNIES COMET - Ripley | BERTHDEE MUNRO

BLACK & ORANGE TEMPLEDOG - Shumakov

BODY: Bronze Skittle tube (see page 80)
WING: First layer, hot orange SLF hank and polar fox dyed hot orange with two strands orange-yellow Mirage. Second layer, polar fox dyed black with a few strands of black and red Angel Hair. Third layer, polar fox dyed black with a few strands of black and red Angel Hair. Fourth layer, polar fox dyed black with a few strands of black Angel Hair. The last wing tied in Templedog style (see page 26)
COLLAR HACKLE: Badger cock dyed orange, tied in between third and fourth wing layers.
CHEEKS: Jungle Cock
HEAD: Black

BLACK & RED WADDINGTON

TAG: Oval silver tinsel
RIB: Oval silver tinsel
BODY: Black floss
WING: Black bucktail tied in above shank - red bucktail tied in below shank
HEAD: Black

BLACK & SILVER EGGHEAD ZONKER

TAG: Oval silver tinsel and hot orange Antron
TAIL: Purple hackle fibres
RIB: Oval silver tinsel for body plus nylon for securing zonker strip
UNDERBODY: White floss
BODY: Rear two-thirds, silver tinsel - front third, black floss
BODY HACKLE: Black cock
FRONT HACKLE: Black cock
WING: Black rabbit zonker strip or similar secured with nylon rib
HEAD: Black, chartreuse and flame Glo-Bug yarn

BLACK & SILVER TEMPLEDOG - Angus

TAG: Oval silver tinsel and fluo yellow Antron
TAIL: Fluorescent yellow Antron
RIB: Oval silver tinsel
BODY: rear half - wide silver holographic tinsel, Front half black dubbing
UNDERWING: in order - black fox hair, strands of silver and pearl Flashabou, holographic silver Angel Hair, four or five strands of peacock herl
COLLAR HACKLE: Natural Guinea fowl, tied in between underwing and overwing.
OVERWING: Long black fox hair tied Templedog style (see page 26)
CHEEKS: Jungle Cock
HEAD: Black

BLACK & YELLOW TUBE

RIB: Oval silver tinsel
BODY: Black floss
WING: Two equal bunches of yellow and black hair (yellow below, black above)
HEAD: Black

BLACK BEAR - Smith

TAIL: Two thin sections of black feather such as dyed swan or goose
BODY: Black wool
WING: Black bear hair extending to end of tail
THROAT: Black bear hair extending to end of hook
HEAD: Black

BLACK BEAR BROWN HACKLE

TAG: Oval silver tinsel
RIB: Oval silver tinsel
BODY: Black wool
WING: Black bear or similar hair
COLLAR HACKLE: Two turns brown cock sloping backwards
HEAD: Black

BLACK BEAR GREEN BUTT - Doak

TAG: Oval silver tinsel and green floss
TAIL: Black hackle fibres
RIB: Oval silver tinsel
BODY: Black floss or wool
WING: Black bear or squirrel hair
CHEEKS: Jungle cock
THROAT: Black cock hackle
HEAD: Black

BLACK BEAR GREEN BUTT - Duncan

TAG: Fine oval silver tinsel and fluorescent green floss
RIB: Fine oval silver tinsel
BODY: Black floss
THROAT: Black grizzly
WING: Black bear hair
HEAD: Black

BLACK BOMBER - Aucoin

TAG: Fine round silver tinsel and yellow floss
TAIL: G.P. topping
RIB: Oval silver tinsel
BODY: Black wool
THROAT: Black cock
WING: Black squirrel hair, G.P. topping over
CHEEKS: Jungle cock
HEAD: Black

BLACK DART - Shumakov

BODY: Bronze Skittle tube (see page 77)
WING: First layer, polar fox dyed dark brown with two strands black holographic tinsel and red Twinkle under. Second layer, polar fox dyed dark brown with a few strands of brown and pearl and red Angel Hair. Third layer, polar fox dyed dark brown with a few strands of black, red, copper and brown Angel Hair. Fourth layer, polar fox dyed black with a few strands of black Angel Hair. The last wing tied in Templedog style (see page 26)
COLLAR HACKLE: Black cock and red-brown cock, tied in between third and fourth wing layers.
CHEEKS: Jungle Cock
HEAD: Black

BLACK DOCTOR FLASH

TAG: Oval silver tinsel and fluorescent red Antron or wool
RIB: Oval silver tinsel
BODY: Black floss
THROAT: Black cock
WING: Soft black hair (fox, goat etc.) with two or three strands each of red and blue Flashabou
CHEEKS: Jungle cock
HEAD: Black

BLACK & ORANGE TEMPLEDOG — BLACK & RED WADDINGTON — BLACK & SILVER EGGHEAD ZONKER

BLACK & SILVER TEMPLEDOG — BLACK & YELLOW TUBE — BLACK BEAR

BLACK BEAR BROWN HACKLE — BLACK BEAR GREEN BUTT - Doak — BLACK BEAR GREEN BUTT - Smith

BLACK BOMBER - Aucoin — BLACK DART - Shumakov — BLACK DOCTOR FLASH

BLACK GOLDFINCH

TAG: Oval silver tinsel and orange floss
TAIL: G.P. topping
BUTT: Black ostrich herl
RIB: Oval silver tinsel
BODY: Black floss
BODY HACKLE: Claret cock
THROAT HACKLE: Blue jay
WING: From bottom, yellow, red and yellow hair. G.P. topping over
HEAD: Black

BLACK MARIA

TAG: Oval silver tinsel
TAIL: G.P. topping
RIB: Oval silver tinsel over black body
BODY: Rear half yellow floss, front half black floss
BODY HACKLE: Black cock over black floss
THROAT: Black cock
WING: Sparse black hair
HEAD: Black

BLACK SHEEP

TAG: Oval silver tinsel
BODY: Black wool
THROAT HACKLE: Long blue cock
WING: Yellow under black bucktail, up to 75mm (3") long
CHEEKS: Jungle cock
HEAD: Black

BLACK SPIDER

TAG: Oval silver tinsel and orange floss
TAIL: Black squirrel hair
RIB: Fine oval silver tinsel
BODY: Black wool
THROAT HACKLE: Black cock
WING: Sparse black squirrel hair to bend of hook
HEAD: Black

BLACK TEMPLEDOG

TAG: Oval gold tinsel
BUTT & TAIL: Red Antron yarn
TAIL: Black hackle fibres
RIB: Oval silver tinsel
BODY: Rear half - flat silver tinsel, front half black dubbing
WING: Two layers of black fox with strands of red and rainbow Flashabou tied Templedog
CHEEKS: Jungle cock dyed hot orange. Pearl/black or yellow/black adhesive eyes on Spectratape as alternative
COLLAR HACKLE: Hot orange and black cock
HEAD: Black

BLACK TEMPLEDOG HALFINCHER

BODY: 1/2" brass tube, no dressing
UNDERWING: White polar bear or other stiff hair followed by strands of peacock and fluorescent orange Krystal Flash
WING: Two layers of black fox with strands of red and purple holographic flash. Tied Templedog style (see page 26)
CHEEKS: Yellow/black adhesive eyes on pearl Spectratape
COLLAR HACKLE: Hot orange and black cock
HEAD: Black

BLACK WULFF

TAG: Flat silver tinsel
TAIL: Short G.P. topping
BODY: Black floss
WING: Black bear or similar hair
THROAT: White moose hair
WING: Black moose hair
HEAD: Black

BLACK, SILVER & YELLOW

RIB: Oval silver tinsel
BODY: Flat silver tinsel
WING: Black bear or squirrel hair
CHEEKS: Jungle cock
THROAT: Yellow cock hackle under shank
WING: Sparse bunch of pearl Crystal Hair, black bucktail over
HEAD: Black

BLUE BOY

TAG: Flat silver tinsel and fluorescent white floss
TAIL: Silver pheasant tippet
BUTT: Black wool
RIB: Flat silver tinsel
BODY: Blue floss
THROAT: Grizzly cock
WING: Grey squirrel tail
HEAD: Black

BLUE CHARM

TAG: Oval silver tinsel and golden yellow floss
TAIL: G.P. topping
BUTT: Black ostrich herl
RIB: Oval silver tinsel
BODY: Black wool
COLLAR HACKLE: Blue cock
WING: Red phase squirrel hair
HEAD: Black

BLUE CHARM HAIRY - Mackenzie

TAG: Oval silver tinsel and yellow floss
TAIL: Yellow Antron wool
RIB: Oval silver tinsel
BODY: Black floss
SHOULDER HACKLE: Grey squirrel tail reaching to tip of tail
FRONT HACKLE: Dyed blue hair reaching to hook point
HEAD: Black

Note: In common with all other McKenzie Hairy flies, the tail and both hackles consist of hair fibres wound in a dubbing loop

BLUE DOCTOR

TAG: Oval silver tinsel and fluorescent red Antron or wool
TAIL: Golden pheasant topping
RIB: Oval silver tinsel
BODY: Blue floss
THROAT: Blue cock
WING: Grey squirrel tail
HEAD: Red

BLACK GOLDFINCH | BLACK MARIA | BLACK SHEEP

BLACK SPIDER | BLACK TEMPLEDOG | BLACK TEMPLEDOG HALFINCHER

BLACK WULFF | BLACK, SILVER & YELLOW | BLUE BOY

BLUE CHARM | BLUE CHARM HAIRY - McKenzie | BLUE DOCTOR

BLUE LADY

TAIL: Yellow hair, tied short
RIB: Oval silver tinsel
BODY: Black wool
THROAT HACKLE: Dark Blue
WING: Grey squirrel tail dyed deep blue
CHEEKS: Jungle cock
HEAD: Black

BLUE OPAL

TAG: Flat silver Mylar
TAIL: Golden pheasant tippets
BUTT: Dark blue dyed ostrich herl
RIB: Round silver tinsel
BODY: Fluorescent blue floss with dark blue dyed ostrich herl butt at front
THROAT HACKLE: Grizzle cock
WING: Grey squirrel tail with peacock sword feathers over
HEAD: Black

BLUE RAT - Jorgensen

TAG: Oval gold tinsel
TAIL: Four short peacock sword fibres
RIB: Oval gold tinsel
BODY: Rear half, Silver Doctor blue floss: Front half, peacock herl
VEILING: Length of blue floss over rear body half
WING: Grey fox guard hair
CHEEKS: Jungle cock with blue kingfisher
FRONT HACKLE: Small bunch of grizzle hackle fibres tied over wing, similar bunch as throat
HEAD: Red

BLUE SAPPHIRE

TAG: Oval gold tinsel & yellow floss
TAIL: GP topping
RIB: Fine round or oval gold tinsel
BODY: Black floss
BODY HACKLE: Black & blue from second turn of tinsel
THROAT: Blue cock
WING: Black hair with strands of light blue hair each side. GP topping over
HEAD: Black

BLUE TEMPLEDOG - Urbig

TUBE: 3/4" to 1" copper, aluminium or plastic
BODY: None, use silicone tubing to hold hook in place
WING: White polar bear or arctic fox, dyed blue arctic fox, strands of pearl Flashabou, black arctic fox or goat over
THROAT HACKLE: Blue cock tied in before last wing layer
HEAD: Black

Note: wing tied Templedog style (see page 26)

BO DIDDLEY

TAG: Oval silver tinsel
TAIL: GP tippet
BUTT: Golden yellow floss
RIB: Oval silver
BODY: Black floss
WING: Black bear hair
COLLAR HACKLE: Bright yellow and orange wound together, sloping back
HEAD: Black

BØRRE FLUA - Pettersen

TAG: Oval silver tinsel, yellow floss followed by red floss
TAIL: Dyed red hackle fibres
BUTT: Black ostrich herl
RIB: Oval silver tinsel
BODY: Black floss
THROAT: Blue dyed guinea fowl
WING: Blue dyed guinea fowl under black squirrel tail
HEAD: Black

BOTHAM'S FANCY - O'Reilly

TAG: Oval silver tinsel
RIB: Oval silver tinsel
BODY: DFM fluorescent green floss
THROAT HACKLE: Blue cock
WING: Black squirrel
HEAD: Black

BOURRACH

TAG: Oval silver tinsel
TAIL: Blue hackle point
RIB: Oval silver tinsel
BODY: Flat silver tinsel
THROAT HACKLE: Blue cock, long
WING: Yellow bucktail or squirrel for smaller sizes. Twice body length
HEAD: Black

BUTTERFLY - Ingalls

TAIL: Dyed red hackle fibres, long
BODY: Rusty peacock herl
WING: White goat hair, slightly longer than body, divided and set above body, slanted backwards at 45°
HACKLE: Brown hackle wound as collar, one turn behind wings, one turn in front
HEAD: Black

BUTTERFLY GREEN MACHINE - Somers

TAG: Flat silver tinsel
TAIL: Krystal Flash, tied short
BUTT: Light green fluorescent wool
BODY: Green Machine micro-chenille
WING: Sparse white polar bear, slightly longer than body, splayed and set slightly above body
HACKLE: Sparse brown hackle wound as collar, one turn behind wings, one turn in front
HEAD: Black

BUTTERFLY VARIANT - Duncan

TAG: Oval silver tinsel and fluorescent yellow floss
TAIL: Dyed red hackle fibres, long
BODY: Rusty peacock herl
WING: White polar bear hair, slightly longer than body, divided and set above body, slanted backwards at 45°
HACKLE: Brown hackle wound as collar, two turns in front of wings
HEAD: Black

BLUE LADY | BLUE OPAL | BLUE RAT

BLUE SAPPHIRE | BLUE TEMPLEDOG | BO DIDDLEY

BØRRE FLUA - Pettersen | BOTHAM'S FANCY - O'Reilly | BOURRACH

BUTTERFLY - Ingalls | BUTTERFLY GREEN MACHINE - Somers | BUTTERFLY VARIANT - Duncan

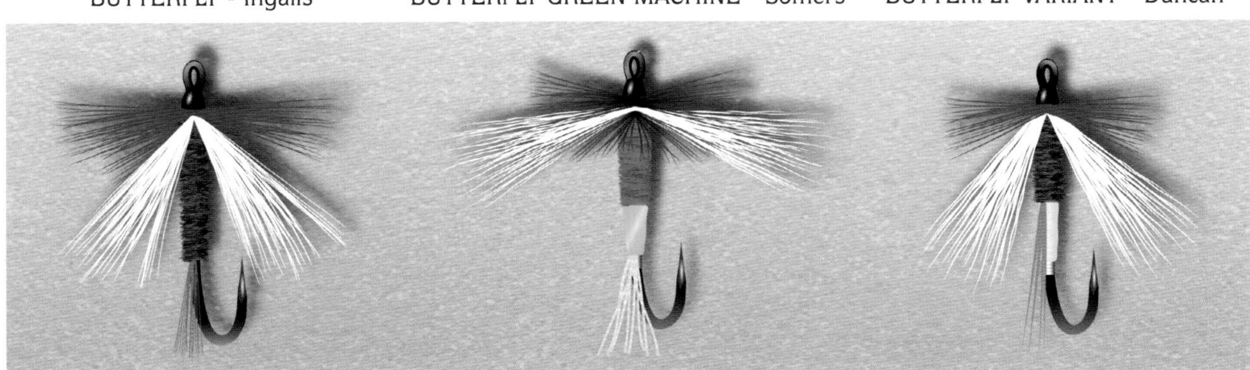

CAINS COPPER

TAG: Oval copper tinsel
TAIL: Dyed fluorescent red hackle fibres
BUTT: Black chenille
RIB: Oval copper tinsel
BODY: Flat copper tinsel
WING: Grey squirrel tail over orange dyed hair
COLLAR HACKLE: Black cock
HEAD: Black

CANADIAN GREEN - Duncan

TAG: Oval silver tinsel
TAIL: Golden pheasant topping
RIB: Oval silver tinsel
BODY: DFM fluorescent green floss
WING: Grey squirrel tail dyed green
COLLAR HACKLE: Yellow cock
HEAD: Black

CANARY

TAG: Oval silver tinsel and yellow floss
TAIL: Golden pheasant topping
BUTT: Black ostrich herl
REAR BODY: Oval silver tinsel
CENTRE HACKLE: Yellow cock
MIDDLE JOINT: Black ostrich herl
FRONT BODY: Oval silver tinsel
HACKLE: Yellow cock
WING: Golden olive mohair with golden pheasant topping over
HEAD: Black

CASCADE SHRIMP - Variant

TAIL: Mixed yellow & orange bucktail with four strands of pearl Crystal Hair. At least length of tube
BODY: Holographic silver Mylar
WING: Black squirrel tail and four strands of pearl Crystal Hair
HACKLE: Four turns each of long yellow & orange cock
HEAD: Black

CHAMELEON - Rattray

TAG: Oval gold tinsel
RIB: Oval or flat gold tinsel
BODY: Rear half, yellow floss. Front half, black floss
WING: Mixed black, yellow and red bucktail with a few strands of pearl Crystal Hair over
HEAD: Black

CHAREST SPECIAL - Charest

TAG: Oval silver tinsel and flat green tinsel
TAIL: Golden pheasant topping
RIB: Oval silver tinsel
BODY: Black floss
WING: Tied in as four bunches equi-spaced along body. Beginning at rear: first bunch - yellow calf tail. Second & third bunches - mixed yellow and pale green calf tail. Fourth bunch - yellow calf tail. Each bunch graduated in length to keep overall wing length equal.
THROAT: Black bear hair
CHEEKS: Jungle cock
HEAD: Black

CHARLOTTE - Peaston

TAG: Oval silver tinsel
TAIL: Five or six strands of golden pheasant tippet with topping over
RIB: Oval silver tinsel
BODY: Flat gold tinsel
BODY HACKLE: Yellow cock
FRONT HACKLES: Yellow cock with blue cock in front
WING: Black squirrel tail
HEAD: Black

CLARET & GRIZZLY

TAG: Oval silver tinsel
TAIL: Golden pheasant topping
RIB: Oval silver tinsel
BODY: Claret dyed seal's fur
BODY HACKLE: Grizzly cock
WING: Grey squirrel tail
CHEEKS: Jungle cock
HEAD: Black

CLARET & JAY

TAG: Oval silver tinsel & orange floss
TAIL: Golden pheasant tippet with topping over
RIB: Oval silver tinsel
BODY: Claret dyed seal's fur
BODY HACKLE: Dark claret cock
THROAT HACKLE: Blue jay
WING: G.P. tippet under brown squirrel tail
HEAD: Black

CLARET KILLER - Baker

TAG: Oval silver tinsel
RIB: Oval silver tinsel
BODY: Claret dyed seal's fur or wool
WING: Grey squirrel tail
COLLAR HACKLE: Black, slanted rearwards
HEAD: Black

COLBURN BLUE

TAG: Oval silver tinsel
TAIL: Grey squirrel tail dyed blue
RIB: Oval silver tinsel
BODY: Medium blue floss tied cigar shape with black ostrich herl butt in centre
WING: Grey squirrel tail dyed blue
COLLAR HACKLE: Light blue cock (dark variant - black cock hackle)
HEAD: Black

Other variants:
Claret Colburn - substitute claret for blue
Orange Colburn - substitute orange for blue

COLBURN SPECIAL

TAG: Oval silver tinsel
TAIL: Black hair over green hair
RIB: Oval silver tinsel
BODY: Fluorescent green floss tied cigar shape with black ostrich herl butt in centre
WING: Black hair over green dyed squirrel hair
COLLAR HACKLE: Yellow cock
HEAD: Black

Pattern as Fulsher & Krom. Bates gives wing as red over green hair

CAINS COPPER | CANADIAN GREEN - Duncan | CANARY

CASCADE SHRIMP - Variant | CHAMELEON - Rattray | CHAREST SPECIAL - Charest

CHARLOTTE - Peaston | CLARET & GRIZZLY | CLARET & JAY

CLARET KILLER - Baker | COLBURN BLUE | COLBURN SPECIAL

COLLIE DOG

TUBE: Plastic or aluminium
BODY: None
WING: Long black goat hair 60 to 100mm (2.5" to 4") long
THROAT HACKLE: black hackle fibres
HEAD: Black

Note:
For heavy spring fishing, tube can be brass

COLLIE DOG VARIANT - Ireland

TUBE: 19mm (3/4") plastic or aluminium
BODY: None
WING: Long black goat hair 60 to 100mm (2.5" to 4") long
THROAT HACKLE: red hackle fibres or bucktail
HEAD: Black

Note:
For heavy spring fishing tube can be 25mm (1") brass

COLLIE DOG VARIANT - Donaldson

TUBE: Plastic
RIB: Silver wire or fine oval silver tinsel over Lurex
BODY: Rear third left undressed. Mid third - lilac Lurex. Front third flat - copper Lurex. Varnish to strengthen Lurex.
WING: Two bunches long black goat hair 60 to 100mm (2.5" to 4") long with strands of fluorescent pink Twinkle between.
HEAD: Black

COMET

TUBE or WADDINGTON
TAIL: Yellow bucktail tied all around shank extending to just beyond hook point
RIB: Oval gold
REAR BODY: Red floss
MID WING: Red bucktail tied all around shank , cloaking tail
RIB: Oval gold
FRONT BODY: Black floss
FRONT WING: Black bucktail cloaking both mid wing and tail
HEAD: Black

COMET FATBACK #1 - McPhail

TUBE: 19mm (3/4") copper tube, fluorescent orange tubing to hold hook in place
TAIL: Fluorescent yellow floss
RIB: Oval silver
BODY: Black floss
WING: First layer - yellow arctic fox. Second layer - long red goats's hair. Third layer - black arctic fox
HACKLE: Yellow and red cock
CHEEKS: Jungle cock
HEAD: Black

Note: wing tied Templedog style (see page 26)

COMET FATBACK #2 - McPhail

TUBE: 19mm (3/4") copper tube
RIB: Oval gold
BODY: Rear half - red floss. Front half - Black floss
WING: First layer - red arctic fox. Second layer - yellow arctic fox. Third layer - long yellow goats's hair. Fourth layer - black arctic fox
HACKLE: Black cock
HEAD: Black

Note: wing tied Templedog style (see page 26)

COPPER KILLER - Doak

TAG: Oval gold tinsel & fluorescent green floss
TAIL: GP red breast feather fibres
BUTT: Fluorescent red floss
RIB: Oval gold tinsel
BODY: Flat copper tinsel
THROAT: Orange cock hackle
WING: Pine squirrel tail
HEAD: Red

COPPER KILLER - Duncan

TAG: Oval copper tinsel & fluorescent green floss
TAIL: GP red breast feather fibres
BUTT: Fluorescent red wool
RIB: Oval copper tinsel
BODY: Flat copper tinsel
THROAT: Hot orange cock hackle
WING: Fiery brown calf tail
HEAD: Fluorescent red

COPPER KILLER - Krom

TAG: Flat silver Mylar dyed orange & fluorescent green floss
TAIL: Partridge body feather fibres
BUTT: Fluorescent red thread
BODY: Silver Mylar tubing dyed orange
THROAT: Orange cock hackle
WING: Red squirrel tail
HEAD: Red

COPPER KILLER - Miner

TAG: Oval copper tinsel & pale green floss
TAIL: Rusty red partridge hackle fibres
BUTT: Bright red floss
RIB: Oval copper tinsel
BODY: Flat copper tinsel
THROAT HACKLE: Bright orange cock hackle applied as collar before wing
WING: Fox squirrel hair
HEAD: Red

COPPER SHRIMP

TAG: Flat copper tinsel
TAIL: Red bucktail and gold Krystal Hair
BUTT: Black ostrich herl
RIB: Oval gold tinsel
BODY: Flat copper tinsel
WING: Orange and yellow bucktail mixed with strands of gold Krystal Flash. Tied above and below shank
HEAD: Red

COSSEBOOM

TAG: Silver tinsel
TAIL: Olive green floss, cut short
RIB: Oval silver tinsel
BODY: Olive green silk floss (Pearsall's #82)
WING: Grey squirrel tail
COLLAR HACKLE: Lemon yellow cock applied after wing. Sloping backwards
CHEEKS: Optional - Jungle cock
HEAD: Red

COLLIE DOG | COLLIE DOG VARIANT - Ireland | COLLIE DOG VARIANT - Donaldson

COMET | COMET FATBACK #1 - McPhail | COMET FATBACK #2 - McPhail

COPPER KILLER - Doak | COPPER KILLER - Duncan | COPPER KILLER - Krom

COPPER KILLER - Miner | COPPER SHRIMP | COSSEBOOM

COSSEBOOM - Black

TAG: Silver tinsel
TAIL: Black floss, cut short
RIB: Oval silver tinsel
BODY: Black floss
WING: Grey squirrel tail
COLLAR HACKLE: Black cock applied after wing. Sloping backwards
CHEEKS: Optional - Jungle cock
HEAD: Red

COSSEBOOM - Duncan

TAG: Oval silver tinsel
TAIL: Dark green floss, cut short
RIB: Oval silver tinsel
BODY: Dark green floss
WING: Grey squirrel tail
COLLAR HACKLE: Yellow cock applied after wing. Sloping backwards
HEAD: Red

COSSEBOOM - Fluorescent Green

TAG: Flat silver tinsel & chinese red floss
RIB: Oval silver tinsel
BODY: Fluorescent green floss
WING: Grey squirrel tail
COLLAR HACKLE: Yellow cock applied after wing. Sloping backwards
HEAD: Red

COSSEBOOM - Gold

TAG: Silver tinsel
TAIL: Golden pheasant topping
RIB: Oval silver tinsel
BODY: Gold tinsel
WING: Grey squirrel tail with four strands peacock sword feather over
COLLAR HACKLE: Light blue cock applied after wing. Sloping backwards
CHEEKS: Optional - Jungle cock
HEAD: Red

COSSEBOOM - Green Butt Black

TAG: Flat silver tinsel & fluorescent green floss
RIB: Oval silver tinsel
BODY: Black floss
WING: Black squirrel tail
COLLAR HACKLE: Yellow cock applied after wing. Sloping backwards
HEAD: Black

COSSEBOOM - Hair Hackle Black

TAG: Oval silver tinsel & fluorescent orange floss
BODY: Black chenille or wool
WING: Dyed dark brown squirrel tail
COLLAR HACKLE: Yellow dyed deer hair spun after wing. Sloping backwards
HEAD: Red

COSSEBOOM - Krystal

TAG: Flat silver tinsel
RIB: Oval silver tinsel
BODY: Fluorescent chartreuse floss or yarn over flat silver tinsel underbody
WING: 1/3rd. green over 2/3rds. fluorescent green Krystal Flash
COLLAR HACKLE: Yellow hen applied after wing. Sloping backwards
HEAD: Red

COSSEBOOM - Miramichi

TAG: Oval silver tinsel
TAIL: Green floss, cut short
RIB: Oval silver tinsel
BODY: Green floss
WING: Grey squirrel tail
COLLAR HACKLE: Lemon yellow cock applied after wing. Sloping backwards
HEAD: Red

COSSEBOOM - Orange

TAG: Flat gold tinsel
TAIL: Orange floss, cut short
RIB: Flat gold tinsel
BODY: Orange floss
WING: Grey squirrel tail with four strands peacock sword feather over
COLLAR HACKLE: Black cock applied after wing. Sloping backwards
CHEEKS: Optional - Jungle cock
HEAD: Black

COSSEBOOM - Peacock

TAG: Silver tinsel
TAIL: Peacock sword fibres, short
RIB: Oval silver tinsel
BODY: Rear half - gold tinsel. Front half - peacock herl
WING: Grey squirrel tail with a bunch of peacock sword feathers over
THROAT HACKLE: Small bunch of peacock sword feathers
CHEEKS: Optional - Jungle cock
HEAD: Red

COSSEBOOM - Red

TAG: Gold tinsel
TAIL: Red floss, cut short
RIB: Oval gold tinsel
BODY: Red floss
WING: Grey squirrel tail
COLLAR HACKLE: Black cock applied after wing. Sloping backwards
CHEEKS: Optional - Jungle cock
HEAD: Red

COSSEBOOM - Silver

BODY: Silver Mylar tubing attatched at rear of hook with black thread. End flared out to act as tail.
WING: Grey squirrel tail
COLLAR HACKLE: Yellow cock applied after wing. Sloping backwards
HEAD: Black

COSSEBOOM - Black

COSSEBOOM - Duncan

COSSEBOOM - Fluorescent Green

COSSEBOOM - Gold

COSSEBOOM - Green Butt Black

COSSEBOOM - Hair Hackle Black

COSSEBOOM - Krystal

COSSEBOOM - Miramichi

COSSEBOOM - Orange

COSSEBOOM - Peacock

COSSEBOOM - Red

COSSEBOOM - Silver

COSSEBOOM - Winston's Green

TAG: Silver tinsel
TAIL: Olive green floss, cut short
RIB: Oval silver tinsel
BODY: Olive green silk floss (Pearsall's #82)
WING: Grey squirrel tail
COLLAR HACKLE: Lemon yellow cock applied after wing. Sloping backwards
CHEEKS: Optional - Jungle cock
HEAD: Red

COSSEBOOM, YELLOW

TAG: Silver tinsel
TAIL: Yellow floss, cut short
RIB: Oval silver tinsel
BODY: Yellow floss
WING: Grey squirrel tail
COLLAR HACKLE: Grizzly cock applied after wing. Sloping backwards
CHEEKS: Optional - Jungle cock
HEAD: Red

CROSFIELD

TAG: Oval silver tinsel
TAIL: Golden pheasant topping
BODY: Embossed silver tinsel
WING: Grey squirrel tail
THROAT HACKLE: Blue cock
HEAD: Black

CULLMAN'S CHOICE - Wulff

RIB: Oval silver tinsel
BODY: Apple green floss
THROAT: White hackle as beard
WING: Black bear hair with GP topping over
HEAD: Black

DARK MACKEREL

TAIL: Small bunch of GP tippet fibres
RIB: Fine oval silver
BODY: Flat red Lurex
WING: Dyed brown squirrel hair
COLLAR HACKLE: Dark claret hen, long
HEAD: Black

DAWN - Saastamoinen

TAG: Oval silver tinsel, lacquered
TAIL: Yellow hackle fibres
BUTT: Fluorescent orange floss
RIB: Oval silver tinsel & fluorescent green floss
BODY: Rear half - flat silver tinsel. Front half - black & gold crystal seal
BODY HACKLE: Black cock over front body
THROAT: Yellow hackle to hook point
WING: Two hot orange hackles back to back. Strand flat pearl flash each side. 1/3rd. green racoon hair. 2/3rds. brown fox hair over. Small bunch golden brown fox hair over all.
HEAD: Black with fluorescent orange stripe

DAWN, BLACK - Saastamoinen

TAG: Oval gold tinsel, lacquered
TAIL: Fire orange hackle fibres
BUTT: Fluorescent orange floss
RIB: Oval silver tinsel & fluorescent orange floss
BODY: Rear half - flat gold tinsel. Front half - black & gold crystal seal
BODY HACKLE: Black cock over front body
THROAT: Black heron to beyond hook bend
WING: Two fire orange hackles back to back. Strand flat red flash each side. Golden brown fox hair over all.
HEAD: Black with fluorescent orange stripe

DAWN, BLUE - Saastamoinen

TAG: Flat gold tinsel, lacquered
TAIL: Blue & orange hackle fibres
BUTT: Fluorescent red floss
RIB: Oval gold tinsel & fluorescent red floss
BODY: Rear half - flat gold tinsel. Front half - blue crystal seal
BODY HACKLE: Blue cock over front body
THROAT: Blue hackle to hook point
WING: Two blue hackles back to back. Strand flat pearl flash each side. 1/3rd. golden brown fox hair. 2/3rds. brown fox hair.
HEAD: Black with fluorescent blue stripe

DAWN, GREEN - Saastamoinen

TAG: Flat gold tinsel, lacquered
TAIL: Green & orange hackle fibres
BUTT: Fluorescent green floss
RIB: Oval gold tinsel
BODY: Rear half - flat gold tinsel. Front half - green crystal seal
BODY HACKLE: Green cock over front body
THROAT: Green hackle to hook point
WING: Two yellow hackles back to back. Strand flat pearl flash each side. 1/4 white fox hair. 1/4 golden brown fox hair. 1/2brown fox hair.
HEAD: Black with fluorescent orange stripe

DAWN, RED - Saastamoinen

TAG: Flat gold tinsel, lacquered
TAIL: Red hackle fibres
BUTT: Fluorescent red floss
RIB: Oval gold tinsel & fluorescent red floss
BODY: Rear half - flat gold tinsel. Front half - black crystal seal
BODY HACKLE: Black cock over front body
THROAT: Red hackle to hook point
WING: Two red hackles back to back. Strand flat pearl flash each side. 1/3rd. golden brown fox hair. 2/3rds. black fox hair.
HEAD: Black with fluorescent orange stripe

DAWN, THUNDER - Saastamoinen

TAG: Oval gold tinsel & fluorescent orange floss, lacquered
TAIL: Hot orange hackle fibres
BUTT: Fluorescent red floss
RIB: Oval gold tinsel
BODY: Rear half - black floss. Front half - black crystal seal
BODY HACKLE: Orange heron over front body
THROAT: Blue guinea hackle to hook point
WING: Two deep blue hackles back to back. Strand flat pearl flash each side. 1/3rd. green racoon hair. 2/3rds. brown fox hair over.
HEAD: Black with fluorescent orange stripe

DAWN, YELLOW - Saastamoinen

TAG: Flat gold tinsel, lacquered
TAIL: Yellow & green hackle fibres
BUTT: Fluorescent red floss
RIB: Oval gold tinsel
BODY: Rear half - flat silver tinsel. Front half - yellow crystal seal
BODY HACKLE: Yellow cock over front body
THROAT: Yellow hackle to hook point
WING: Two yellow hackles back to back. Strand flat pearl flash each side. 1/3rd. golden brown fox hair. 2/3rds. brown fox hair.
HEAD: Black with fluorescent orange stripe

COSSEBOOM - Winston's Green | COSSEBOOM, YELLOW | CROSFIELD

CULLMAN'S CHOICE - Wulff | DARK MACKEREL | DAWN - Saastamoinen

DAWN, BLACK - Saastamoinen | DAWN, BLUE - Saastamoinen | DAWN, GREEN - Saastamoinen

DAWN, RED - Saastamoinen | DAWN, THUNDER - Saastamoinen | DAWN, YELLOW - Saastamoinen

DENTIST

TAIL: Hot orange calf tail
RIB: Oval gold
BODY: Flat gold tinsel
THROAT HACKLE: Hot orange calf tail
WING: Black squirrel tail
HEAD: Black

DOWN EAST

TAG: Flat silver tinsel
TAIL: GP topping
BUTT: Black ostrich herl
BODY: Grey floss
WING: Reddish-brown fitchtail
COLLAR HACKLE: Orange cock
HEAD: Black

DOWNEASTER

TAG: Flat silver tinsel & fluorescent red floss
TAIL: GP topping
BUTT: Black ostrich herl
RIB: Oval silver tinsel
BODY: Silver grey floss
THROAT HACKLE: Bright orange cock
WING: Black bear hair
HEAD: Black

DREAM - Saastamoinen

TAG: Flat gold tinsel
TAIL: Golden pheasant tippet fibres
BUTT: Black ostrich herl
RIB: Oval gold tinsel
BODY: Golden yellow floss
BODY HACKLE: Yellow cock
THROAT: Fire orange cock hackle
WING: Two fire orange hackles back to back. 1/2 golden brown fox hair. 1/2 brown fox hair.
HEAD: Black

DROWES DAWN - O'Connor

TUBE: 19 - 75mm (3/4 to 3")
TAG: Flat gold tinsel
RIB: Oval gold tinsel
BODY: Rear half - claret floss. Front half - yellow floss
WING: Two bunches of dark claret red bucktail alternating with two bunches of yellow bucktail.
CHEEKS: Jungle cock over the claret hair
HEAD: Black

DUNKELD

TAG: Fine oval gold tinsel
TAIL: GP topping with shorter red hackle fibres over
BUTT: Black ostrich herl
BODY: Embossed gold tinsel
THROAT HACKLE: Bright orange cock
WING: Grey squirrel tail dyed orange
CHEEKS: Jungle cock
HEAD: Black

DUNKELD, HAIRY - Mackenzie

TAG: Oval gold tinsel
TAIL: Yellow Antron wool under red Antron wool, wound
BUTT: Black ostrich herl
BODY: Embossed gold braided Mylar
TRAILING HACKLE: Grey squirrel hair dyed orange, wound
FRONT HACKLE: Hot orange hair, wound
HEAD: Black

Note: In common with all other McKenzie Hairy flies, the tail and both hackles consist of hair fibres wound in a dubbing loop

DUNKELD, IRISH

TAG: Oval gold tinsel
TAIL: GP red breast feather, wound
REAR BODY: Fluorescent green floss
RIB: Oval gold
CENTRE HACKLE: Creamy badger cock
FRONT BODY: Fluorescent green floss
RIB: Oval gold
WINGS: Roofed jungle cock
FRONT HACKLE: Creamy badger
HEAD: Black

DURHAM RANGER - Dupo

TUBE: Plastic
TAG: Fine oval silver tinsel and yellow floss
TAIL: Fluorescent yellow SLF Hanks
BUTT: Black ostrich herl
BODY: 1/2 orange floss, 1/2 hot orange seal's fur
RIB: Oval silver tinsel and small flat silver tinsel
BODY HACKLE: Hot orange cock hackle
THROAT: Black with blue hackle over
WING: Black, orange, black Artic fox with Flashabou, Four strands peacock herl over
CHEEKS: Jungle cock with blue hackle tip over
HEAD: Black

Note: wing tied Templedog style (see page 26)

DUSTY MILLER, HAIRWING

TAG: Oval silver tinsel & yellow floss
TAIL: GP topping with shorter red hackle fibres
BUTT: Black ostrich herl
RIB: Oval silver tinsel
BODY: Rear 2/3rds. embossed silver tinsel, front 1/3rd. orange floss
BODY HACKLE: Golden olive over orange floss (optional)
THROAT: Guinea fowl wound as collar
WING: Brown polar bear hair with a GP topping each side
CHEEKS: Jungle cock
HEAD: Black

EDITOR - Leventon

RIB: Fluorescent yellow nylon
BODY: Flat pearl Lurex over an underbody of white floss
THROAT: Blue dyed cock hackle tied as collar and swept back
WING: Black bucktail
CHEEKS: Jungle cock
HEAD: Black

EDITOR WADDINGTON - Leventon

RIB: Fluorescent yellow nylon
BODY: Flat pearl Lurex over an underbody of white floss
WING: Black bucktail all around shank
THROAT: Blue dyed cock hackle tied as collar and swept back
CHEEKS: Jungle cock
HEAD: Black

DENTIST | DOWN EAST | DOWNEASTER

DREAM - Saastamoinen | DROWES DAWN - O'Connor | DUNKELD

DUNKELD, HAIRY - McKenzie | DUNKELD, IRISH | DURHAM RANGER - Dupo

DUSTY MILLER | EDITOR - Leventon | EDITOR WADDINGTON - Leventon

ED'S HIGHLANDER - Myers

TAG: Oval silver tinsel and yellow-orange floss
TAIL: GP topping with barred wood duck over
BUTT: Black ostrich herl
RIB: Oval silver tinsel
BODY: Rear 1/3rd. rusty orange floss. Front 2/3rds. green highlander dubbing or wool
BODY HACKLE: Green cock over front body
THROAT: Yellow, wound and pulled down
WING: Yellow under orange under red bucktail. Each section with a few strands of Krystal flash of the same colour
CHEEKS: Jungle cock
HEAD: Black

EM-TE-FLUGOR

TAG: Gold tinsel
TAIL: GP topping
RIB: Flat gold tinsel
BODY: Blended red-brown and green wool
THROAT: Black cock hackle
WING: Cinnamon dyed polar bear with a furnace hackle each side. Strands peacock sword fibres over all
HEAD: Black

ETERNAL OPTIMIST - Williams

BODY: Pearl Mylat tubing, fastened at rear end of body with red silk. End frayed out to make tail
THROAT: Yellow bucktail
WING: Goat's hair dyed dark green
CHEEKS: Jungle cock
HEAD: Black

FAST EDDIE - Headley

TAG: Flat gold tinsel
RIB: Oval gold tinsel
BODY: Flat gold tinsel
THROAT: Hot orange hackle fibres or squirrel hair
WING: Green over yellow squirrel hair or bucktail
HEAD: Red

FAST EDDIE, WADDINGTON

TAIL: Yellow bucktail bound to treble with red fluoresent floss (Glo-Brite #5)
RIB: Oval gold tinsel
BODY: Flat gold tinsel
WING: Yellow under orange under green bucktail. All round shank
HEAD: Red

FIREBALL - Ingvarsson

TAG: Flat gold tinsel
TAIL: GP tippet fibres
RIB: Oval gold tinsel
BODY: Rear half - golden-yellow floss. Front half - purple floss
WING: Dyed red squirrel tail with two strands red Flashabou
COLLAR HACKLE: Scarlet cock hackle
HEAD: Black

FOXTON BADGER - Foxton

TUBE: Brass, aluminium or plastic 12-50mm (1/2"- 2")
RIB: Flat silver followed by oval silver tinsel
BODY: Black floss
WING: Well marked white-tipped badger hair
COLLAR HACKLE: Cock hackle dyed kingfisher blue
HEAD: Black

FRAFJORDSELVA

RIB: Oval gold tinsel
BODY: Pearl Mylar tinsel
WING: Grey squirrel tail in two bunches, the second shorter, to obtain barred effect
COLLAR HACKLE/HEAD: Long fibred scarlet seal's fur in a dubbing loop to produce a collar and then a muddler head

FULKRO - Fulsher & Krom

TAG: Flat silver tinsel & fluorescent orange floss
TAIL: Dyed red calf tail
RIB: Oval silver tinsel
BODY: Black wool
THROAT HACKLE: Brown
WING: Red squirrel tail
HEAD: Black

GALWAY BLACK & YELLOW

TAG: Oval gold tinsel
TAIL: G.P. topping
RIB: Oval gold tinsel
BODY: Flat gold tinsel
THROAT HACKLE: Lemon yellow cock, long
WING: Black squirrel tail
HEAD: Black

GALWAY GREEN

TAG: Oval silver tinsel
TAIL: Black squirrel tail
RIB: Oval silver tinsel
BODY: Yellow floss
THROAT HACKLE: Yellow bucktail tied as beard
WING: Bucktail dyed Green Highlander
HEAD: Black

GARRY DOG

TAG: Oval silver tinsel & yellow floss
TAIL: GP topping with red hackle tips over
RIB: Oval silver tinsel
BODY: Black floss
THROAT HACKLE: Guinea fowl dyed blue
WING: Yellow over red bleached squirrel hair
HEAD: Black

ED'S HIGHLANDER - Myers | EM-TE-FLUGOR | ETERNAL OPTIMIST - Williams

FAST EDDIE - Headley | FAST EDDIE, WADDINGTON | FIREBALL - Ingvarsson

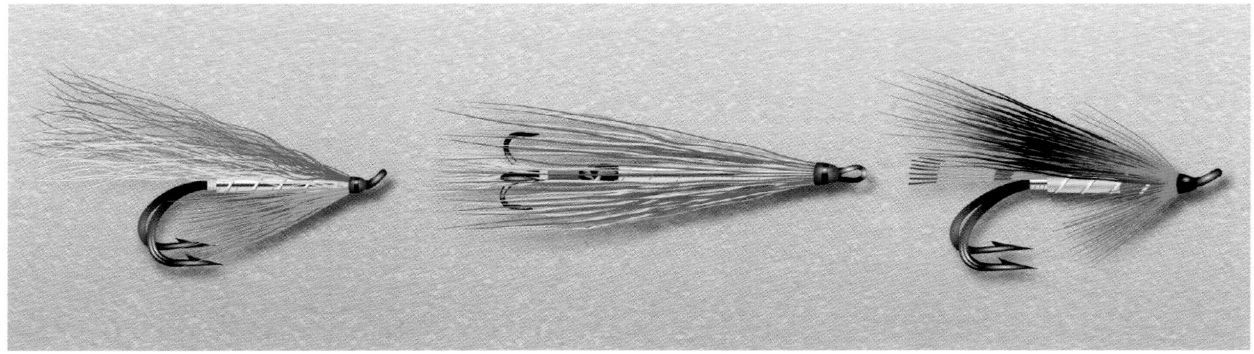

FOXTON BADGER - Foxton | FRAFJORDSELVA | FULKRO - Fulsher & Krom

GALWAY BLACK & YELLOW | GALWAY GREEN | GARRY DOG

GARRY DOG, VARIANT - McPhail

TAG: Oval silver tinsel
RIB: Oval silver
BODY: Black floss
THROAT: Mixed blue & black bucktail
WING: Red bucktail & holographic silver tinsel under yellow goar hair
CHEEKS: Silver adhesive eyes
HEAD: Black

GARRY DOG FATBACK #1 - McPhail

TUBE: 19mm (3/4") copper tube, fluorescent orange or yellow tubing to hold hook in place
TAG: Oval silver tinsel
RIB: Oval silver tinsel
BODY: Holographic silver Mylar
HACKLE: Red cock
WING: Red arctic fox with yellow goat over, red & yellow tinsel between
CHEEKS: Jungle cock dyed red
HEAD: Black

Notes: wing tied Templedog style (page 26)

GARRY DOG FATBACK #2 - McPhail

TUBE: 19mm (3/4") copper tube
TAG: Oval silver tinsel
RIB: Oval silver tinsel
BODY: Black floss
HACKLE: Guinea fowl dyed blue
WING: Red arctic fox under yellow arctic fox under yellow goat. Strands of gold Crystal Flash over
HEAD: Black

Notes: wing tied Templedog style (page 26)

GARRY DOG, GOLDEN - Donaldson

RIB: Oval silver
BODY: Flat gold tinsel
WING: Red bucktail under red Crystal Hair under yellow bucktail
HEAD: Black

GARRY DOG, MIRAMICHI

TAG: Oval silver tinsel & yellow floss
TAIL: GP topping
RIB: Oval silver
BODY: Black wool
WING: Mixed red & yellow calftail
COLLAR HACKLE: Blue dyed cock, tied as collar sloping backwards
HEAD: Black

GARRY DOG, MULTI WING

TAG: Oval silver tinsel & yellow floss
TAIL: GP topping
RIB: Oval silver
BODY: Black wool
WING: Three bunches of calf tail spaced along body. Red at rear, orange in centre and yellow at front.
THOAT: Blue dyed cock
HEAD: Black

GEORDIE GREEN - Williams

BODY: Green Mylar
THOAT: Yellow bucktail to hook bend
WING: Yellow bucktail, long with strands of yellow Crystal Hair
HEAD: Black

GLÖDHÄCK

TAG: Fluorescent red floss
RIB: Oval silver
BODY: Black floss or wool
HACKLE: Black cock
WING: Black arctic fox hair
HEAD: Black

GLOW FLY - Donaldson

BODY: Veniard's Colour Glow Pearl Mylar tubing - red
WING: Orange bucktail under pink Crystal Hair under magenta bucktail
HEAD: Black

GOAT

TAG: Oval silver tinsel
TAIL: GP topping
BUTT: Black seal's fur
RIB: Oval silver
BODY: Light grey seal's fur
HACKLE: Yellow cock
WING: Yellow goat or squirrel hair
HEAD: Black

GOLD FEVER, VARIANT - Krom

TAG: Flat gold Mylar & yellow floss
TAIL: Black hackle fibres
BUTT: Black tying thread
BODY: Gold Mylar tubing
THROAT: Guinea fowl body feather
WING: Grey squirrel tail over yellow dyed squirrel tail
HEAD: Black

GOLD SHEEP - Dupo

BODY: Gold Mylar tinsel
THROAT: Yellow marabou, full and long
RIB: Flat silver tinsel - wound opposite spiral over palmer hackle
WING: Bear hair dyed hot orange with long sheeps hair dyed fluorescent yellow over. Strands of yellow Flashabou
CHEEKS: Jungle cock
HEAD: Red

GARRY DOG VARIANT - McPhail | GARRY DOG FATBACK #1 - McPhail | GARRY DOG FATBACK #2 - McPhail

GARRY DOG, GOLDEN - Donaldson | GARRY DOG, MIRAMICHI | GARRY DOG, MULTI WING

GEORDIE GREEN - Williams | GLODHACK | GLOW FLY - Donaldson

GOAT | GOLD FEVER, VARIANT - Krom | GOLD SHEEP - Dupo

GOLDEN FOX - Freeman

TAG: Flat gold tinsel
TAIL: Barred wood duck
RIB: Oval gold tinsel
BODY: Flat gold tinsel
WING: Grey squirrel tail
COLLAR HACKLE: Long hen dyed golden olive, wound as collar and swept back
HEAD: Black

GOLDIE (Gold Kenny's Killer)

TAG: Oval gold tinsel
TAIL: GP tippet fibres or yellow hackle fibres
RIB: Oval gold tinsel
BODY: Flat gold tinsel
THROAT: Yellow cock hackle
WING: Black squirrel tail
HEAD: Black

GOSHAWK

TAG: Oval gold tinsel & orange floss
TAIL: GP topping with Ibis and peacock fibres over
BUTT: Black ostrich herl
RIB: Oval gold tinsel
BODY: Black floss
BODY HACKLE: Claret cock
THROAT: Blue jay
WING: Yellow mohair with two GP toppings over
HEAD: Black

GOSHAWK, MODERN HAIRWING

TAG: Oval gold tinsel
TAIL: GP topping with red hackle fibres over
RIB: Oval gold tinsel
BODY: Black floss or seal's fur
THROAT: Rich claret cock tied as collar
WING: Yellow bucktail
HEAD: Black

GREEN & ORANGE TEMPLEDOG

TAG: Oval silver tinsel
BUTT/TAIL: Fluorescent yellow Antron
RIB: Oval silver tinsel
BODY: Rear 1/2 flat green holographic tinsel. Front 1/2 black seal's fur
BODY HACKLE: Silver badger cock
WING: In this order: orange fox, strands of red & pearl flash. Strands of orange Angel hair, four or five strands of peacock herl. Long black fox over all.
FRONT HACKLE: Black cock, tied in before black overwing.
CHEEKS: Jungle cock
HEAD: Black

GREEN-BLACK HIGHLANDER

TAG: Oval gold tinsel
BUTT/TAIL: Fluorescent green Antron
RIB: Oval gold tinsel
BODY: Rear 2/3rds. flat embossed gold tinsel. Front 1/3rd. black seal's fur
BODY HACKLE: One yellow and one green highlander hackle, wound together.
WING: In this order: yellow polar bear, strands of yellow Krystal Flash & green Flashabou. Yellow then green then hot orange then dark brown fox hair. Four strands bronze peacock herl. Black fox hair 2/3rds wing length over.
CHEEKS: Jungle cock
HEAD: Black

GREEN BRAHAN (EMERALD STOAT)

TAG: Oval silver tinsel
TAIL: Yellow hackle fibres with sparse lime Crystal Hair
RIB: Oval silver tinsel followed by fluorescent lime green floss (Glo-Brite #12)
BODY: Green Lurex
HACKLE: Black cock
WING: Black squirrel
HEAD: Black

GREEN ERLING

TAG: Oval silver tinsel & fluorescent green floss
TAIL: GP topping
BUTT: Black ostrich herl
BODY: Rear 1/3rd - 8 yellow & 8 strands olive floss braided. Front 2/3rds - mix of green/olive/peacock/peacock black Ice dubbing
WING: In this order: green SLF hanks mixed with green arctic fox, Ferry brown and black arctic fox mixed with peacock Angel Hair
FRONT HACKLE: Green cock with GP body feather dyed black over
HEAD: Black

GREEN HIGHLANDER

TAG: Oval silver tinsel
TAIL: Yellow hackle fibres
RIB: Oval silver tinsel
BODY: Rear 1/3rd - yellow floss. Front 2/3rds - green floss
THROAT: Mixed green and yellow hackle fibres
WING: Orange hackle fibres under fluorescent lime Twinkle under brown squirrel hair
HEAD: Black

GREEN HIGHLANDER - Donaldson

BODY: Veniard's Colour Glow Pearl Mylar tubing. Green
WING: Green bucktail under strands of lime Crystal Hair under yellow then green bucktail
HEAD: Black

GREEN HIGHLANDER, HAIRY - Mackenzie

TAG: Oval silver tinsel & yellow floss
TAIL: Yellow hair or Antron wool, wound
RIB: Oval silver tinsel
BODY: Rear 1/2 - yellow floss. Front 1/2 - green highlander dubbing
TRAILING HACKLE: Grey squirrel hair dyed orange, wound over front 1/2 of body, grey squirrel dyed orange at front
FRONT HACKLE: Yellow hair, wound
HEAD: Black

Note: In common with all other Mackenzie Hairy flies, the tail and both hackles consist of hair fibres wound in a dubbing loop

GREEN HIGHLANDER - Jorgensen

TAG: Oval silver tinsel & yellow floss
TAIL: GP topping
BUTT: Black ostrich herl
RIB: Oval silver tinsel
BODY: Rear 1/4 - yellow floss. Front 3/4 - bright green seal's fur
BODY HACKLE: Grass green over seal's fur
WING: Strands GP tippet. Small bunch yellow, orange & green polar bear tied in together. Brown bucktail over
COLLAR HACKLE: Bright yellow hackle over wing
CHEEKS: Jungle cock
HEAD: Black

GOLDEN FOX - Freeman | GOLDIE (Gold Kenny's Killer) | GOSHAWK

GOSHAWK HAIRWING | GREEN & ORANGE TEMPLEDOG | GREEN-BLACK HIGHLANDER

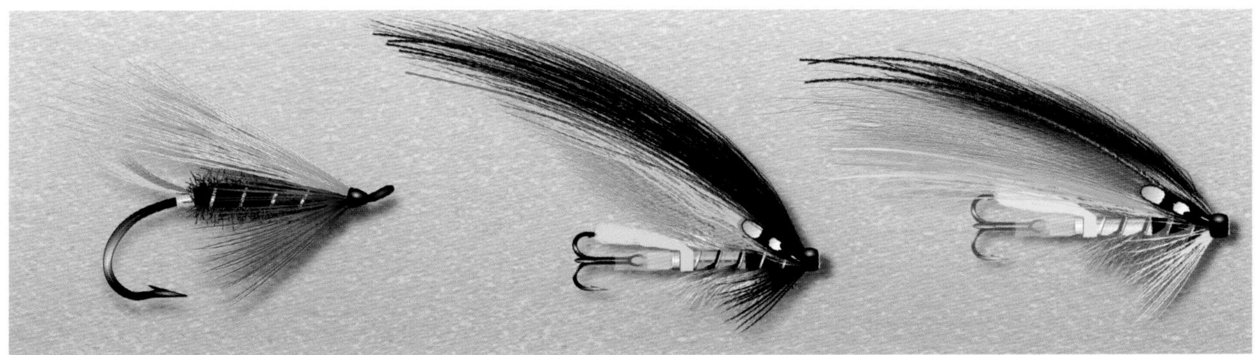

GREEN BRAHAN | GREEN ERLING | GREEN HIGHLANDER

GREEN HIGHLANDER - Donaldson | GREEN HIGHLANDER, HAIRY - Mackenzie | GREEN HIGHLANDER - Jorgensen

GREEN HIGHLANDER - Marriner

TAG: Oval silver tinsel & yellow floss
TAIL: GP topping
BUTT: Black ostrich herl
RIB: Oval silver tinsel
BODY: Rear 1/4 - yellow floss. Front 3/4 - bright green seal's fur
BODY HACKLE: Grass green over seal's fur
WING: Strands GP tippet. Small bunch yellow, orange & green polar bear tied in together. Brown bucktail over
COLLAR HACKLE: Bright yellow hackle over wing
CHEEKS: Jungle cock
HEAD: Black

GREEN HIGHLANDER - McPhail

TAG: Oval silver tinsel & yellow floss
TAIL: GP topping
BUTT: Black ostrich herl
RIB: Oval silver tinsel
BODY: Rear 1/4 - yellow floss. Front 3/4 - bright green seal's fur
BODY HACKLE: Grass green over seal's fur
WING: Strands GP tippet. Small bunch yellow, orange & green polar bear tied in together. Brown bucktail over
COLLAR HACKLE: Bright yellow hackle over wing
CHEEKS: Jungle cock
HEAD: Black

GREEN HIGHLANDER - Shumakov

TAG: Oval silver tinsel & yellow floss
TAIL: GP topping
BUTT: Black ostrich herl
RIB: Oval silver tinsel
BODY: Rear 1/4 - yellow floss. Front 3/4 - bright green seal's fur
BODY HACKLE: Grass green over seal's fur
WING: Strands GP tippet. Small bunch yellow, orange & green polar bear tied in together. Brown bucktail over
COLLAR HACKLE: Bright yellow hackle over wing
CHEEKS: Jungle cock
HEAD: Black

GREEN MAMBA - Rattray

RIB: Medium oval silver tinsel
BODY: None
UNDERWING: Silver Flashabou
WING: Quartered - yellow above and below, green at sides.
HEAD: Black

GREEN THING

TAG: Flat silver tinsel
TAIL: GP tippet fibres
BUTT: Black ostrich herl
RIB: Fine oval silver over rear body
REAR BODY: Flat silver tinsel
FRONT BODY: Green Highlander seal's fur dubbing - well picked out
WING: Brown squirrel tail
THROAT HACKLE: Green Highlander dyed cock
HEAD: Black

GREEN WING TEMPLEDOG - Angus

TAG: Oval silver tinsel
BUTT/TAIL: Fluorescent green Antron
RIB: Oval silver tinsel
BODY: Rear 1/2 flat silver holographic tinsel. Front 1/2 black seal's fur dubbing
BODY HACKLE: Silver badger cock
WING: In this order: yellow fox, strands of green, silver & pearl flash. Four or five strands of peacock herl. Long green dyed fox over all.
FRONT HACKLE: Black cock, tied in before green overwing.
CHEEKS: Jungle cock
HEAD: Black

GRIZZLY KING, Modern

TAG: Oval silver tinsel
TAIL: Dyed red GP topping
RIB: Oval gold tinsel
BODY: Fluorescent green floss
WING: Grey squirrel
FRONT HACKLE: Grizzly cock, wound as collar
HEAD: Black

GRIZZLY KING, Original

TAG: Oval silver tinsel
TAIL: Red Ibis or Goose or red hackle fibres
RIB: Oval silver tinsel
BODY: Dark green floss or wool
WING: Grey squirrel or black & white bucktail mixed
FRONT HACKLE: Grizzly cock, wound as collar
HEAD: Black

GULLNØKK - Steen

TAG: Flat gold tinsel
TAIL: GP topping with dyed red hackle fibres over
RIB: Oval gold tinsel
REAR BODY: Flat gold tinsel
FRONT BODY: Bronze peacock herl
BODY HACKLE: Hot orange cock over peacock herl
THROAT HACKLE: Guinea fowl
WING: Brown squirrel tail with strands of gold Crystal Hair over
HEAD: Black

HAGGIS - Wulff

TAG: Oval silver tinsel
RIB: Oval silver tinsel
BODY: Black wool
THROAT: Yellow hackle fibres tied as beard
WING: Black hair with topping over - optional underwing of long black bucktail for riffled fly
HEAD: Black

HAIRWING NEPTUNE

TAG: Oval silver tinsel
TAIL: GP topping
RIB: Oval silver tinsel
BODY: Rear 2/3rds. flat silver tinsel. Front 1/3rd. peacock herl
WING: Black Krystal Flash with black squirrel tail over
FRONT HACKLE: Guinea fowl, wound as collar and slanted rearwards
HEAD: Black

HAIRY MARY

TAG: Oval gold tinsel
TAIL: Yellow hackle fibres or GP topping
RIB: Oval gold tinsel
BODY: Black floss
THROAT: Mid blue cock
WING: Barred brown squirrel or fine brown bucktail
HEAD: Black

GREEN HIGHLANDER - Marriner | GREEN HIGHLANDER - McPhail | GREEN HIGHLANDER - Shumakov

GREEN MAMBA - Rattray | GREEN THING | GREEN WING TEMPLEDOG - Angus

GRIZZLY KING, Modern | GRIZZLY KING, Original | GULLNØKK - Steen

HAGGIS - Wulff | HAIRWING NEPTUNE | HAIRY MARY

HAIRY MARY - IRISH

TAG: Oval silver tinsel & golden yellow floss
TAIL: GP topping
RIB: Oval silver tinsel
BODY: Black floss
THROAT: Kingfisher blue cock
WING: Grey squirrel
HEAD: Black

HALPIN

TAG: Oval silver tinsel
TAIL: GP topping
BUTT: Red wool
RIB: Oval silver tinsel
BODY: Black floss
BODY HACKLE: Dyed red cock
THROAT: Pale blue dun
WING: Grey squirrel with GP topping over
HEAD: Red

HASLAM - Buchanan

TAIL: GP topping
RIB: Oval silver tinsel
BODY: Flat silver tinsel
THROAT: Guinea fowl dyed blue
WING: Brown squirrel or fine brown bucktail
HORNS: Blue macaw
HEAD: Black

HEATHERLIE - Gaunt-Baker

TAG: Oval silver tinsel
RIB: Oval silver tinsel - closely spaced
BODY: Rear 3/4 - Black floss, front 1/4 - red floss
WING: Orange bucktail under yellow bucktail with strands of gold Crystal Hair over
FRONT HACKLE: Magenta cock
HEAD: Black

HEGGELI HAIRWING - Furuly

TAG: Flat silver tinsel
TAIL: GP tippets
RIB: Oval silver tinsel
BODY: Flat silver tinsel
THROAT: Brown cock hackle, wound
WINGS: Brown arctic fox hair
CHEEKS: Jungle cock
HEAD: Black

HERB JOHNSON SPECIAL

RIB: Flat silver tinsel
BODY: Black wool
THROAT: White bucktail extending beyond hook bend
WING: Bright yellow bucktail extending beyond hook bend, on each side two strands red & blue fluorescent floss. Bunch of yellow dyed brown bucktail over
HEAD: Large, painted silver with yellow eye & black pupil

ICE MAIDEN - Vipond

BODY: Pearl Mylar tubing fastened at rear with red tying thread
WING: Layer of fluorescent yellow or chartreuse bucktail, all round. Thin layer of light blue bucktail over. Finally a thin layer of white bucktail.
HEAD: Black

ICY BLUE

TAG: Flat silver tinsel & fluorescent blue floss
TAIL: GP topping
RIB: Oval silver tinsel
BODY: Flat silver tinsel
THROAT HACKLE: Blue cock
WING: Grey squirrel hair dyed blue over white
HEAD: Black

INFLUENCE - Lauzon

TAG: Oval gold tinsel & bright red wool
TAIL: GP topping
RIB: Oval gold tinsel
BODY: Black floss
WING: Bright green polar bear, sparse
COLLAR HACKLE: Yellow, wound and slanted backwards
HEAD: Black

IRISHMAN'S CLARET

TAG: Oval gold tinsel
TAIL: GP tippets (dyed hot orange for preference)
BODY: Dark claret seal's fur
BODY HACKLE: Dark claret cock
RIB: Oval gold tinsel
WING: Bronze mallard
FRONT HACKLE: Long dark claret hen in front of wing
HEAD: Black

JAKE'S SHRIMP

TAIL: Fluorescent orange bucktail with four strands copper mobile over - at least hook length.
BODY: Rear half - wound copper mobile, front half - Globrite #4 scarlet floss
RIB: Oval gold tinsel
WING: Fluorescento range bucktail with four strands copper mobile over, to extend to end of tail
EYE: One jungle cock feather, split and tied on top of wing
HEAD: Red

JAMIE'S FANCY

BODY: Black floss
RIB: Flat embossed silver
WING: Yellow bucktail under sky blue under black
HEAD: Black

HAIRY MARY - IRISH | HALPIN | HASLAM - Buchanan

HEATHERLIE - Gaunt-Baker | HEGGELI HAIRWING - Furuly | HERB JOHNSON SPECIAL

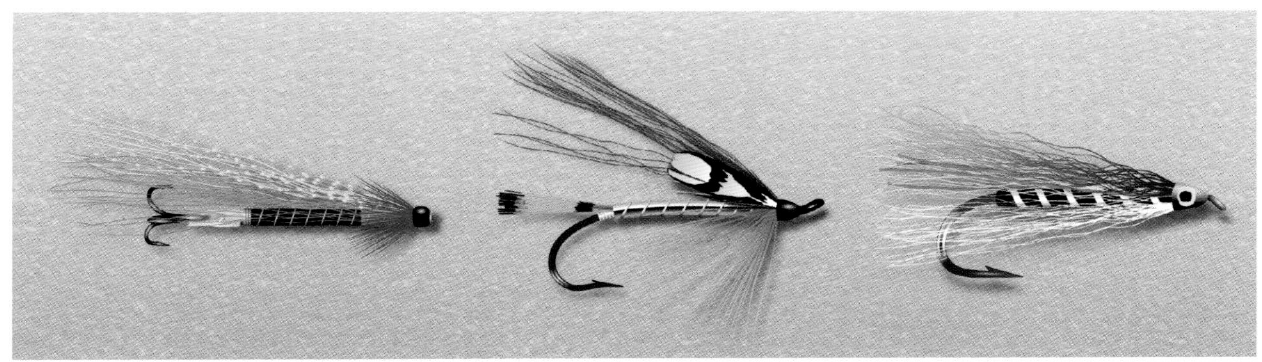

ICE MAIDEN - Vipond | ICY BLUE | INFLUENCE - Lauzon

IRISHMAN'S CLARET | JAKE'S SHRIMP | JAMIE'S FANCY

JANSSONS

TAG: Fine silver tinsel
TAIL: Peacock sword feathers
BODY: Rear half, lime-green fluorescent Antron with strands extending back to tail. Front half, black wool
RIB: Oval silver tinsel over black wool
WING: Grey fox guard hair
COLLAR HACKLE: Grizzle cock
HEAD: Black

JEANNIE

TAG: Oval silver tinsel
TAIL: GP crest or yellow hackle fibres
BODY: Rear half - yellow floss. Front half - black floss
RIB: Oval silver tinsel
THROAT HACKLE: Black cock
WING: Brown squirrel
CHEEKS: Jungle cock
HEAD: Black

JEANNIE, NAVER - McKay

TAG: Oval silver tinsel
BODY: Flat silver tinsel
RIB: Oval silver tinsel
WING: Yellow bucktail
CHEEKS: Jungle cock
HEAD: Black

KARASJOHKA SPECIAL

TAG: Fine silver tinsel & fluorescent red floss
TAIL: Red over brown fox tail
BUTT: Black ostrich herl
BODY: Rear half - fluorescent red floss. Front half - black floss
RIB: Oval silver tinsel
WING: Black over brown fox tail, shorter orange fox overall
THROAT HACKLE: Natural Guinea fowl
CHEEKS: Jungle cock
HEAD: Black

KATIE'S KILLER - Ross

BODY: Medium flat pearl tinsel
RIB: Medium oval gold tinsel
WING: Dyed red goat hair over yellow goat hair with three or four strands of yellow Crystal Hair. Extending 50mm beyond hook for sizes 4 to 8, 25mm beyond for sizes 10 and 12
CHEEKS: Jungle cock
HEAD: Red

KENMORE GOLD

TAIL: GP topping, very long
BODY: Flat gold tinsel
RIB: Fine oval gold tinsel
WING: Orange over yellow dyed squirrel tail
FRONT HACKLE: Orange cock
CHEEKS: Jungle cock
HEAD: Red

KENNY'S KILLER

TAG: Fine oval silver
TAIL: GP tippet or yellow hackle fibres
BODY: Flat silver tinsel
RIB: Oval silver tinsel
WING: Black squirrel
THROAT HACKLE: Rich yellow cock
HEAD: Black

KENYAMAN

TAIL: GP topping
BODY: Wide oval silver tinsel
WING: Yellow goat or squirrel hair
COLLAR HACKLE: Long black hen, wound full
HEAD: Black

KERR'S SUNBURST - McPHAIL

TAG: Oval gold tinsel
BODY: Holographic gold tinsel
RIB: Oval gold tinsel
WING: Bright orange bucktail, gold holographic tinsel, flame-orange goat hair over
THROAT HACKLE: Bright orange bucktail
CHEEKS: Fluorescent adhesive orange eyes
HEAD: Fluorescent orange

KERRY BLUE - Davis

TAG: Flat silver tinsel
TAIL: GP crest
BODY: Rear half - blue Lurex. Front half - red Lurex
RIB: Oval silver tinsel
WING: Black squirrel, twice body length with GP topping over
THROAT HACKLE: Black bucktail extending to hook point
HEAD: Black

KEYSER FINDHORN - Keyser

TAG: Oval silver tinsel
BODY: Black floss
RIB: Oval silver tinsel
WING: Orange dyed fallow tail, teardrop shaped, twice the length of the shank
THROAT HACKLE: Blue cock, liberally applied to hook points
HEAD: Black

KEYSER SPEY - Keyser

TAG: Oval gold tinsel
BODY: Black floss
RIB: Oval gold tinsel
WING: Orange dyed fallow tail, teardrop shaped, twice the length of the shank
THROAT HACKLE: Black cock, liberally applied to hook points
HEAD: Black

JANSSONS | JEANNIE | JEANNIE, NAVER - McKay

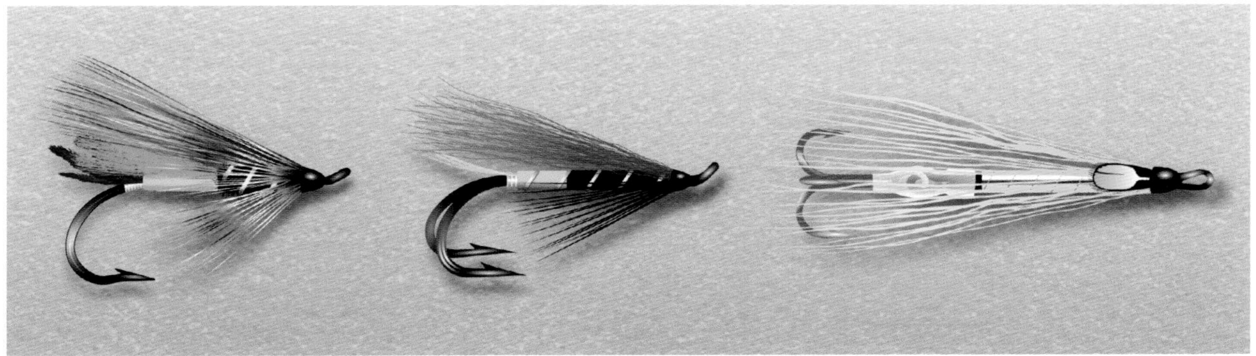

KARASJOHKA SPECIAL | KATIE'S KILLER - Ross | KENMORE GOLD

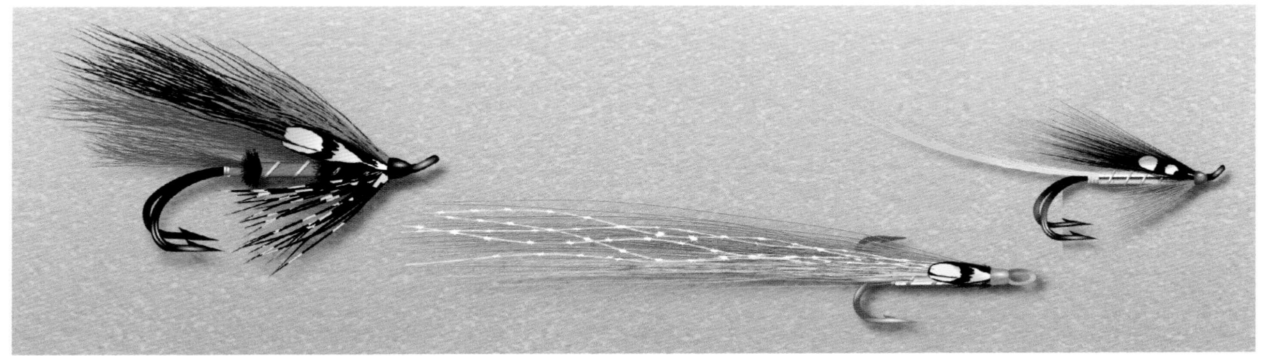

KENNY'S KILLER | KENYAMAN | KERR'S SUNBURST - McPHAIL

KERRY BLUE - Davis | KEYSER FINDHORN | KEYSER SPEY

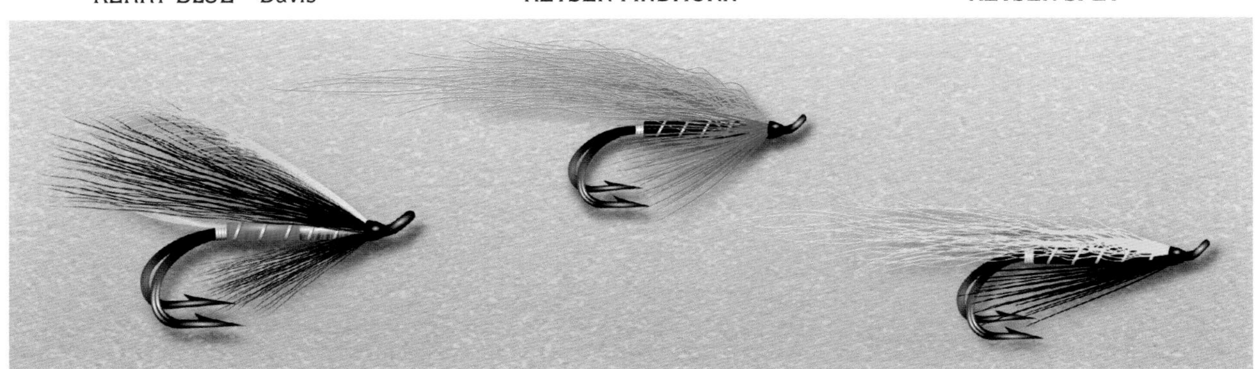

KOLA BOTTLE TUBE #1 - Fairgrieve

TUBE: Loop bottleneck brass tube
TAG: Red Antron
TAIL: Two or three stripped hackle stalks
BODY: Brass tube
WING: Black arctic fox with strands of silver & red holographic tinsel
THROAT HACKLE: Black cock
CHEEKS: Jungle cock
HEAD: Red

KOLA BOTTLE TUBE #2 - Fairgrieve

TUBE: Loop bottleneck brass tube
TAG: Red Antron
TAIL: Two or three stripped hackle stalks
BODY: Brass tube
WING: Black arctic fox with strands of silver & red holographic tinsel
THROAT HACKLE: Red cock
CHEEKS: Jungle cock
HEAD: Red

KOTKAN KERTTU

TAG: Oval silver tinsel and yellow floss
TAIL: GP topping
BUTT: Red wool
BODY: Flat silver tinsel
RIB: Oval silver tinsel
THROAT HACKLE: Blue cock
WING: From bottom - blue, yellow, red & black fox hair, each section with matching strands of Crystal Hair over
HEAD: Black

KYLIE - Donaldson

TAG: Fine oval silver tinsel
TAIL: Longish orange hackle fibres
BUTT: Black floss
BODY: Rear half - flat copper tinsel. Front half - black floss
RIB: Fine oval silver tinsel over copper only
HACKLE: Orange cock
THROAT: Sparse, dyed blue Guinea fowl.
WING: Orange hackle fibres under black squirrel
HEAD: Black

KYLIE WADDINGTON - Donaldson

TAG: Flat silver tinsel
BUTT: Black floss
BODY: Rear half - flat copper tinsel. Front half - black floss
RIB: Fine oval silver tinsel over copper only
THROAT: Sparse, dyed blue Guinea fowl.
WING: Fluorescent orange Twinkle under orange bucktail. Sparse bunches of black bucktail above and below
HEAD: Black

LADY AMHERST - Hairwing

TAG: Fine oval silver tinsel and yellow floss
TAIL: GP topping
BUTT: Black herl
BODY: Flat silver tinsel
RIB: Oval silver tinsel
HACKLE: Orange cock
THROAT: Teal, grizzle or wigeon
WING: Grey squirrel
CHEEKS: Fans of fluorescent blue floss
HEAD: Black

LADY EWE - Mateer

TAG: Flat silver tinsel
TAIL: GP topping
BODY: Rear half - blue Lurex. Front half - silver Lurex
RIB: Fine oval silver tinsel
THROAT: Dyed blue Guinea fowl.
WING: White Twinkle under black bucktail, twice body length
HEAD: Black

LADY JOAN - Wulff

TAG: Fine oval gold tinsel
TAIL: GP topping (optional)
BODY: Burnt orange floss
RIB: Oval gold tinsel (tight turns)
THROAT: Light yellow hen
WING: Black bear under grey squirrel with GP topping over
HEAD: Black

LAERDAL - Hairwing

TAG: Fine oval silver tinsel
TAIL: GP topping
BUTT: Black herl
BODY: Rear half - grey seal's fur. Front half - black sael's fur
RIB: Oval gold tinsel
THROAT: Black cock
WING: Grey squirrel with GP topping over
CHEEKS: Jungle cock
HEAD: Black

LAWSON - Frodin

TAG: Fine oval gold tinsel and red floss
TAIL: Black fox hair
BODY: Rear half - oval gold tinsel. Front half - black floss
BODY HACKLE: Orange cock over black floss
THROAT: Black cock
WING: Black fox hair
HEAD: Black

LAWSON - Dupo

TAG: Fine oval gold tinsel
TAIL: Black fox hair over orange floss
BODY: Rear 2/3rds - Flat gold tinsel. Front 1/3rd. - black seal's fur, well picked out
RIB: Oval gold tinsel
THROAT: Black fox hair under orange cock
WING: Black fur Zonker strip, extending well beyond hook bend, fastened along body by ribbing
CHEEKS: Jungle cock
HEAD: Black

LAWSON - Zonker

TAG: Fine oval gold tinsel and red floss
TAIL: Black fox hair
BODY: Rear half - oval gold tinsel. Front half - black floss
BODY HACKLE: Orange cock over black floss
THROAT: Black cock
WING: Black fox hair
HEAD: Black

KOLA BOTTLE TUBE #1- Fairgrieve | KOLA BOTTLE TUBE #2- Fairgrieve |  KOTKAN KERTTU

KYLIE WADDINGTON - Donaldson | KYLIE WADDINGTON - Donaldson | LADY AMHERST - Hairwing

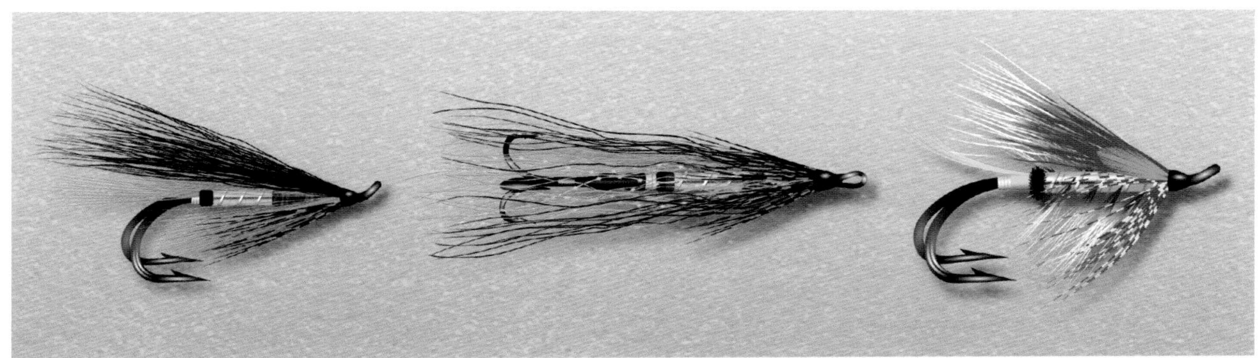

LADY EWE - Mateer | LADY JOAN - Wulff | LAERDAL - Hairwing

LAWSON - Frodin | LAWSON - Dupo | LAWSON - Zonker

LAXA BLUE

TAG: Fine flat silver tinsel & fluorescent orange floss
TAIL: GP topping
BUTT: Black herl
BODY: Flat silver tinsel or pale blue floss
RIB: Oval silver tinsel
THROAT: Blue cock
WING: Light blue dyed bucktail
HEAD: Black

LAXA BLUE, VARIANT

TAG: Fine flat silver tinsel & fluorescent orange floss
TAIL: GP topping
BUTT: Fluorescent red floss
BODY: Bright light blue floss
RIB: Oval silver tinsel
WING: Light blue dyed squirrel or fox hair
COLLAR HACKLE: Light blue dyed cock tied full
HEAD: Black

LEGO - Shumakov

TUBE: Shumakov 13mm Skittle tube
BODY: Tube
WING: From bottom - Yellow dyed Arctic fox with strands of orange-yellow Mirage, red dyed Arctic fox with strands of black & red Angel Hair, dark brown dyed Arctic fox with strands of black & red Angel Hair, dyed black Arctic fox - the last layer tied in Templedog style. Strands of peacock herl overall
FRONT HACKLE: Red-brown dyed badger cock
CHEEKS: Jungle cock
HEAD: Black

LEMON & GREY

TAG: Fine flat silver tinsel
TAIL: GP topping
BUTT: Black seal's fur
BODY: Light grey seal's fur
RIB: Oval silver tinsel
THROAT: Yellow cock
WING: One part orange under two parts brown squirrel tail
HEAD: Black

LEMON GREY - Hairwing

TAG: Silver tinsel and fluorescent orange floss
TAIL: GP topping
BUTT: Fluorescent red floss
BODY: Bright light blue floss
RIB: Oval silver tinsel
WING: Light blue dyed squirrel or fox hair
COLLAR HACKLE: Light blue dyed cock tied full
HEAD: Black

LESLIE PETERS - Peters

TAIL: GP topping
BUTT: Fluorescent red floss
BODY: Yellow seal's fur
RIB: Oval gold tinsel
WING: Grey squirrel dyed brown or off-black
THROAT HACKLE: Yellow cock
HEAD: Yellow tying thread

LILLEY KILLER - Lilley

TAIL: GP tippets, long
BODY: Bright orange floss
RIB: Medium flat silver tinsel
WING: Underwing GP tippets tied flat to meet tail. Overwing orange bucktail
THROAT HACKLE: Orange hen
CHEEKS: Jungle cock
HEAD: Red

LOGIE - MODERN

TAG: Silver tinsel
TAIL: GP topping
BODY: Rear 2/5ths - yellow floss. Front 3/5ths - red floss
RIB: Oval silver tinsel
THROAT HACKLE: Light blue cock
WING: Yellow under brown squirrel hair
HEAD: Black

LOGIE - ORIGINAL

TAG: Silver tinsel
TAIL: GP topping
BODY: Claret floss
RIB: Oval silver tinsel
THROAT HACKLE: Light blue cock
WING: Yellow under brown squirrel hair
CHEEKS: Jungle cock
HEAD: Black

L.T. SPECIAL - Tracy

TAG: Copper Diamond Braid & fluorescent orange floss
BODY: Copper Diamond Braid
WING: Orange bucktail under Kelly green bucktail with a few strands of copper Krystal Flash
COLLAR HACKLE: Two turns of yellow cock under two turns wine red cock
HEAD: Fluorescent orange

MAR LODGE - Hairwing

TAG: Silver tinsel
TAIL: GP topping
BODY: Claret floss
RIB: Oval silver tinsel
THROAT HACKLE: Light blue cock
WING: Yellow under brown squirrel hair
CHEEKS: Jungle cock
HEAD: Black

MARIUS

TAG: Silver tinsel
TAIL: GP topping
BODY: Claret floss
RIB: Oval silver tinsel
THROAT HACKLE: Light blue cock
WING: Yellow under brown squirrel hair
CHEEKS: Jungle cock
HEAD: Black

LAXA BLUE | LAXA BLUE, VARIANT | LEGO - Shumakov

LEMON & GREY | LEMON GREY - Hairwing | LESLIE PETERS - Peters

LILLEY KILLER - Lilley | LOGIE - MODERN | LOGIE - ORIGINAL

L.T. SPECIAL - Tracy | MAR LODGE - Hairwing | MARIUS

McDERMOTT'S BADGER

TAG: Oval silver tinsel
TAIL: GP topping
BODY: Flat silver tinsel
RIB: Oval silver tinsel
HACKLE: Yellow cock
WING: Badger hair
CHEEKS: Jungle cock
HEAD: Black

MICKEY FINN

BODY: Flat silver tinsel
RIB: Oval silver tinsel
THROAT HACKLE: Light blue cock
WING: From bottom - Yellow under red under yellow bucktail
HEAD: Black

MILL POOL SPECIAL

TAG: Oval silver tinsel & fluorescent green floss
TAIL: GP topping
BUTT: Fluorescent red floss
BODY: Black wool
RIB: Oval silver tinsel
WING: Red squirrel tail
COLLAR HACKLE: Brown cock
HEAD: Black

MOODY BRAGG

TAG: Oval gold tinsel
RIB: Oval gold tinsel
BODY: Black floss
WING: Mixed black & red bucktail with strands of silver Flashabou
HEAD: Black

MOOSE BOGAN - Belaieff

TAG: Oval gold tinsel
RIB: Oval gold tinsel
BODY: Flat copper Mylar
WING: Squirrel tail dyed Highlander green
COLLAR: Fluorescent green chenille
HEAD: Red

MOSQUITO, BLACK - Sutherland

TAG: Oval silver tinsel
REAR FIN: Square of metallised foil, folded into triangle and tied around tube to point upwards.
RIB: Oval silver tinsel
BODY: Black floss
FRONT FIN: Square of metallised foil, folded into triangle and tied around tube to give two downward slanting fins
HACKLE: Black cock
WING: Black Arctic fox
CHEEKS: Jungle cock
HEAD: Black

MOY GREEN - Downey

TAG: Oval silver tinsel
TAIL: GP topping
RIB: Oval silver tinsel
BODY: Flat silver tinsel
HACKLE: Hot orange cock
WING: Squirrel tail dyed Highlander green
HEAD: Black

MUNRO, GOLD - Donaldson

TAG: Oval gold tinsel
TAIL: Orange hackle fibres
RIB: Oval gold tinsel
BODY: Flat gold tinsel
HACKLE: Orange cock with blue guinea fowl over
WING: Squirrel tail dyed yellow
HEAD: Black

MUNRO KILLER

TAG: Oval gold tinsel
TAIL: Orange hackle fibres
RIB: Oval gold tinsel
BODY: Black floss
HACKLE: Orange cock with blue guinea fowl over
WING: Squirrel tail dyed yellow
HEAD: Black

Dressings in the south of Scotland may dispense with the tail fibres and the under hackle of orange cock at the throat.

MUNRO, HAIRY - Mackenzie

TAG: Oval gold tinsel
TAIL: Orange dyed hair
RIB: Oval gold tinsel
BODY: Black floss
FRONT HACKLE (1): Squirrel tail dyed yellow
FRONT HACKLE (2): Orange dyed hair followed by squirrel tail dyed kingfisher blue
HEAD: Black

MUNRO, DARK

TAG: Oval gold tinsel
TAIL: GP topping
RIB: Oval gold tinsel
BODY: Black floss
HACKLE: Orange cock with blue guinea fowl over
WING: Bleached squirrel tail dyed yellow under black squirrel
HEAD: Black

MURMANSK KILLER

TAG: Oval gold tinsel
TAIL: Yellow bucktail
RIB: Oval gold tinsel
BODY: Flat copper tinsel
THROAT HACKLE: Yellow cock
WING: Squirrel tail dyed orange with strands of yellow Twinkle over
HEAD: Black

McDERMOTT'S BADGER | MICKEY FINN | MILL POOL SPECIAL

MOODY BRAGG | MOOSE BOGAN - Belaieff | MOSQUITO, BLACK - Sutherland

MOY GREEN - Downey | MUNRO, GOLD - Donaldson | MUNRO KILLER

MUNRO, HAIRY - Mackenzie | MUNRO, DARK | MURMANSK KILLER

NAMSEN HAIRWING

TAG: Oval silver tinsel & yellow floss
TAIL: GP topping with red swan or goose over
RIB: Oval silver tinsel
BODY: Seal's fur in four equal divisions, from back - yellow, red-brown, blue-green, black
HACKLE: Black cock, full
UNDERWING: Combed out strands of yellow, red and blue floss
WING: Brown hair with natural grey squirrel tail over
HEAD: Black

NIGHT HAWK HAIRWING

TAG: Oval silver tinsel & yellow floss
TAIL: GP topping
RIB: Oval silver tinsel
BODY: Flat silver tinsel
HACKLE: Black cock
WING: Black hair
SIDES: Jungle cock with blue dyed hackle tip over
HEAD: Red

NIPISIGUIT GREY HAIRWING

TAG: Oval gold tinsel & yellow floss
TAIL: GP topping
BUTT: Peacock herl
RIB: Oval gold tinsel
BODY: Grey muskrat or seal's fur
HACKLE: Grizzle cock
WING: Black-Brown bear hair
HEAD: Black

NORA CRIENA

TAG: Oval silver tinsel & yellow floss
TAIL: GP topping with GP tippets over
BUTT: Black ostrich herl
RIB: Oval silver tinsel
BODY HACKLE: Light furnace over seal's fur
BODY: Three turns yellow floss then yellow seal's fur
HACKLE: Golden olive cock
WING: Golden olive mohair with GP topping over
HEAD: Black

NORTH POLE - McPHAIL

TAG: Silver holographic tinsel
TAIL: Blue-green Reflection
RIB: Oval silver tinsel
BODY: Wound blue-green Reflection
HACKLE: Sunburst yellow cock
WING: Yellow and blue Arctic fox with strands of blue-green Reflection between
HEAD: River green Lite-Brite

NORTHERN DOG

TAG: Flat silver tinsel
RIB: Oval silver tinsel
BODY: Black floss
WING: Four strands pearl Crystal Hair doubled and divided either side. Orange under yellow bucktail
HEAD: Red with black band

NORWAY #1

TAG: Flat silver tinsel
TAIL: Glo-Brite fluorescent orange floss #4
RIB: Oval silver tinsel
BODY: Red Mylar
HACKLE: Black hen
WING: Fluorescent yellow bucktail with black Arctic fox over
CHEEKS: Fluorescent yellow goose biots
HEAD: Fire orange

NORWAY #2

TAG: Flat silver tinsel
TAIL: Glo-Brite fluorescent green floss #12
RIB: Oval silver tinsel
BODY: Rear half - Glo-Brite #12 floss. Front half - black floss
HACKLE: Black hen
WING: Strands UV pearl Krystal Flash with fluorescent orange Arctic fox over
CHEEKS: Jungle cock
HEAD: Black

NORWEGIAN WOOD - Shumakov

TAG: Oval silver tinsel, fluorescent green and fluorescent red floss
TAIL: Yellow floss
BUTT: Black ostrich herl
RIB: Oval silver tinsel
BODY: Rear half - flat silver tinsel. Front half - black seal's fur - orange dyed badger palmered over black seal's fur
WING: Yellow Arctic fox, yellow Crystal Hair, green Arctic fox, pearl Crystal Hair, black Arctic fox
COLLAR HACKLE: Light green cock over Guinea fowl
CHEEKS: Jungle cock
HEAD: Black

ORANGE & BLUE

RIB: Flat silver tinsel
BODY: Black floss
WING: Orange bucktail under blue bucktail
HEAD: Black

ORANGE & GOLD TEMPLEDOG

TAG: Oval silver tinsel & orange Antron
RIB: Oval gold tinsel
BODY HACKLE: Orange cock
BODY: Rear half - flat gold tinsel. Front half-black floss
THROAT HACKLE: Black cock
WING: Orange fox tail, strands of orange Crystal Hair, black fox tail over
CHEEKS: Jungle cock
HEAD: Black

ORANGE BLOSSOM - Bigaouette

TAG: Oval silver tinsel with orange floss
TAIL: GP topping
BUTT: Black ostrich herl
BODY: Rear half - silver tinsel. Front half - yellow seal's fur
RIB: Oval silver tinsel over seal's fur
WING: Mixed white and light brown bucktail
COLLAR HACKLE: Two orange cock hackles extending to hook point, tied full
CHEEKS: Jungle cock
HEAD: Black

NAMSEN HAIRWING | NIGHT HAWK HAIRWING | NIPISIGUIT GREY HAIRWING

NORA CRIENA | NORTH POLE - McPHAIL | NORTHERN DOG

NORWAY #1 | NORWAY #2 | NORWEGIAN WOOD - Shumakov

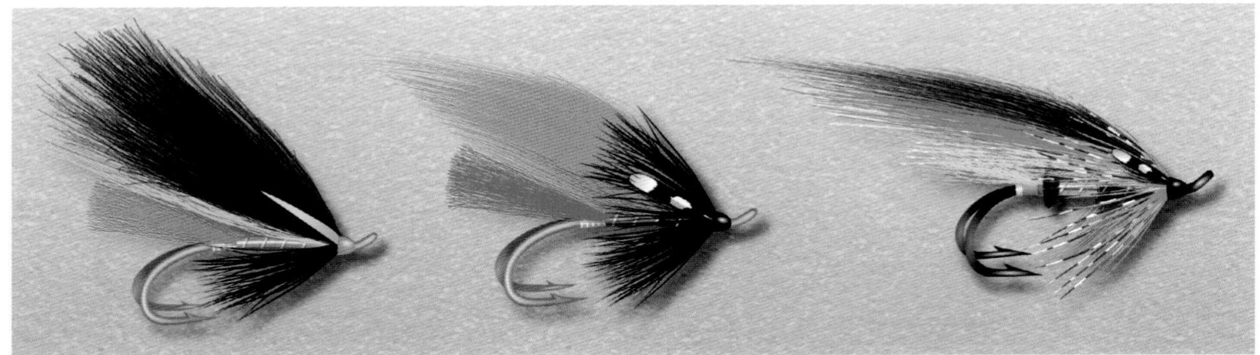

ORANGE & BLUE | ORANGE & GOLD TEMPLEDOG | ORANGE BLOSSOM - Bigaouette

ORANGE BOURRACH

TAG: Oval silver tinsel
TAIL: Yellow hackle fibres
BODY: Flat silver tinsel
RIB: Oval silver tinsel
THROAT HACKLE: Blue cock
WING: Orange bucktail or bleached squirrel dyed orange
HEAD: Black

OWENMORE

TAG: Oval silver tinsel
TAIL: GP topping with Jungle cock over
BUTT: Black ostrich herl
BODY: Five joints alternate yellow and black floss. At each joint two turns silver tinsel
MANES: Mohair at each joint, starting from back - medium claret, dark red, dark claret, very dark red, mixture of yellow, brown & red
HACKLE: Olive cock hackle, red GP rump, blue jay over
WING: GP tippets, GP tail, bronze mallard, GP topping over
HORNS: Blue macaw
HEAD: Black

PALSBU

TAG: Flat gold tinsel & yellow floss
TAIL: Red ibis and brown turkey
BODY: Bronze peacock herl
RIB: Oval gold tinsel
HACKLE: Red game cock
WING: Dark brown hair with GP topping over
CHEEKS: Jungle cock
HEAD: Black

PEATY MAN - McPHAIL

TAG: Oval gold tinsel
BODY: Flat gold tinsel
RIB: Oval gold tinsel
WING: Tango orange Arctic fox with black goat hair over, top layer tied Templedog style. Optional strands of Gold Crystal Flash
HACKLE: Yellow cock
CHEEKS: Jungle cock
HEAD: Black

PEER GYNT

TAG: Oval silver tinsel with yellow floss
TAIL: GP topping with crimson hackle fibres over
BUTT: Black ostrich herl
RIB: Oval silver tinsel
BODY: Flat silver tinsel
BODY HACKLE: crimson cock
THROAT HACKLE: Natural Guinea fowl
WING: Brown tipped, black hair with gold Krystal Flash over
CHEEKS: Jungle cock
HEAD: Black

PHANTOM - Baylis

TAG: Fine oval gold tinsel with fluorescent orange floss
TAIL: GP topping
BUTT: Black ostrich herl
BODY: Rear body, yellow Phentex. Centre Butt of fluorescent orange floss with black ostrich herl. Front body - wound chartreuse Krystal Flash
RIB: Oval silver tinsel over rear and front body
WING: Black squirrel tail with strands of pink Krystal Flash
COLLAR HACKLE: Black cock
HEAD: Red

PINOCCHIO - Shumakov

TUBE: Shumakov 13mm Skittle tube
BODY: Tube
WING: From bottom - Brown dyed Arctic fox with strands of orange-yellow Mirage, brown dyed Arctic fox with strands of copper & dark brown Angel Hair, dark brown dyed Arctic fox with strands of black & red Angel Hair, dyed dark brown Arctic fox - the last layer tied in Templedog style. Strands of brown Rippleflash overall
FRONT HACKLE: Brown dyed badger cock
CHEEKS: Jungle cock
HEAD: Black

PONOI GREEN

TAG: Oval silver tinsel
TAIL: Black squirrel
BUTT: Fluorescent green floss
BODY: Black floss
RIB: Oval silver tinsel
THROAT HACKLE: Blue cock
WING: Black squirrel hair over six strands of green Krystal Flash
HEAD: Black

PONOI RED

TAG: Oval silver tinsel
TAIL: Black hackle fibres
BUTT: Fluorescent red
BODY: Black floss
RIB: Oval silver tinsel
THROAT HACKLE: Black hen
WING: Red bucktail, six strands of gold Krystal Flash, black squirrel over
HEAD: Black

POT SCRUBBER

TAG: Oval silver tinsel
TAIL: GP topping
BODY: Flat copper tinsel
RIB: Oval silver tinsel
THROAT HACKLE: Brown cock
WING: Grey squirrel tail
HEAD: Black

PRIEST

TAG: Oval silver tinsel
TAIL: Light blue dun hackle fibres
BODY: Fluorescent white wool
RIB: Oval silver tinsel
WING: White calf tail
COLLAR HACKLE: Light blue dun cock
HEAD: White

PRINGLE'S BADGER - Pringle

BODY: Black floss
RIB: Flat silver tinsel
WING: Badger hair
CHEEKS: Hackle tips in orange, red, yellow or blue
HEAD: Black

ORANGE BOURRACH | OWENMORE | PALSBU

PEATY MAN - McPHAIL | PEER GYNT | PHANTOM - Baylis

PINOCCHIO - Shumakov | PONOI GREEN | PONOI RED

POT SCRUBBER | PRIEST | PRINGLE'S BADGER - Pringle

PURPLE & COPPER - Larsen
BODY: Braided copper Mylar tubing
WING: Three layers. From bottom - purple dyed Arctic fox, purple dyed Polar bear, black Icelandic sheep hair
HEAD: Black

PURPLE McBAIN - McBain
TAG: Fine oval gold tinsel
BODY: Purple floss
RIB: Oval gold tinsel
THROAT HACKLE: Purple cock
WING: Black squirrel tail over bleached squirrel dyed yellow
HEAD: Black

RAINBOW WARRIOR
TAG: Fine oval gold tinsel
TAIL: Bleached squirrel hair dyed orange
BODY: Black floss
RIB: Oval gold
WING: Tied in in two separate bunches (manes). Centre of body - grey squirrel dyed blue. Front - Grey squirrel dyed yellow
COLLAR HACKLE: Blue, orange or yellow cock
HEAD: Black

RAT - Thomson
TAG: Fine oval silver tinsel
TAIL: GP topping
BODY: Peacock herl
RIB: Oval silver tinsel
WING: Grey fox hair
COLLAR HACKLE: Grizzle cock
CHEEKS: Optional. Jungle cock
HEAD: Red

RAT, BLACK
TAG: Flat silver tinsel
TAIL: GP topping
BODY: Black seal's fur
RIB: Flat silver tinsel
WING: Grey fox hair
COLLAR HACKLE: Grizzle cock
CHEEKS: Optional. Jungle cock
HEAD: Red

RAT, BLACK KRYSTAL - Baylis
TAG: Oval gold tinsel
TAIL: GP topping dyed black
BUTT: Black ostrich herl
BODY: Rear half - black Krystal Flash. Front half - peacock herl
VEIL: Black Krystal Flash over rear body
RIB: Oval gold tinsel
WING: Black squirrel hair over four strands black Krystal Flash
COLLAR HACKLE: Black cock
HEAD: Black ostrich herl and black thread

RAT, BROWN
TAG: Oval silver tinsel
TAIL: Two short barred wood duck feathers
BODY: Fiery brown seal's fur
RIB: Flat gold tinsel
WING: Grey fox hair
COLLAR HACKLE: Grizzle cock
CHEEKS: Optional. Jungle cock
HEAD: Red

RAT, COPPER - Howard
TAG: Flat silver tinsel
TAIL: GP topping
BODY: Black seal's fur
RIB: Flat silver tinsel
WING: Grey fox hair
COLLAR HACKLE: Grizzle cock
CHEEKS: Optional. Jungle cock
HEAD: Red

RAT, FLUORESCENT GREEN - Solo
TAG: Oval gold tinsel
TAIL: Peacock sword
BODY: Rear half - fluorescent green floss. Front half - fluorescent green seal's fur
VEIL: Fluorescent green floss over rear body
RIB: Oval gold tinsel over seal's fur only
WING: Grey squirrel dyed fluorescent green over strands of fluorescent green Krystal Flash
COLLAR HACKLE: Fluorescent green dyed grizzle cock
HEAD: Fluorescent green

RAT, GOLD
TAG: Flat silver tinsel
TAIL: GP topping dyed red
BODY: Flat gold tinsel
RIB: Oval silver tinsel
WING: Grey fox hair
COLLAR HACKLE: Grizzle cock
CHEEKS: Optional. Jungle cock
HEAD: Red

RAT, GREY
TAG: Flat gold tinsel
TAIL: GP topping
BODY: Grey fox underfur
RIB: Flat gold tinsel
WING: Grey fox hair
COLLAR HACKLE: Grizzle cock
CHEEKS: Optional. Jungle cock
HEAD: Red

RAT, KING
TAG: Oval silver tinsel
TAIL: Peacock herl over yellow floss
BODY: Rear half - flat silver tinsel. Front half - bronze peacock herl
VEIL: Yellow floss top & bottom over rear body
RIB: Oval gold tinsel
WING: Grey fox hair
COLLAR HACKLE: Grizzle cock
HEAD: Black

PURPLE & COPPER - Larsen   PURPLE McBAIN - McBain   RAINBOW WARRIOR

RAT - Thomson   RAT, BLACK   RAT, BLACK KRYSTAL - Baylis

RAT, BROWN   RAT, COPPER - Howard   RAT, FLUORESCENT GREEN - Solo

RAT, GOLD   RAT, GREY   RAT, KING

RAT, PURPLE - Sturrock

TAG: Oval silver tinsel
TAIL: Fluorescent chartreuse floss
BODY: Dark purple floss
RIB: Oval silver tinsel over front half of body
WING: Grey squirrel dyed purple
COLLAR HACKLE: Purple cock
HEAD: Red

RAT, RED

TAG: Oval silver tinsel
TAIL: Two short barred wood duck feathers
BODY: Red seal's fur
RIB: Flat gold tinsel
WING: Grey fox hair
COLLAR HACKLE: Grizzle cock
CHEEKS: Optional. Jungle cock
HEAD: Red

RAT, REED'S GREEN - Reed

TAG: Fluorescent red wool
BODY: Rear half - fluorescent green floss
Front half - peacock herl
VEIL: Fluorescent green floss
RIB: Oval silver tinsel over rear body only
WING: Grey fox hair
COLLAR HACKLE: Grizzle cock dyed bright yellow
HEAD: Red

RAT, REED'S ORANGE - Reed

TAG: Fluorescent green wool
BODY: Rear half - fluorescent orange floss. Front half - peacock herl
VEIL: Fluorescent orange floss
RIB: Oval silver tinsel over rear body only
WING: Grey fox hair
COLLAR HACKLE: Grizzle cock dyed bright yellow
HEAD: Red

RAT, RUSTY

TAG: Oval gold tinsel
TAIL: Peacock sword fibres
BODY: Rear half - bright yellow floss. Front half - peacock herl
VEIL: Bright yellow floss
RIB: Oval gold tinsel
WING: Grey fox hair
COLLAR HACKLE: Grizzle cock
CHEEKS: Optional. Jungle cock
HEAD: Black

RAT, SILVER

TAG: Flat silver tinsel
TAIL: GP topping dyed red
BODY: Flat silver tinsel
RIB: Oval gold tinsel
WING: Grey fox hair
COLLAR HACKLE: Grizzle cock
CHEEKS: Optional. Jungle cock
HEAD: Red

REBECCA - Peaston

TAG: Oval silver tinsel
RIB: Oval silver tinsel
BODY: Flat silver tinsel with three or four turns of black ostrich herl at front
BODY HACKLE: Scarlet cock
HACKLE: Scarlet cock
WING: Orange squirrel with scarlet goat hair over
HEAD: Black

RED ABBEY

TAG: Oval silver tinsel
TAIL: Red Ibis, swan or small bunch of red bucktail
RIB: Oval silver tinsel
BODY: Red floss or wool
HACKLE: Brown cock
WING: Light brown squirrel or bucktail
CHEEKS: Jungle cock
HEAD: Black

RED BUTT

TAG: Oval silver tinsel & red Antron
RIB: Oval silver tinsel
BODY: Black Antron
THROAT HACKLE: Black cock
WING: Black Arctic fox
CHEEKS: Jungle cock
HEAD: Black

RED COW

TAIL: Red-Brown hair fibres
RIB: Oval silver tinsel
BODY: Red-brown dubbed hair
THROAT HACKLE: Red-brown hair
WING: Red-Brown hair
HEAD: Black

RED DEVIL - McPhail

BODY: Brass tube
WING: Grey fox hair
CHEEKS: Dyed red squirrel hair or bucktail tips
HEAD: Red

RED TEMPLEDOG - Norling

TAG: Oval silver tinsel
BUTT: Fluorescent orange Antron
RIB: Oval silver tinsel
UNDERBODY: White floss
BODY: Rear 2/3rds - flat silver tinsel. Front 1/3rd - fluorescent orange Antron
WING: From bottom - hot-orange polar bear, fluorescent hot orange Krystal Flash, strands of silver, gold and red Ripple Flash, two long jungle cock feathers, hot orange fox hair with Flashabou dubbing in chartreuse, yellow, red, pearl and orange combed into the fox hair
BODY HACKLE: Hot orange cock
FRONT HACKLE: Black cock
HEAD: Black

RAT, PURPLE - Sturrock RAT, RED RAT, REED'S GREEN - Reed

RAT, REED'S ORANGE - Reed RAT, RUSTY RAT, SILVER

REBECCA - Peaston RED ABBEY RED BUTT

RED COW RED DEVIL - McPHAIL RED TEMPLEDOG - Norling

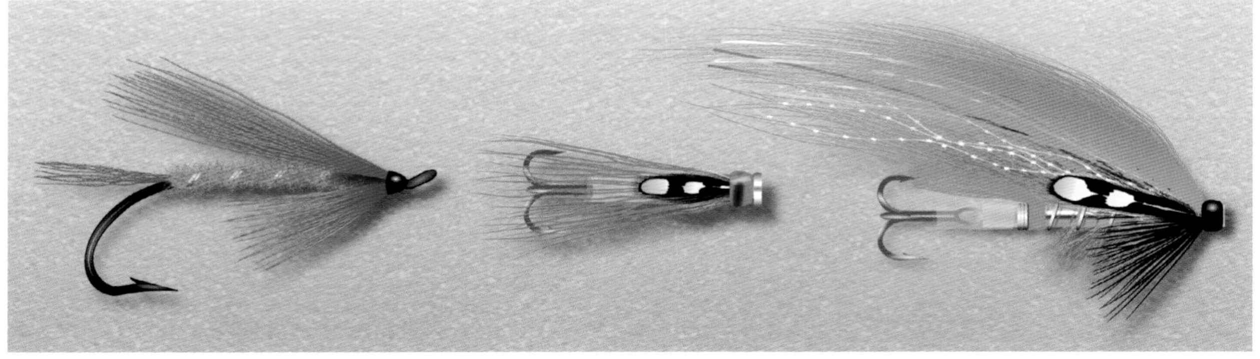

REIPPU

TAG: Oval gold tinsel & fluorescent yellow floss
TAIL: GP topping
BUTT: Fluorescent red floss
RIB: Oval gold tinsel
BODY: Claret floss
HACKLE: Natural Guinea fowl
WING: Grey squirrel dyed green
HEAD: Black

REYNARD BLACK - Fulsher

TAG: Oval silver tinsel & black floss
TAIL: Guinea fowl fibres
RIB: Oval silver tinsel
BODY: Black wool
WING: Red fox hair
COLLAR HACKLE: Black cock
HEAD: Black

REYNARD BLUE - Fulsher

TAG: Oval silver tinsel & fluorescent blue floss
TAIL: Guinea fowl fibres
RIB: Oval gold tinsel
BODY: Flat silver tinsel
WING: Red fox hair
COLLAR HACKLE: Bright blue cock
HEAD: Black

REYNARD GREEN - Fulsher

TAG: Oval silver tinsel & fluorescent green floss
TAIL: Guinea fowl fibres
RIB: Oval silver tinsel
BODY: Flat gold tinsel
WING: Red fox hair
COLLAR HACKLE: Bright green cock
HEAD: Black

REYNARD ORANGE - Fulsher

TAG: Oval silver tinsel & fluorescent orange floss
TAIL: Guinea fowl fibres
RIB: Oval gold tinsel
BODY: Flat silver tinsel
WING: Red fox hair
COLLAR HACKLE: Bright orange cock
HEAD: Black

REYNARD YELLOW - Fulsher

TAG: Oval gold tinsel & fluorescent yellow floss
TAIL: Guinea fowl fibres
RIB: Oval silver tinsel
BODY: Flat gold tinsel
WING: Red fox hair
COLLAR HACKLE: Bright yellow cock
HEAD: Black

RIVER PHILIP COPPER

BODY: Copper Diamond Braid
THROAT HACKLE: Sparse red calf tail
WING: Copper Krystal Flash under orange bucktail
HEAD: Black

ROGER'S FANCY

TAG: Oval silver tinsel & fluorescent yellow floss
TAIL: Peacock sword fibres
RIB: Oval silver tinsel
BODY: Fluorescent green floss
WING: Grey fox hair
COLLAR HACKLE: Bright Green cock
HEAD: Black

ROGIE - Brown

RIB: Oval silver tinsel
BODY: Green Lurex
WING: Grey fox hair
COLLAR HACKLE: Black over orange over yellow bucktail
HEAD: Black

ROYAL CHARM - Farago

TAG: Oval gold tinsel & fluorescent green floss
TAIL: GP topping
BUTT: Black ostrich herl
RIB: Oval gold tinsel
BODY: Royal blue floss
WING: Short GP tippets under grey squirrel hair
COLLAR HACKLE: Kingfisher blue cock
HEAD: Black

SANDEEL STREAMER - Buckland

BODY: Detached silver Mylar tube
WING: Generally working from light at the bottom to dark - white, pearl, olive, green, blue, peacock Crystal hair mixed with Fishair or other synthetic fibres. Long grizzle hackle overall. All hair secured with thread windings and then with Loctite superglue.
EYES: 3D wiggle eyes mounted on hook.
HEAD: Built up with nail varnish - various colours

This is just a sample tie. The form is more important than the tying details

SHEILA - Mathieson

TAG: Oval gold tinsel
RIB: Oval gold tinsel
BODY: Flat gold tinsel
THROAT HACKLE: Hot orange cock
WING: Black squirrel or fine bucktail
HEAD: Black

REIPPU | REYNARD BLACK - Fulsher | REYNARD BLUE - Fulsher

REYNARD GREEN - Fulsher | REYNARD ORANGE - Fulsher | REYNARD YELLOW - Fulsher

RIVER PHILIP COPPER | ROGER'S FANCY | ROGIE - Brown

ROYAL CHARM - Farago | SANDEEL STREAMER - Buckland | SHEILA - Mathieson

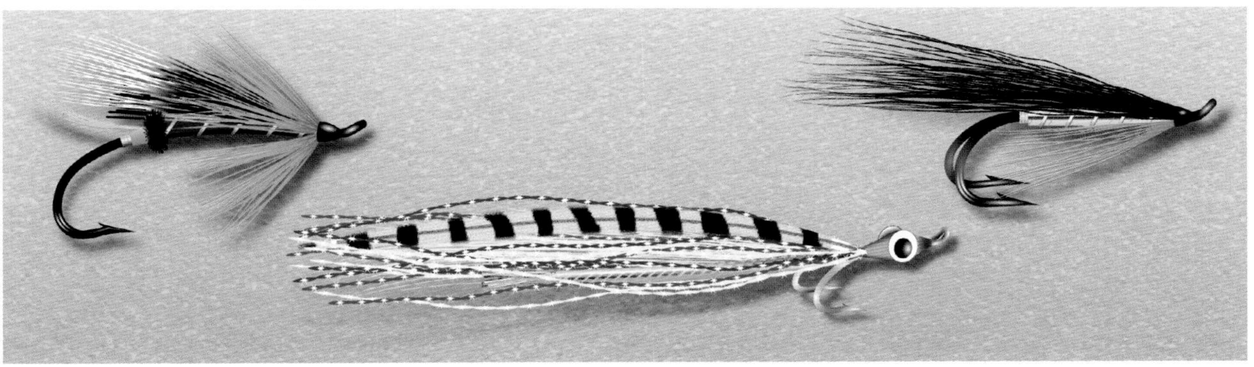

SILVER BADGER

TAG: Oval silver tinsel & yellow floss
TAIL: GP topping
BUTT: Black ostrich herl
RIB: Oval silver tinsel
BODY: Flat silver tinsel
THROAT HACKLE: Kingfisher blue cock
WING: Badger hair
HEAD: Black

SILVER BLUE

TAG: Oval silver tinsel & yellow floss
TAIL: GP topping
RIB: Oval silver tinsel
BODY: Flat silver tinsel
THROAT HACKLE: Light blue cock
WING: Grey squirrel tail
HEAD: Red

SILVER CANARY

TAG: Oval silver tinsel & yellow
TAIL: GP topping, GP tippets, chatterer
BUTT: Black ostrich herl
BODY: Flat silver tinsel
CENTRE BUTT: yellow cock and black ostrich herl
FRONT HACKLE: Indigo blue cock
WING: Golden olive mohair with GP topping over
CHEEKS: Jungle cock with chatterer or kingfisher over
HEAD: Black

SILVER DOWNEASTER - Miner

TAG: Oval silver tinsel
TAIL: GP topping
BUTT: Black ostrich herl
RIB: Oval silver tinsel
BODY: Flat silver tinsel
THROAT HACKLE: Bright orange cock
WING: Black squirrel or bear hair
HEAD: Black

SILVER ERRIFF

TAG: Flat gold tinsel
TAIL: GP topping
BUTT: Black ostrich herl
RIB: Oval silver tinsel
BODY: Flat silver tinsel
THROAT HACKLE: Kingfisher blue cock
WING: Badger hair with GP topping over
HEAD: Black

SILVER GREY EPOXY HEAD

TAG: Oval silver tinsel
BUTT: Fluorescent green Antron
RIB: Oval silver tinsel
BODY: Flat silver tinsel
WING: From bottom - yellow polar bear, fluorescent yellow Krystal Flash, yellow, white & green fox hair, Flashabou in chartreuse, green and yellow combed into fox hair, strands of bronze peacock herl, brown fox hair overall
CHEEKS: Red 3D eyes
HEAD: 5 min clear Epoxy

SILVER GREY FATBACK

TAG: Oval silver tinsel & golden yellow floss
RIB: Oval silver tinsel
BODY: Flat silver tinsel
BODY HACKLE: Badger cock
THROAT HACKLE: Teal or widgeon
WING: From bottom - yellow, green and brown fox hair. Last layer tied in Templedog style
CHEEKS: Jungle cock
HEAD: Black

SILVER MONKEY, VARIANT - Krom

TAG: Flat silver tinsel & fluorescent red floss
TAIL: GP topping
BUTT: Black tying thread
BODY: Silver Mylar tubing
THROAT HACKLE: Grizzle hen
WING: Silver monkey hair over fluorescent green floss
HEAD: Black

SILVER WILKINSON

TAG: Oval silver tinsel & golden yellow floss
TAIL: GP topping
BUTT: Red wool
RIB: Oval silver tinsel
BODY: Flat silver tinsel
THROAT HACKLE: Magenta cock
WING: Strands of red, blue & yellow floss combed out, dyed brown squirrel hair over
HEAD: Red

SKAIDI

TAG: Oval silver tinsel
TAIL: Green floss
RIB: Oval silver tinsel
BODY: Flat silver tinsel
THROAT HACKLE: Green cock
WING: Grey squirrel dyed green
HEAD: Black

SPATE SPECIAL

RIB: Oval gold tinsel
BODY: Black floss
WING: Orange bucktail
CHEEKS: Jungle cock
HEAD: Black

SPEY GILLIE

TAG: Oval silver tinsel
RIB: Oval silver tinsel
BODY: Rear half - yellow floss. Front half - black floss
COLLAR HACKLE: Orange cock with black cock in front
WING: Yellow Arctic fox under black Arctic fox with five strands of Crystal Hair in between
HEAD: Black

SILVER BADGER SILVER BLUE SILVER CANARY

SILVER DOWNEASTER - Miner SILVER ERRIFF SILVER GREY EPOXY HEAD

SILVER GREY FATBACK SILVER MONKEY VARIANT - Krom SILVER WILKINSON

SKAIDI SPATE SPECIAL SPEY GILLIE

SPRING TUBE

TAG: Oval gold tinsel & fluorescent red floss
RIB: Oval gold tinsel
BODY: Black floss
COLLAR HACKLE: Light blue cock
WING: Black Arctic fox under yellow Arctic fox with, optionally, strands of pearl Crystal Hair over
HEAD: Black

SQUIRREL TAIL

TAG: Oval silver tinsel
RIB: Oval silver tinsel
BODY: Black wool or floss
THROAT HACKLE: Brown cock
WING: Red Squirrel tail
HEAD: Black

SQUIRREL TAIL - Duncan

TAG: Fine oval silver tinsel
RIB: Fine oval silver tinsel
BODY: Black floss
HACKLE: Fiery brown cock
WING: Pine squirrel tail
HEAD: Black

STOAT, FLUORESCENT RED

TAG: Oval silver tinsel & Glo-Brite #4 floss
TAIL: Fluorescent red goose biots
RIB: Oval silver tinsel
BODY: Flat silver tinsel
WING: Strands of UV pearl Krystal Flash with black stoat's tail over
COLLAR HACKLE: Fluorescent red cock
HEAD: Black

STOAT, LONGTAIL

TAG: Oval silver tinsel
TAIL: Long black bucktail & calf tail with a few strands of pearl Krystal Flash
RIB: Pearl Lurex
BODY: Black floss
HACKLE: Orange cock with dyed blue guinea fowl over
WING: Black squirrel with peacock sword feathers over
HEAD: Black

STOAT, PEARLY

BODY: Flat pearl Lurex over varnished underbody of white tying silk. Body varnished over for protection
WING: Sparse black squirrel over pearl Crystal Hair
HEAD: Black

STOAT, PEARLY - WADDINGTON

BODY: Flat pearl Lurex over varnished underbody of white tying silk. Body varnished over for protection
WING: Black squirrel over pearl Crystal Hair
HEAD: Black

STOAT, SILVER

TAG: Oval silver tinsel
TAIL: GP topping or yellow hackle fibres
RIB: Oval silver tinsel
BODY: Flat silver tinsel
THROAT HACKLE: Black cock
WING: Black squirrel
HEAD: Black

STOAT, STINCHAR

WING: Black squirrel tail around whole shank
COLLAR HACKLE: Hot orange cock
HEAD: Black

STOAT, THUNDER

TAG: Oval gold tinsel
TAIL: GP topping
RIB: Oval gold tinsel
BODY: Black floss
HACKLE: Hot orange cock with blue dyed guinea fowl over
WING: Black squirrel tail
HEAD: Black

STOAT, THUNDER - IRISH

TAG: Oval gold tinsel
TAIL: Yellow over red hackle fibres
RIB: Oval gold tinsel
BODY: Black floss
HACKLE: Hot orange cock with blue dyed guinea fowl over, tied as collar
WING: Black squirrel tail
CHEEKS: Jungle cock
HEAD: Black

STOAT'S TAIL

TAG: Oval silver tinsel
TAIL: GP topping
RIB: Oval silver tinsel
BODY: Black floss
THROAT HACKLE: Black cock
WING: Black squirrel
HEAD: Black

SPRING TUBE

SQUIRREL TAIL

SQUIRREL TAIL - Duncan

STOAT, FLUORESCENT RED

STOAT, LONGTAIL

STOAT, PEARLY

STOAT, PEARLY - WADDINGTON

STOAT, SILVER

STOAT, STINCHAR

STOAT, THUNDER

STOAT, THUNDER - IRISH

STOAT'S TAIL

STOAT'S TAIL, HOLOGRAPHIC - McPhail

TAG: Silver wire
RIB: Silver wire
BODY: Holographic silver tinsel
THROAT: Black bucktail
WING: Black bucktail under holographic silver tinsel and black goat hair
CHEEKS: Black & silver adhesive eyes
HEAD: Black

SUNNY DAY - Shumakov

TUBE: Shumakov 13mm Skittle tube
BODY: Tube
WING: From bottom - Hot orange SLF hanks under natural badger with strands of orange-yellow Mirage, brown dyed Arctic fox with strands of holographic & silver Angel Hair, dyed dark brown Arctic fox - the last layer tied in Templedog style. Strands of brown Rippleflash overall
FRONT HACKLE: Badger cock
CHEEKS: Jungle cock
HEAD: Black

SUNRAY SHADOW - Brooks

TUBE: from 25 to 50mm (1" to 2") long plastic
WING: Bunch of brown bucktail, a few strands bronze peacock herl, long black goat over
HEAD: Black

SUNRAY SHADOW, VARIANT

TUBE: from 25 to 50mm (1" to 2") long plastic
WING: Bunch of yellow goat hair, long black goat hair, a few strands bronze peacock herl over
HEAD: Black

SWEDISH KILLER

TAG: Oval silver tinsel
RIB: Oval silver tinsel over black chenille
BODY: Rear 1/3rd - yellow chenille. Front 2/3rds - black chenille
HACKLE: Light blue cock
WING: Black squirrel tail
HEAD: Deer hair, spun and clipped

SWEEP

TAG: Oval gold tinsel
TAIL: GP tippets
RIB: Oval gold tinsel
BODY: Black floss
HACKLE: Black cock
WING: Black squirrel tail
CHEEKS: Kingfisher
HEAD: Black

TADPOLE, GRAESSER

RIB: Oval gold tinsel
BODY: Rear half - yellow floss. Front half - red floss
MID-WING: Long yellow squirrel or bucktail
WING: Long black bucktail
HEAD: Red

TADPOLE, SILVER

RIB: Oval gold tinsel
BODY: Rear half - flat silver tinsel. Front half - red floss
MID-WING: Long yellow squirrel or bucktail, above and below
WING: Black bucktail, above & below
HEAD: Red

TADPOLE, TWEED

TAG: Oval gold tinsel
TAIL: Yellow bucktail
RIB: Flat gold tinsel
BODY: Red floss
WING: Black bucktail
HEAD: Red

TANA

TAG: Oval gold tinsel
TAIL: GP topping
BUTT: Black ostrich herl
RIB: Oval gold tinsel
BODY: Flat silver tinsel
BODY HACKLE: Yellow cock over front half of body
THROAT: Natural guinea fowl
WING: White tipped, brown hair with GP topping over
CHEEKS: Jungle cock
HEAD: Black

TANA, VARIANT

TAG: Flat gold tinsel
BUTT: Black floss
RIB: Oval silver tinsel
BODY: Flat silver tinsel
WING: Yellow bucktail under white bucktail with natural guinea fowl hackle overall
HEAD: Black

TARNISHED SILVER

TAG: Flat silver gold tinsel
TAIL: GP topping
RIB: Oval gold tinsel
BODY: Rear half - flat copper tinsel. Front half - flat silver tinsel
THROAT HACKLE: Black cock
WING: Red squirrel tail
HEAD: Black

STOAT'S TAIL, HOLOGRAPHIC | SUNNY DAY - Shumakov | SUNRAY SHADOW - Brooks

SUNRAY SHADOW, VARIANT | SWEDISH KILLER | SWEEP

TADPOLE, GRAESSER | TADPOLE, SILVER | TADPOLE, TWEED

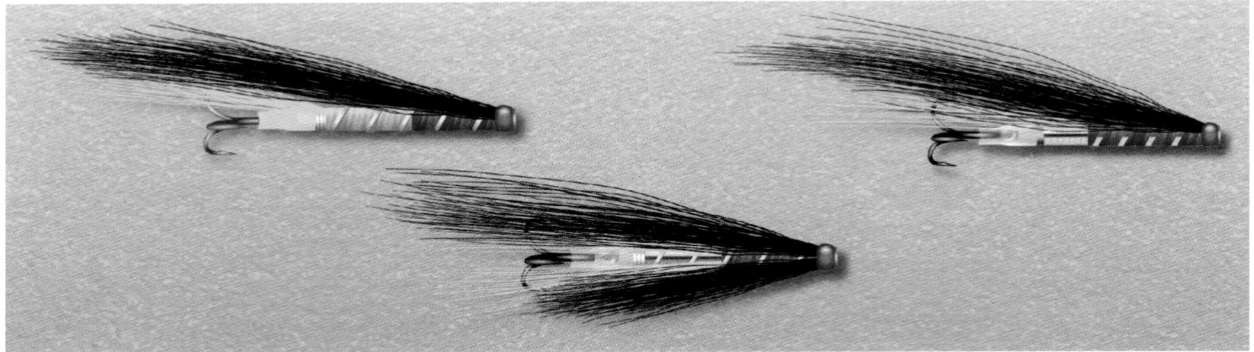

TANA | TANA, VARIANT | TARNISHED SILVER

TAYLOR SPECIAL

TAG: Oval silver tinsel
TAIL: Three or four peacock sword feathers
RIB: Oval silver tinsel over front body only
BODY: Rear half - Fluorescent green floss. Front half - peacock herl
VEIL: Fluorescent green floss over rear body reaching to tail
WING: Unbleached grey squirrel tail dyed green
HACKLE: Yellow cock, tied as collar
HEAD: Black

TEMPLEDOG, ORIGINAL

TAG: Oval gold tinsel
BUTT: Fluorescent orange or red Antron yarn
RIB: Oval gold tinsel
BODY: Rear 2/3rds - flat gold tinsel. Front 1/3rd - black floss
BODY HACKLE: Bager cock dyed orange
THROAT HACKLE: Black or blue cock
WING: Dark brown fox and four strands of peacock herl under a bunch of black fox, 2/3rds. wing length. Flank with strands of rainbow and red Flashabou
CHEEKS: Jungle cock, natural or dyed orange
HEAD: Black

TEXAS JACK

TAG: Oval silver tinsel & fluorescent red floss
TAIL: GP topping
RIB: Oval silver tinsel
BODY: Grey seal's fur
THROAT HACKLE: Natural guinea fowl
WING: Black bear hair
HEAD: Black

THUNDER & LIGHTNING, CLASSIC

TAG: Oval gold tinsel & red floss
BUTT: Black ostrich herl
RIB: Oval gold tinsel
BODY: Black floss
BODY HACKLE: Orange over front half of body
HACKLE: Orange cock under blue dyed Guinea fowl
WING: Pale orange under black under yellow
CHEEKS: Jungle cock
HEAD: Black

THUNDER & LIGHTNING, TUBE

TAG: Oval gold tinsel
RIB: Oval gold tinsel
BODY: Black floss
WING: Pale orange bucktail, tied top and bottom only
HACKLE: Blue jay, sparse
CHEEKS: Jungle cock
HEAD: Black

THUNDER & LIGHTNING, SCOTTISH

TAG: Oval gold tinsel & yellow floss
TAIL: Yellow & red hackle fibres
RIB: Oval gold tinsel
BODY: Black floss
THROAT HACKLE: Orange cock with blue dyed guinea fowl over, tied as collar
WING: Brown squirrel over orange hackle fibres
HEAD: Black

THUNDERFLASH

BODY: Oval glod timsel
HACKLE: Three full turns orange cock set at 45 degrees
UNDERWING: Four or five strands gold Lureflash extending to bend of hook
WING: Sparse black squirrel tail
OVERWING: Six fibres pearl Krystal Flash longer than squirrel hair
HEAD: Black

THURSO DEMON

TAG: Oval gold tinsel
TAIL: GP topping
RIB: Oval gold tinsel
BODY: Flat gold tinsel
HACKLE: Orange cock
WING: Brown squirrel tail
CHEEKS: Jungle cock
HEAD: Black

THURSO DOG

TAG: Oval silver tinsel
TAIL: GP topping
BUTT: Glo-Brite fluorescent floss #12
RIB: Oval gold tinsel
BODY: Black floss
HACKLE: Kingfisher blue bucktail
WING: Green over orange bucktail with four strands fluorescent green Lureflash Twinkle
CHEEKS: Jungle cock
HEAD: Black

THVERA BLUE

TAG: Oval silver tinsel
TAIL: GP tippet fibres
RIB: Oval silver tinsel
BODY: Horizon Blue DRF floss
THROAT HACKLE: Blue cock
WING: Black squirrel tail
CHEEKS: Jungle cock
HEAD: Black

THVERA BLUE, VARIANT

TAG: Oval silver tinsel & yellow floss
TAIL: Yellow hackle fibres
RIB: Oval silver tinsel
BODY: Pale blue floss
THROAT HACKLE: Light blue cock
WING: Black squirrel tail
CHEEKS: Grey squirrel tail dyed light blue
HEAD: Black

TOPOL - Shumakov

TUBE: Shumakov 13mm Skittle tube
BODY: Tube
WING: From bottom - Arctic fox dyed orange with strands of orange-yellow Mirage. Golden olive dyed Arctic fox with strands of black, copper & olive Angel Hair. Dark golden olive dyed Arctic fox with strands of black, copper & olive Angel Hair - the last layer tied in Templedog style. Strands of brown Rippleflash overall
FRONT HACKLE: Orange-brown dyed badger cock
CHEEKS: Jungle cock
HEAD: Black

TAYLOR SPECIAL | TEMPLEDOG, ORIGINAL | TEXAS JACK

THUNDER & LIGHTNING, CLASSIC | THUNDER & LIGHTNING, TUBE | THUNDER & LIGHTNING, SCOTTISH

THUNDERFLASH | THURSO DEMON | THURSO DOG

THVERA BLUE | THVERA BLUE, VARIANT | TOPOL - Shumakov

TORRENT RIVER SPECIAL

TAG: Oval silver tinsel
RIB: Oval silver tinsel
BODY: Fluorescent white floss
WING: White polar bear or calf tail
HACKLE: One turn soft furnace sloping backwards
HEAD: White

TOSH

BODY: Black floss
THROAT HACKLE: Yellow cock
WING: Black squirrel tail
CHEEKS: Jungle cock
HEAD: Black

TOSH, GOLD

RIB: Oval gold tinsel
BODY: Flat gold tinsel
UNDERWING: Hot orange Crystal Hair
WING: Black squirrel tail
HEAD: Black

TOSH, MODERN

TAG: Oval silver tinsel
TAIL: Yellow hackle fibres
RIB: Oval silver tinsel
BODY: Black floss
THROAT HACKLE: Yellow cock
WING: Black squirrel tail
HEAD: Black

TOSH TUBE

BODY: Black floss
WING: Quartered bunches black & yellow hair
HEAD: Black

UNDERTAKER - Duncan

TAG: Fine oval gold tinsel
BUTT: Green stretch Nylon and red stretch Nylon
RIB: Fine oval gold tinsel
BODY: Peacock herl
WING: Black bear hair
HACKLE: Black grizzly
HEAD: Black

VALDUM

TAG: Oval silver tinsel & red floss
TAIL: Red hackle fibres
BUTT: Black ostrich herl
RIB: Black floss
BODY: Flat silver tinsel
THROAT HACKLE: Black cock
WING: Black squirrel tail
CHEEKS: Jungle cock
HEAD: Black

VAMBECK

TAG: Oval silver tinsel
TAIL: GP topping
RIB: Oval silver tinsel
BODY: Flat silver tinsel
HACKLE: Black cock doubled and tied as collar
WING: Black squirrel tail
CHEEKS: Jungle cock
HEAD: Black

VEIDLIST

TAG: Oval silver tinsel
TAIL: GP topping
BUTT: Black and red ostrich herl
RIB: Oval silver tinsel
BODY: Flat silver tinsel
FRONT TAG: Scarlet ostrich herl
HACKLE: Blue cock
WING: Yellow squirrel tail
HEAD: Black

WATSON'S FANCY

TAG: Oval silver tinsel
TAIL: GP topping
RIB: Oval silver tinsel
BODY: Rear half - red seal's fur. Front half - black seal's fur
HACKLE: Black hen
WING: Black squirrel tail
CHEEKS: Jungle cock
HEAD: Black

WEASEL - Rattray

TAG: Oval silver tinsel
TAIL: Yellow hackle fibres
RIB: Medium flat silver
BODY: Black floss (body should have equal widths of black & silver). Complete body protected with three coats of clear varnish
HACKLE: Black henny (soft) cock
WING: Sparse black squirrel tail over three or four strands of pearl Krystal Flash
HEAD: Black

WHALIN GALEN

TAG: Oval silver tinsel
TAIL: Red hackle fibres
RIB: Oval silver tinsel
BODY: Light grey rabbit fur
WING: Grey squirrel tail
HACKLE: Light blue cock, tied as collar
HEAD: Yellow

TORRENT RIVER SPECIAL | TOSH | TOSH, GOLD

TOSH, MODERN | TOSH TUBE | UNDERTAKER - Duncan

VALDUM | VAMBECK | VEIDLIST

WATSON'S FANCY | WEASEL - Rattray | WHALIN GALEN

WHITEWING, TUBE

RIB: Oval silver tinsel
BODY: Black floss
WING: Equal segments of white, blue and red bucktail
HEAD: Black

WILLIE GUNN, GOLD

RIB: Oval embossed gold tinsel
BODY: Flat gold tinsel
WING: Mixed black, yellow and orange bucktail
HEAD: Black

WILLIE GUNN, LONGWING

TAG: Oval gold tinsel
RIB: Oval gold tinsel
BODY: Black floss
WING: Strands of pearl Flashabou. Black bucktail over mixed yellow and orange bucktail. All twice the length of the body
HEAD: Black

WILLIE GUNN, TEMPLEDOG

TAG: Oval gold tinsel & fluorescent yellow Antron yarn
TAIL: Fluorescent yellow Antron yarn
RIB: Oval gold tinsel
BODY: Rear half - wide black holographic tinsel. Front half - Black dubbing
BODY HACKLE: Badger cock dyed hot orange
WING: In order: yellow fox, orange fox with strands of red, orange & pearl Mirage around. Four or five strands peacock herl
FRONT HACKLE: Guinea fowl dyed orange
OVER WING: Long black fox hair
CHEEKS: Jungle cock
HEAD: Black

WILLIE GUNN, TUBE

RIB: Oval gold tinsel
BODY: Black floss
WING: Mixed orange and yellow bucktail with sparse black bucktail over
HEAD: Black

WILLIE GUNN, VARIANT - McDonald

TAG: Oval gold tinsel
RIB: Oval gold tinsel
BODY: Black floss
WING: Yellow, orange and purple bucktail mixed
HEAD: Black

WILLIE GUNN, VARIANT - McPhail

TAG: Oval gold tinsel
RIB: Oval gold tinsel
BODY: Black floss
THROAT: Black bucktail
WING: Mixed yellow & orange bucktail, gold holographic tinsel. Black bucktail over
CHEEKS: Adhesive gold eyes
HEAD: Black

WRINGER

TAG: Flat silver tinsel & golden yellow floss
TAIL: GP topping
BUTT: Black ostrich herl
RIB: Oval silver tinsel
BODY: Black floss
THROAT HACKLE: Medium blue cock
WING: Grey squirrel tail dyed red under same amount dyed yellow
HEAD: Black

YELLOW & ORANGE TEMPLEDOG

BUTT: Yellow wool
RIB: Oval silver tinsel
BODY: Flat silver tinsel
BODY HACKLE: Badger cock dyed orange
WING: White polar bear hair, yellow Icelandic sheep hair, orange Icelandic sheep hair. Six strands peacock herl over
FRONT HACKLE: Badger cock dyed orange
CHEEKS: Jungle cock
HEAD: Black

YELLOW BADGER

BODY: Flat silver tinsel
WING: Badger hair dyed yellow
HEAD: Black

YELLOW DOG

RIB: Oval silver tinsel
BODY: Red floss
WING: Yellow bucktail
HEAD: Black

YOKANGA GOLD

TAG: Oval gold tinsel
RIB: Oval gold tinsel
BODY: Flat gold tinsel
THROAT HACKLE: Orange cock
WING: Black squirrel tail over six strands of gold Krystal Flash
HEAD: Black

WHITEWING, TUBE — WILLIE GUNN, GOLD — WILLIE GUNN, LONGWING

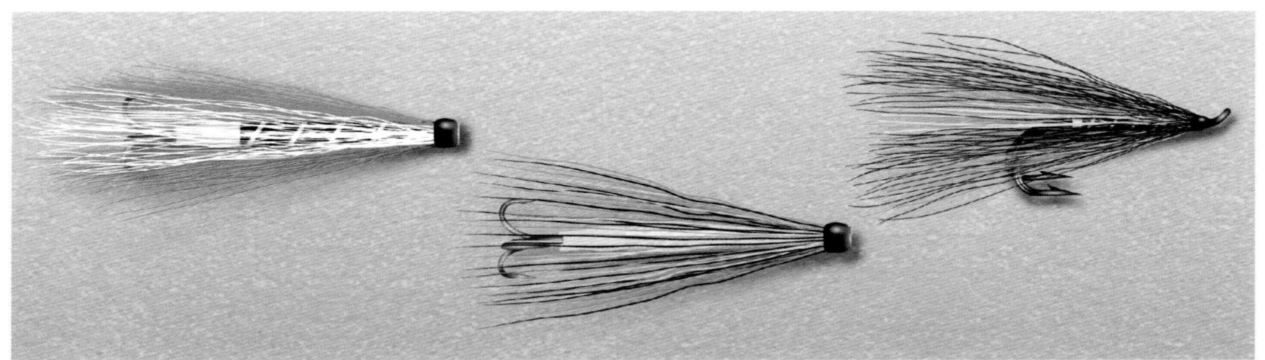

WILLIE GUNN, TEMPLEDOG — WILLIE GUNN, TUBE — WILLIE GUNN, VARIANT - McDonald

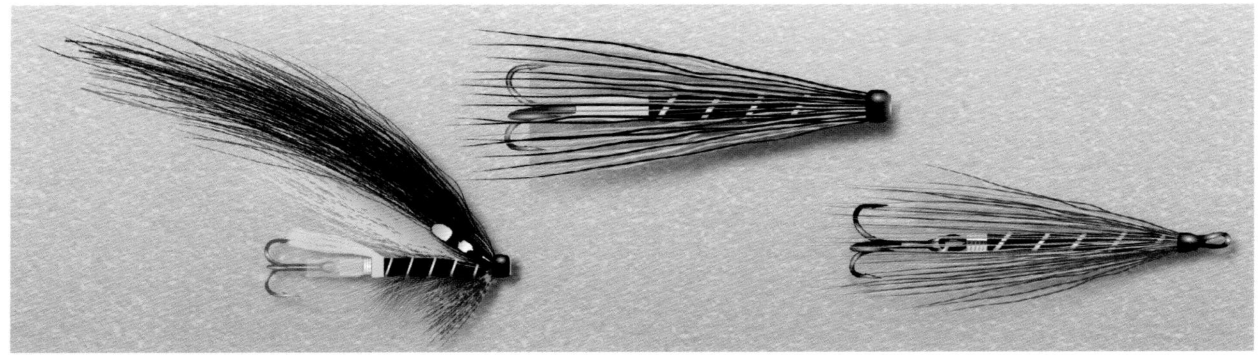

WILLIE GUNN, VARIANT - McPhail — WRINGER — YELLOW & ORANGE TEMPLEDOG

YELLOW BADGER — YELLOW DOG — YOKANGA GOLD

YOKANGA GOLD, FOXWING

TAG: Oval gold tinsel
RIB: Oval gold tinsel
BODY: Flat gold tinsel
THROAT HACKLE: Orange cock
WING: Black Arctic fox over orange Arctic fox. Strands of gold Krystal Flash between. Top wing tied Templedog style
CHEEKS: Jungle cock
HEAD: Black

YO-YO - Charest

TAG: Oval silver tinsel & green floss
TAIL: GP topping
RIB: Oval silver tinsel
BODY: Rear third - fluorescent purple floss. Middle third - pale green floss. Front third - black floss
THROAT: Black bear hair
WING: In three parts spaced along body at joints: rear - green goose biots top & bottom with pale green calf tail wing above. Centre - green goose biots top & bottom with orange calf tail wing above. Front - Yellow calf tail
CHEEKS: Jungle cock
HEAD: Black

ZONKER

BODY: Gold Mylar tubing
RIB: Oval gold tinsel
WING: Black rabbit zonker strip secured with turns of rib, extending well beyond end of hook
HACKLE: Hot orange rabbit strip, wound and stroked back over body
HEAD: Black

YOKANGA GOLD, FOXWING

YO-YO - Charest

ZONKER

ADMIRAL - Rogers

TAIL: Red hackle fibres
RIB: Oval gold tinsel
BODY: Red wool
HACKLE: Red cock
WING: White bucktail
HEAD: Black

AKROYD, VARIANT - Halyk

TAG: Oval silver tinsel
RIB: Oval gold tinsel
BODY: Rear half - orange seal's fur. Front half - black seal's fur
HACKLE: Black saddle or schlappen
WING: Brown squirrel hair
COLLAR HACKLE: Teal flank
HEAD: Black

AL'S SPECIAL - Knudson

TAG: Oval gold tinsel
TAIL: Red hackle fibres
RIB: Oval silver tinsel
BODY: Yellow chenille
HACKLE: Red cock
WING: White bucktail
HEAD: Black

AS SPECIFIED #2 - Lingren

TAG: Oval gold tinsel & purple floss
TAIL: Purple hackle fibres
RIB: Oval gold tinsel
BODY: Rear 1/3rd. - purple floss. Front 2/3rds. - purple seal's fur
BODY HACKLE: sparse black hackle (one side stripped)
THOAT: Two turns widgeon or teal
WING: Black squirrel tail
HEAD: Black

BEADHEAD SQUIRRELS - Valk

TAIL: Black, natural or orange squirrel
RIB: Oval gold tinsel
BODY: Ultra chenille - black, orange and chartreuse
WING: Black, natural or orange squirrel tail
COLLAR HACKLE: Hoffman chickabou in olive grizzly, white, purple or burnt orange
HEAD: Gold bead

(refer to plate 29 on page 136)

BI-COLOUR POLAR BEAR MATUKA - McNeese

TAG: Flat silver tinsel
TAIL: Polar bear, orange at base, purple at tips
RIB: Oval silver tinsel
BODY: Hot orange seal's fur
WING: Polar bear dyed orange at bottom, purple at tips, tied in at four positions along body. A few strands of purple Krystal flash are added to each wing.
COLLAR HACKLE: Orange dyed guinea fowl
CHEEKS: Jungle cock
HEAD: Red

BLACK & BLUE - Van Egan

TAG: Oval gold tinsel & yellow floss (alternate: blue seal's fur)
TAIL: GP topping
RIB: Oval silver tinsel
BODY: Black floss or seal's fur
HACKLE: Bright blue cock
WING: Small bunches of blue, yellow & red polar bear with brown bucktail over. Optional GP topping over
CHEEKS: Jungle cock
HEAD: Black

BLACK & RED MATUKA - Mackenzie

TAG: Small dubbing ball of gold Lite-Brite
TAIL: Squirrel hair dyed black
RIB: Oval gold tinsel
BODY: Red dubbing
BACK HACKLE: Pre-formed squirrel hair dyed black
HEAD HACKLE: Grey squirrel hair dyed red
HEAD: Black

BLACK BEAR - Knudson

TAG: Oval silver tinsel
TAIL: Mixed black & red hackle fibres
RIB: Oval silver tinsel
BODY: Black chenille
HACKLE: Red & black cock wound together
WING: Black bucktail
HEAD: Black

BLACK BUTT BLACK - Lingren

TAG: Oval silver tinsel & black floss
TAIL: Guinea fowl fibres
RIB: Oval silver tinsel
BODY: Rear 1/3rd. - black floss. Front 2/3rds. - black seal's fur
BODY HACKLE: From 2nd turn of ribbing. Sparse black hackle with one side stripped.
THROAT HACKLE: Two turns natural guinea fowl
WING: Black squirrel tail
HEAD: Black

BLACK DIAMOND - Lemire

TAG: Oval silver tinsel
RIB: Oval silver tinsel
BODY: Black floss
THROAT HACKLE: Guinea fowl
UNDERWING: Grey squirrel tail over four peacock sword fibres.
OVERWING: Guinea fowl fibres
CHEEKS: Jungle cock
HEAD: Black

BLACK GORDON - Gordon

TAG: Oval gold tinsel
RIB: Oval gold tinsel
BODY: Rear 1/3rd. - red floss. Front 2/3rds. - black floss
HACKLE: Black cock
WING: Black bucktail
HEAD: Black

ADMIRAL - Rogers | AKROYD, VARIANT - Halyk | AL'S SPECIAL - Knudson

AS SPECIFIED #2 - Lingren | BEADHEAD SQUIRRELS - Valk | BI-COLOUR POLAR BEAR MATUKA

BLACK & BLUE - Van Egan | BLACK & RED MATUKA - Mackenzie | BLACK BEAR - Knudson

BLACK BUTT BLACK - Lingren | BLACK DIAMOND - Lemire | BLACK GORDON - Gordon

BLACK MATUKA

TAG: Small dubbing ball of gold Lite-Brite
TAIL: Squirrel hair dyed black
RIB: Oval silver tinsel
BODY: Rear 3/4 - black dubbing. Front 1/4 red dubbing
BACK HACKLE: Pre-formed squirrel hair dyed black
HEAD HACKLE: Grey squirrel hair dyed black
HEAD: Black

BLACK OPTIC - Prey

RIB: Oval gold tinsel
BODY: Oval gold tinsel
HACKLE: Black cock
WING: Black bucktail
HEAD: Split brass bead painted black with white iris

BLACK PHASE SPEY - Howell

RIB: Oval gold tinsel
BODY: Rear half - flat gold tinsel. Front half - black floss
TAIL: Short tuft of orange polar bear at junction of body halves
SPEY HACKLE: Black heron
WING: Orange polar bear
CHEEKS: Jungle cock
HEAD: Black

BLUE CHARM, VARIANT

RIB: Oval silver tinsel
BODY: Black floss
THROAT HACKLE: Blue dyed guinea fowl
WING: Red, yellow & black bucktail, polar bear or synthetic hair
HEAD: Black

BLUE DRAIN - Darling

BODY: Light blue Diamond Braid
BODY HACKLE: Medium blue saddle hackle
THROAT HACKLE: Grey mallard or teal flank
WING: White polar bear over blue Krystal Flash
HEAD: Black

BOSS

TAIL: Black buckstail at least as long as hook shank
RIB: Flat silver tinsel
BODY: Black chenille
HACKLE: Red cock
HEAD: Silver bead chain eyes

BRAD'S BRAT - Bradner

TAG: Oval gold tinsel
TAIL: Orange & white bucktail
RIB: Flat gold tinsel
BODY: Rear half - orange wool. Front half - red wool
HACKLE: Brown cock
WING: Orange bucktail over white bucktail
CHEEKS: Jungle cock
HEAD: Black

CATNIP - Kustich

TAG: Oval silver tinsel
BODY: Orange dubbing
HACKLE: Orange Hoffman soft hackle
WING: Yellow calf tail
HEAD: Black

CLARET & BLACK - Lingren

TAG: Oval gold tinsel & claret floss
BUTT: Black ostrich herl
TAIL: Small hen neck feather dyed red-orange
RIB: Oval gold tinsel
BODY: Rear 1/3rd. - claret floss. Front 2/3rds. - dark claret seal's fur
BODY HACKLE: Sparse black hackle with one side stripped
THROAT HACKLE: Two turns of widgeon of pintail flank
WING: Black squirrel tail
HEAD: Black

COAL CAR - Kaufmann

TAG: Oval silver tinsel
TAIL: Black hackle fibres
RIB: Oval silver tinsel
BODY: Rear half - fluorescent orange & fire orange wool. Front half - black chenille
HACKLE: Black cock
WING: Black squirrel tail over strands of black Krystal Flash
HEAD: Black

COMET, BLACK

TAG: Oval gold tinsel
TAIL: Black bucktsail at least as long as hook shank
RIB: Flat silver tinsel
BODY: Black chenille
HACKLE: Black cock
HEAD: Silver bead chain eyes

COMET, GOLD

TAIL: Fluorescent orange polar bear at least as long as hook shank
BODY: Embossed gold tinsel
HACKLE: Fluorescent yellow & orange cock wound together
HEAD: Silver bead chain eyes

BLACK MATUKA | BLACK OPTIC - Prey | BLACK PHASE SPEY - Howell

BLUE CHARM, VARIANT | BLUE DRAIN - Darling | BOSS

BRAD'S BRAT - Bradner | CATNIP - Kustich | CLARET & BLACK - Lingren

COAL CAR - Kaufmann | COMET, BLACK | COMET, GOLD

COMET, ORANGE

TAIL: Fluorescent orange polar bear at least as long as hook shank
BODY: Oval silver tinsel
HACKLE: Fluorescent orange cock
HEAD: Silver bead chain eyes

COQUIHALLA ORANGE - Brayshaw

TAG: Oval gold tinsel
TAIL: GP tippet fibres
BUTT: Black ostrich herl
RIB: Oval gold tinsel
BODY: Rear half - oarange floss. Front half - orange polar bear underhair
THROAT HACKLE: Red cock
WING: White over orange polar bear
HEAD: Black

COQUIHALLA SILVER - Brayshaw

TAIL: GP tippet fibres
BUTT: Red floss
RIB: Oval silver tinsel
BODY: Flat silver tinsel
THROAT HACKLE: Red cock
WING: White over orange polar bear
HEAD: Black

DEAN RIVER LANTERNS

TAIL: Squirrel tail dyed black, as long as body
BODY: Underbody of flat silver tinsel. Edge Bright dyed fluorescent green, orange, red, yellow & chartreuse
HACKLE: Fluorescent cock dyed to match body
WING: Black squirrel tail
CHEEKS: Jungle cock
HEAD: Black

(refer to plate 24 page 126)

DEER CREEK - Arnold

TAG: Oval silver tinsel
TAIL: Red hackle fibres
RIB: Oval silver tinsel
BODY: Flat silver tinsel
WING: Purple Arctic fox tied above & below hook
HACKLE: Silver Doctor blue, tied as collar
HEAD: Black

DEL COOPER - Kennedy

TAG: Oval silver tinsel
TAIL: Red hackle fibres
RIB: Oval silver tinsel
BODY: Purple wool
WING: White bucktail
HACKLE: Red cock, wound as collar
HEAD: Black

DESCHUTES MADNESS - McNeese

TAG: Flat silver tinsel
TAIL: GP topping
RIB: Oval silver tinsel
BODY: Black floss
HACKLE: Purple
WING: White polar bear or pearl Krystal Flash
CHEEKS: Jungle cock
HEAD: Black

FALL FAVOURITE - Silvius

BODY: Flat silver tinsel
HACKLE: Red cock
WING: Orange bucktail
HEAD: Black

FIERY BROWN - Brooks

TAG: Flat gold tinsel
RIB: Oval gold tinsel
BODY: Blended fur from ear & cheek of rabbit, dyed hot orange
WING: Fiery brown woodchuck guard hairs
HACKLE: Fiery brown cock
HEAD: Black

FLAT CAR - Kaufmann

TAG: Oval silver tinsel
TAIL: Black hackle fibres
BUTT: Fluorescent green wool
RIB: Oval silver tinsel
BODY: Black chenille
HACKLE: Black cock
WING: Black Arctic fox with a few strands of black & pearl Krystal Flash under
CHEEKS: Jungle cock
HEAD: Black

FREIGHT TRAIN - Kaufmann

TAG: Oval silver tinsel
TAIL: Purple hackle fibres
RIB: Oval silver tinsel
BODY: Rear 1/3rd - fluorescent flame wool. Middle 1/3rd. - fluorescent red wool. Front 1/3rd - black chenille
HACKLE: Purple cock
WING: White calf tail
HEAD: Black

FREIGHT TRAIN, KRYSTAL FLASH

TAG: Oval silver tinsel
TAIL: Purple hackle fibres
RIB: Oval silver tinsel
BODY: Rear 1/3rd - fluorescent flame wool. Middle 1/3rd. - fluorescent red wool. Front 1/3rd - black chenille
HACKLE: Purple cock
WING: Pearl over blue Krystal Flash
HEAD: Black

COMET, ORANGE

COQUIHALLA ORANGE - Brayshaw

COQUIHALLA SILVER - Brayshaw

DEAN RIVER LANTERNS

DEER CREEK - Arnold

DEL COOPER - Kennedy

DESCHUTES MADNESS - McNeese

FALL FAVOURITE - Silvius

FIERY BROWN - Brooks

FLAT CAR - Kaufmann

FREIGHT TRAIN - Kaufmann

FREIGHT TRAIN, KRYSTAL FLASH

GARDENER - Lemire

TAG: Oval gold tinsel & red floss
TAIL: GP tippet fibres over GP topping
RIB: Flat silver tinsel
BODY: Body in three parts, from rear: yellow, green & Cambridge blue seal's fur. Well picked out
THROAT HACKLE: Long black cock
WING: Grey squirrel tail, divided into two bunches, low on either side of body
CHEEKS: Jungle cock, tied drooping
HEAD: Black

GENERAL MONEY #1

TAG: Oval silver tinsel
TAIL: GP red breast feather fibres
RIB: Oval silver tinsel
BODY: Rear half - oval silver tinsel. Front half - black polar bear underfur or seal's fur
BODY HACKLE: Long red cock over front of body
WING: Orange squirrel tail
COLLAR HACKLE: Long red cock
CHEEKS: Jungle cock
HEAD: Black

GENERAL MONEY #2

TAG: Oval gold tinsel
TAIL: GP topping
RIB: Oval gold
BODY: Rear half - black floss. Front half - black polar bear underfur or seal's fur
BODY HACKLE: Long yellow cock over front of body
WING: Red squirrel tail
COLLAR HACKLE: Long badger hackle dyed bright yellow
CHEEKS: Jungle cock
HEAD: Black

GOLDEN DEMON

TAG: Oval gold tinsel
TAIL: GP topping
RIB: Oval gold tinsel
BODY: Flat gold tinsel
HACKLE: Hot orange cock
WING: Brown squirrel tail
CHEEKS: Jungle cock
HEAD: Black

GREASE LINER - Lemire

TAIL: Dark deer body fibres
BODY: Dark brown seal's fur
HACKLE: Grizzle cock, sparse
WING: Dark deer body fur, tie down leaving butts flared. Trim butt to about 3mm (1/4")
long

HARRY KARI BUCKTAIL - Lemire

TAG: Oval gold tinsel
TAIL: Red hackle fibres
RIB: Narrow black chenille
BODY: Yellow chenille
HACKLE: Pheasant shoulder
WING: Black squirrel tail
HEAD: Black

HOWARD NORTON SPECIAL

TAG: Oval silver tinsel
TAIL: Fluorescent orange polar bear, at least as long as hook shank
RIB: Oval silver tinsel
BODY: Fluorescent flame chenille
HACKLE: Fluorescent orange cock
HEAD: Silver bead chain eyes

ICE BLUE

TAG: Oval silver tinsel & light blue floss
TAIL: GP topping
RIB: Oval silver tinsel
BODY: Flat silver tinsel
HACKLE: Kingfisher blue cock
WING: Grey squirrel dyed blue over white polar bear
HEAD: Black

IMPROVED GOVERNOR

TAG: Oval gold tinsel
TAIL: Red hackle fibres
RIB: Oval gold tinsel over rear body
BODY: Rear 2/3rds. - red floss. Front 1/3rd. - peacock herl
HACKLE: Black cock
WING: Dark brown bucktail
CHEEKS: Jungle cock
HEAD: Black

KALAMA SPECIAL - Abrams

TAIL: Red hackle fibres
BODY: Yellow chenille
BODY HACKLE: Badger cock palmered
WING: White bucktail
HEAD: Black

KALEIDOSCOPE - Balek

TAIL: Red hackle fibres
BODY: Underbody of purple floss overwound with pearl Flashabou
WING: White calf tail with purplel Krystal Flash over
HACKLE: Blue & purple saddle hackles wound together
HEAD: Black

KISPIOX BRIGHT - York

TAG: Oval silver tinsel
TAIL: Red calf tail with a few strands of yellow Krystal Flash
RIB: Oval silver tinsel
BODY: Purple chenille
HACKLE: Hot orange cock
WING: White bucktail with yellow bucktail over
HEAD: Black

GARDENER - Lemire | GENERAL MONEY #1 | GENERAL MONEY #2

GOLDEN DEMON | GREASE LINER - Lemire | HARRY KARI BUCKTAIL - Lemire

HOWARD NORTON SPECIAL | ICE BLUE | IMPROVED GOVERNOR

KALAMA SPECIAL - Abrams | KALEIDOSCOPE - Balek | KISPIOX BRIGHT - York

KISPIOX DARK - York

TAG: Oval gold tinsel
TAIL: Black bucktail
RIB: Oval gold tinsel
BODY: Green floss
HACKLE: Grizzly cock
WING: Black bucktail with strands of black Krystal Flash
HEAD: Black

LADY GODIVA - Olsen

TAIL: Red & white hackle fibres
BUTT: Red chenille
RIB: Flat silver tinsel
BODY: Yellow seal's fur or wool
WING: Red over white bucktail
HEAD: Black

LADY HAMILTON - Wahl

TAIL: Red goose primary strips
RIB: Oval silver tinsel
BODY: Red floss
WING: Red-orange over white bucktail
HEAD: Large black, with white iris and black pupil

LEMIRE'S WINTER FLY - Lemire

TAG: Flat silver tinsel
TAIL: Salmon & red hackle fibres
RIB: Medium flat silver tinsel
BODY: Salmon coloured dubbing
HACKLE: Salmon coloured, long & soft
WING: White polar bear or goat, sparse
CHEEKS: Jungle cock
HEAD: Red

LORD HAMILTON - Wahl

TAIL: Red goose primary strips
RIB: Oval silver tinsel
BODY: Yellow floss
WING: Red-orange over white bucktail
HEAD: Large black, with white iris and black pupil

LOW WATER GREEN - York

BODY: Insect green wool, slim
HACKLE: Furnace cock
WING: White calf tail
HEAD: Black

MACK'S CANYON - Stewart

TAG: Oval silver tinsel
TAIL: Orange & white hackle fibres
RIB: Oval silver tinsel
BODY: Rear 1/3rd. - hot orange seal's fur or wool. Front 2/3rds. - black seal's fur or wool
HACKLE: Black cock
WING: White bucktail with topping of orange bucktail
CHEEKS: Jungle cock
HEAD: Black

MACK'S CANYON, BLUE - Melody

RIB: Oval gold tinsel
BODY: Rear 1/3rd. - hot orange seal's fur. Front 2/3rds. - black seal's fur
HACKLE: Light blue cock
WING: Black bucktail with topping of orange bucktail
HEAD: Black

MACK'S CANYON, DARK

TAG: Oval gold tinsel
RIB: Oval gold tinsel
BODY: Rear 1/3rd. - hot orange wool. Front 2/3rds. - black wool
HACKLE: Black cock
WING: Black bucktail with topping of orange bucktail
CHEEKS: Jungle cock
HEAD: Black

MARABOU MADNESS - Shewey

TAG: Flat silver tinsel
TAIL: Purple hackle fibres
BODY: Underbody of fluorescent orange floss. Front half overwound with dark purple plastic (Cactus) chenille
HACKLE: Purple cock
WING: Purple Arctic fox, then purple Krystal Flash , then purple Arctic fox, then four or five strands of purple Flashabou each side
HEAD: Red

McKENZIE SAPPHIRE #1 - Brooks

TAG: Oval silver tinsel & yellow floss
TAIL: Blue hackle fibres
RIB: Flat silver tinsel
BODY: Black seal's fur
BODY HACKLE: Bright blue cock
COLLAR HACKLE: Bright blue cock
WING: Underwing, four strands each of red, yellow, light blue & green bucktail. Soft white hair over
HEAD: Black

McKENZIE SAPPHIRE #2 - Brooks

TAG: Oval silver tinsel & yellow floss
TAIL: Blue hackle fibres
RIB: Flat silver tinsel
BODY: Black seal's fur
BODY HACKLE: Bright blue cock
COLLAR HACKLE: Bright blue cock
WING: Underwing, four strands each of red, yellow, light blue & green bucktail. Black squirrel tail over
CHEEKS: Jungle cock (optional)
HEAD: Black

KISPIOX DARK - York | LADY GODIVA - Olsen | LADY HAMILTON - Wahl

LEMIRE'S WINTER FLY - Lemire | LORD HAMILTON - Wahl | LOW WATER GREEN - York

MACK'S CANYON - Stewart | MACK'S CANYON, BLUE - Melody | MACK'S CANYON, DARK

MARABOU MADNESS - Shewey | McKENZIE SAPPHIRE #1 - Brooks | McKENZIE SAPPHIRE #2 - Brooks

McLEODS UGLY - McLeod

TAIL: Red hackle fuzz from base of hackle (or marabou)
RIB: Oval silver tinsel
BODY: Black chenille
BODY HACKLE: Grizzle cock palmered
WING: Black bucktail
HEAD: Black

McNEESE MADNESS - McNeese

TAG: Flat silver tinsel
TAIL: Fluorescent orange floss
RIB: Four turns of purple plastic (Cactus) chenille, counter wrap with silver wire.
BODY: Fluorescent orange floss
HACKLE: Hot pink Krystal Flash with purple cock over
WING: Hot purple polar bear mixed with purple Krystal Flash
CHEEKS: Jungle cock
HEAD: Black

MONTREAL #1

TAIL: Claret hackle fibres
RIB: Oval gold tinsel
BODY: Claret wool
HACKLE: Claret cock
WING: Grey squirrel tail
HEAD: Black

MONTREAL #2

TAIL: Red hackle fibres
RIB: Oval gold tinsel
BODY: Red wool
HACKLE: Red cock
WING: Brown bucktail
HEAD: Black

NIGHT DANCER - Amato

TAG: Oval silver tinsel
TAIL: Red hackle fibres
RIB: Flat silver tinsel
BODY: Black floss
HACKLE: Deep purple
WING: Black calf or bucktail
CHEEKS: Jungle cock
HEAD: Black

NIGHT DANCER, VARIANT

TAG: Oval silver tinsel
TAIL: Red hackle fibres
RIB: Flat silver tinsel
BODY: Black seal's fur
WING: Black Arctic fox
HACKLE: Deep purple
HEAD: Black

NITE OWL - Silvius

TAIL: Yellow hackle fibres
BUTT: Two turns of red chenille
BODY: Oval silver tinsel
HACKLE: Orange cock
WING: White bucktail
HEAD: Black

OCTOBER SPEY - Stetzer

TAG: Oval gold tinsel
RIB: Oval gold tinsel
BODY: Rear half - orange floss. Front half - hot orange seal's fur
BODY HACKLE: Badger hackle dyed hot orange
WING: Brown squirrel tail
COLLAR HACKLE: Mallard or teal flank dyed hot orange
HEAD: Black

OLIVE MATUKA - Mackenzie

TAG: Small dubbing ball of gold Lite-Brite
TAIL: Grey squirrel hair dyed olive
RIB: Oval gold tinsel
BODY: Rear 3/4 - olive dubbing. Front 1/4 red dubbing
BACK HACKLE: Pre-formed squirrel hair dyed olive
HEAD HACKLE: Grey squirrel hair dyed olive
HEAD: Black

PALE PEARL - McNeese

TAG: Flat silver tinsel
TAIL: GP topping dyed red
RIB: Oval silver tinsel
BODY: Purple Poly Flash tinsel
HACKLE: Long purple cock or pintail flank dyed purple
WING: White polar bear over six strands pearl Krystal Flash. Overwing, small bunch bluish-purple polar bear
CHEEKS: Jungle cock
HEAD: Black

PALE PERIL - McNeese

TAG: Flat silver tinsel
TAIL: GP topping dyed purple
RIB: Oval silver tinsel
BODY: Flat silver tinsel
HACKLE: Long purple cock
WING: Purple over white polar bear
CHEEKS: Jungle cock
HEAD: Black

PATRICIA - Stetzer

TAG: Oval gold tinsel
TAIL: Claret hackle fibres
RIB: Oval gold tinsel
BODY: Claret seal's fur
HACKLE: Claret cock
WING: White polar bear
HEAD: Black

McLEODS UGLY - McLeod | McNEESE MADNESS - McNeese | MONTREAL #1

MONTREAL #2 | NIGHT DANCER - Amato | NIGHT DANCER, VARIANT

NITE OWL - Silvius | OCTOBER SPEY - Stetzer | OLIVE MATUKA

PALE PEARL - McNeese | PALE PERIL - McNeese | PATRICIA - Stetzer

PATRIOT - Amato

TAG: Oval silver tinsel
TAIL: Red hackle fibres
RIB: Oval silver tinsel
BODY: Yellow floss
HACKLE: Deep purple cock
WING: White calf or bucktail
HEAD: Black

PEACOCK UNDERTAKER - Arnold

TAG: Flat silver tinsel
TAIL: GP topping
RIB: Oval silver tinsel
BODY: Rear 1/3rd. - yellow floss. Middle 1/3rd. - orange floss. Front 1/3rd. - peacock herl
WING: Green bucktail with green peacock sword fibres over
HACKLE: Guinea fowl dyed light blue
HEAD: Black

PEARL & BLACK MATUKA - Mackenzie

TAG: Small dubbing ball of pearl Lite-Brite
TAIL: Squirrel hair dyed black
RIB: Oval silver tinsel
BODY: Rear 3/4 -pearl Lite-Brite. Front 1/4 red dubbing
BACK HACKLE: Pre-formed squirrel hair dyed black
HEAD HACKLE: Grey squirrel hair dyed black
HEAD: Black

PEARL & BLUE MATUKA - Mackenzie

TAG: Small dubbing ball of pearl Lite-Brite
TAIL: Grey squirrel hair
RIB: Oval silver tinsel
BODY: Rear 3/4 -pearl Lite-Brite. Front 1/4 red dubbing
BACK HACKLE: Pre-formed Grey squirrel hair
HEAD HACKLE: Grey squirrel hair dyed blue
HEAD: Black

PURPLE BRAT - McNeese

TAG: Flat silver tinsel
TAIL: GP topping dyed red
RIB: Oval silver
BODY: Rear 1/3rd. - half & half fluorescent orange floss and fluorescent red floss. Front 2/3rds - hot purple seal's fur.
HACKLE: Long hot purple from 2nd turn of ribbing
WING: Hot orange polar bear with a few strands of orange Krystal FlashBlack. Purple polar bear over
CHEEKS: Jungle cock
HEAD: Black

PURPLE BUNNY SPEY - Kustich

RIB: Round copper
BODY: Purple Haze SLF
WING: Purple dyed rabbit Zonker strip fastened matuka style with ribbing
HACKLE: Long purple schlappen
HEAD: Black

PURPLE FLASH - Kaufmann

TAG: Oval silver tinsel
TAIL: Purple hackle fibres
RIB: Oval silver tinsel
BODY: Purple chenille
HACKLE: Purple cock
WING: Underwing - two or three strands of wine, pearl, lime green & purple Krystal Flash. Purple Arctic fox over
HEAD: Black

PURPLE JESUS - Miltenberger

TAIL: Purple bucktail with fuchia Flashabou over
BODY: Fluorescent pink yarn
BODY HACKLE: Purple saddle hackle
WING: Purple bucktail
HACKLE: Deep purple saddle
HEAD: Red

PURPLE OCTOBER - Kustich

TAG: Oval silver tinsel
RIB: Oval silver tinsel
BODY: Purple dubbing
HACKLE: Purple burnt goose with orange dyed pheasant rump over
WING: Purple Arctic fox
HEAD: Black

PURPLE PERIL - McLeod

TAG: Oval silver tinsel
TAIL: Purple hackle fibres
RIB: Oval silver tinsel
BODY: Purple floss, wool or dubbing
HACKLE: Purple cock
WING: Natural brown bucktail
HEAD: Black

PURPLE POLAR BEAR MATUKA - McNeese

TAG: Flat silver tinsel
TAIL: Long purple polar bear with four strands of purple Krystal Flash
RIB: Oval silver tinsel
BODY: Purple seal's fur
WING: Polar bear dyed purple, tied in at four positions along body. A few strands of purple Krystal flash are added to each wing.
COLLAR HACKLE: Long purple dyed mallard flank
CHEEKS: Jungle cock
HEAD: Red

PURPLE UGLY - Miltenberger

TAIL: Wine red calf tail
RIB: Flat silver tinsel
BODY: Purple yarn
HACKLE: Fluorescent red saddle hackle
WING: Wine red calf tail
HEAD: Silver bead chain eyes

PATRIOT - Amato | PEACOCK UNDERTAKER - Arnold | PEARL & BLACK MATUKA - Mackenzie

PEARL & BLUE MATUKA - Mackenzie | PURPLE BRAT - McNeese | PURPLE BUNNY SPEY - Kustich

PURPLE FLASH - Kaufmann | PURPLE JESUS - Miltenberger | PURPLE OCTOBER - Kustich

PURPLE PERIL - McLeod | PURPLE POLAR BEAR MATUKA - McNeese | PURPLE UGLY - Miltenberger

RED PHASE SPEY - Howell

RIB: Oval silver tinsel
BODY: Rear half - flat silver tinsel. Front half - red floss
SPEY HACKLE: Black heron
WING: Red polar bear
HEAD: Black

Note: Purple Phase Spey replaces red above with purple.

RICK'S REVENGE - Shewey

TAIL: Hot pink fluorescent floss
RIB: Oval silver tinsel over front body
BODY: Rear half - fluorescent pink floss. Front half - purple seal's fur or goat dubbing
MID-WING: Fluorescent hot pink floss
HACKLE: Purple cock
WING: Blue over purple over white polar bear or calf tail
CHEEKS: Jungle cock
HEAD: Red

ROSE PETAL - Gobin

TAG: Oval silver tinsel
RIB: Oval silver tinsel
BODY: Rear 1/3rd. - fluorescent pink floss. Front 2/3rds. - light claret seal's fur
BODY HACKLE: Long pink saddle over front body
WING: White bucktail
COLLAR HACKLE: Guinea fowl
HEAD: Black

ROSS MATUKA - Mackenzie

TAG: Small dubbing ball of pearl Lite-Brite
TAIL: Orange dyed, black tipped woodchuck hair with grey squirrel hair over
RIB: Oval silver tinsel
BODY: Rear 3/4 -pearl Lite-Brite. Front 1/4 red dubbing
BACK HACKLE: Pre-formed squirrel hair
HEAD HACKLE: Grey squirrel hair dyed black
HEAD: Black

ROYAL FLUSH - Arnold

TAG: Flat silver tinsel
RIB: Flat silver tinsel
BODY: Navy blue chenille
WING: Bright red Arctic fox above and below shank
HEAD: Black

SALMON FLY

TAIL: Fluorescent white bucktail at least as long as hook shank
BODY: Embossed silver tinsel
HACKLE: Fluoresent red cock
HEAD: Silver bead chain eyes

SIGNAL LIGHT - Kaufmann

TAG: Oval silver tinsel
TAIL: Purple hackle fibres
RIB: Oval silver tinsel
BODY: In three parts: Flame fuzzy wool, fluorescent green fuzzy wool, black chenille
HACKLE: Purple cock
WING: Underwing - four strands each of pearl, wine, lime green & blue Krystal Flash. Black arctic fox over
HEAD: Black

SKPADE

TAIL: Natural brown bucktail
BODY: Black sparkle chenille
WING: White bucktail
HACKLE: Black cock
HEAD: Black

SKUNK, COASTAL - Jackson

TAIL: Red hackle fibres
BODY: Chenille made by twisting silver tinsel together with strands of peacock & ostrich herl. Tied slimly
HACKLE: Black cock
WING: White polar bear
HEAD: Red

SKUNK, DESCHUTES

TAG: Oval silver tinsel & red floss
TAIL: Red hackle fibres
RIB: Oval silver tinsel
BODY: Black chenille
HACKLE: Yellow cock with mallard flank over
WING: Brown squirrel tail
HEAD: Black

SKUNK, GREEN BUTT

TAIL: Red hackle fibres
BUTT: Fluorescent green chenille
RIB: Oval silver tinsel
BODY: Black chenille
HACKLE: Black cock
WING: White polar bear
HEAD: Black

SKUNK, INLAND - Jackson

TAIL: Red hackle fibres
BODY: Chenille made by twisting silver tinsel together with strands of peacock & ostrich herl. Tied quite fat & bulky
HACKLE: Black cock
WING: White polar bear
HEAD: Red

RED PHASE SPEY - Howell   RICK'S REVENGE - Shewey   ROSE PETAL - Gobin

ROSS MATUKA - Mackenzie   ROYAL FLUSH - Arnold   SALMON FLY

SIGNAL LIGHT - Kaufmann   SKPADE   SKUNK, COASTAL - Jackson

SKUNK, DESCHUTES   SKUNK, GREEN BUTT   SKUNK, INLAND - Jackson

SKUNK, ORIGINAL

TAIL: Red hackle fibres
RIB: Oval silver tinsel
BODY: Black chenille
HACKLE: Black cock
WING: White polar bear
HEAD: Black

SKUNK, PURPLE - Stonebreaker

TAIL: Grey squirrel tail
BUTT: Fluorescent green chenille
RIB: Oval silver tinsel
BODY: Purple chenille
HACKLE: Purple cock
WING: Grey squirrel tail
HEAD: Black

SKUNK, SUPER

TAG: Oval silver tinsel & fluorescent red floss
TAIL: Red hackle fibres
RIB: Oval silver tinsel
BODY: Black floss
HACKLE: Dark brown cock tied as collar
WING: White bucktail
CHEEKS: Jungle cock
HEAD: Black

SKUNK, VARIANT - Gordon

BODY: Rear half - yellow wool. Front half - black wool
HACKLE: Black cock
WING: Black squirrel tail over white bucktail
HEAD: Black

SKYKOMISH SUNRISE

TAG: Oval silver tinsel
TAIL: Yellow & red hackle fibres
RIB: Flat silver tinsel
BODY: Red wool or chenille
HACKLE: Red & yellow mixed
WING: White bucktail
HEAD: Black

SKYKOMISH YELLOW - McLeod

TAG: Oval silver tinsel
TAIL: Yellow & red hackle fibres
RIB: Flat silver tinsel
BODY: Yellow wool or chenille
HACKLE: Red & yellow mixed
WING: White bucktail
HEAD: Black

SPAWNING PURPLE - McNeese

TAG: Flat silver tinsel
TAIL: Long hot orange polar bear with strands of orange Krystal Flash
RIB: Oval gold tinsel
BODY: Hot orange seal's fur
HACKLE: Hot orange cock with purple cock and guinea fowl over, tied as collar
WING: Purple Arctic fox
HEAD: Red

SPAWNING PURPLE, VARIANT

TAG: Flat silver tinsel
TAIL: Long hot orange polar bear with strands of orange Krystal Flash
RIB: Oval gold tinsel
BODY: Flame orange floss
WING: Purple Arctic fox tied in as four or five separate spikes, spaced along body
COLLAR HACKLE: Purple cock with orange dyed guinea fowl over, tied as collar
CHEEKS: Jungle cock
HEAD: Red

SPRING FAVOURITE - York

TAIL: Red calf tail
BUTT: Green wool
BODY: Red chenille
HACKLE: Red cock
WING: Orange calf tail over strands of orange Krystal Flash
HEAD: Red

SPRINGER GREEN

TAG: Flat silver tinsel & fluorescent light green floss
RIB: Flat silver tinsel
BODY: Rear half - light green fluorescent wool. Front half - deep fluorescent green wool
HACKLE: Toucan orange dyed hen
THROAT: Barred wood duck breast
WING: White brown Arctic fox
CHEEKS: Highlander green dyed hackle tips
HEAD: Black

ST. ESTEPHE

TAG: Oval gold tinsel
TAIL: Claret hackle fibres
RIB: Oval gold tinsel
BODY: Claret seal's fur
HACKLE: Claret cock
WING: Black Arctic fox
HEAD: Black

STEELHEAD CHARLIES - Wagoner

UNDERBODY: Flat silver tinsel
BODY: Black floss
HACKLE: Edge Brite dyed fluorescent red, orange, green, yellow or chartreuse
WING: Squirrel tail dyed black or to match body
EYES: Nickel plated on top of fly

Note: Refer to plate 24 page 126

SKUNK, ORIGINAL | SKUNK, PURPLE - Stonebreaker | SKUNK, SUPER

SKUNK, VARIANT - Gordon | SKYKOMISH SUNRISE | SKYKOMISH YELLOW - McLeod

SPAWNING PURPLE - McNeese | SPAWNING PURPLE, VARIANT | SPRING FAVOURITE - York

SPRINGER GREEN - Johnson | ST. ESTEPHE | STEELHEAD CHARLIES - Wagoner

STEELHEAD PETITES - Valk

TAG: Flat gold tinsel
RIB: Flat gold tinsel
BODY: Uni-Stretch in wine, purple, black, blue, orange & olive
THORAX: Peacock herl
WING: Antron yarn in clear, chartreuse, yellow & olive
HACKLE: Hoffman chickabou in pink, purple, black, blue, grizzle & olive
HEAD: Black

Note: Refer to plate 28 on page 135

STEELHEAD RATS - Brooks

TAG: Oval gold tinsel
TAIL: Fiery brown fox squirrel fibres
RIB: Oval gold tinsel
BODY: Rear 1/3rd - fluorescent green floss, rest peacock herl
HACKLE: Grizzly, palmered over peacock herl
WING: Black & white barred woodchuck hair
COLLAR: Natural black hen, two turns
HEAD: Black

For other variants: change body colour to - fluorescent flame, orange, blue or grey
Refer to plate 22 on page 123

STEELHEAD STINGER, BLACK - Yarnot

BODY: Rear half - flat silver tinsel. Front half - black seal's fur
COLLAR HACKLE: Black cock
WING: White Arctic fox
HEAD: Black

STEELHEAD STINGER, ORANGE - Yarnot

BODY: Rear half - fluorescent orange floss. Front half - fluorescent orange seal's fur
COLLAR HACKLE: Red & orange hackles wound together
WING: White Arctic fox
HEAD: Black

STEWART

TAG: Flat gold tinsel
TAIL: GP tippet fibres
RIB: Oval gold tinsel
BODY: Black floss
HACKLE: Hot orange cock with blue dyed guinea fowl over, tied as collar
WING: Black squirrel tail with orange bucktail over
HEAD: Black

STILLAGUAMISH SPECIAL

TAG: Oval silver tinsel
TAIL: Red & white hackle fibres
RIB: Oval silver tinsel
BODY: Yellow wool palmered with yellow cock hackle.
HACKLE: Red cock
WING: Mixed red & white bucktail
CHEEKS: Jungle cock
HEAD: Black

STRATMAN FANCY - McNeese

TAG: Flat silver tinsel
TAIL: GP topping dyed purple
RIB: Oval silver tinsel
BODY: Purple tinsel
BODY HACKLE: Hot orange pintail flank wound from middle of body
THROAT: Purple dyed pintail flank
WING: Four strands each pearlescent orange & purple Krystal Flash, purple polar bear over
CHEEKS: Jungle cock
HEAD: Red

SUMMER FLING - Shewey

TAG: Flat silver tinsel
TAIL: Purple over orange hackle fibres
RIB: Oval silver tinsel
BODY: Rear 1/4 - hot pink Cactus chenille, 1/4 hot orange Cactus chenille, 1/2 purple Cactus chenille
HACKLE: Dark purple then two turns of guinea fowl dyed red
WING: Purple over orange polar bear
HEAD: Red

SUSTUT BOSS - Miltenberger

TAIL: Thick tag of fluorescent cerise or pink yarn
RIB: Flat gold tinsel
BODY: Black chenille
WING: Black bear hair with pearl Flashabou over
HEAD: Bead chain eyes with red thread

SUSTUT SUNRISE - Miltenberger

TAIL: Purple bucktail with fuschia Flashabou over
RIB: Flat gold tinsel
BODY: Fluorescent flame chenille
HACKLE: Deep purple saddle
WING: Purple bucktail
HEAD: Red

TARTAN, VARIANT - Lemire

TAG: Flat gold tinsel
TAIL: GP red rump
RIB: Oval gold tinsel
BODY: Rear half - orange seal's fur. Front half - scarlet seal's fur
HACKLE: Badger cock with teal at front
WING: Grey squirrel tail divided into two bunches and tied low each side of body
HEAD: Black

THOMSON SPECIAL - York

TAG: Oval silver tinsel
TAIL: Brown calf tail
RIB: Oval silver tinsel
BODY: Black wool
HACKLE: Grizzly cock
WING: Black calf tail with brown calf tail over
HEAD: Orange

STEELHEAD PETITES - Valk | STEELHEAD RATS - Brooks | STEELHEAD STINGER, BLACK - Yarnot

STEELHEAD STINGER, ORANGE - Yarnot | STEWART | STILLAGUAMISH SPECIAL

STRATMAN FANCY - McNeese | SUMMER FLING - Shewey | SUSTUT BOSS - Miltenberger

SUSTUT SUNRISE - Miltenberger | TARTAN, VARIANT - Lemire | THOMSON SPECIAL - York

THOR - Pray

TAIL: Orange hackle fibres
BODY: Red chenille
HACKLE: Brown cock
WING: White bucktail
HEAD: Black

TRANQUILISER - Kennedy

TAG: Flat gold tinsel
TAIL: Yellow over red hackle fibres
RIB: Flat silver tinsel
BODY: Purple seal's fur
WING: White tipped black hair
HACKLE: Claret cock
HEAD: Black

TRINITY, CHRISTMAS - Garrett

TAG: Flat gold tinsel
TAIL: GP topping dyed hot orange
RIB: Flat gold tinsel
BODY: Three "balls" of fluorescent dubbing, separated by ribbing. Colours from rear, orange, flame & lime green
HACKLE: Lime green and flame cock
WING: White polar bear or bucktail
HEAD: Purple

TRINITY, HOT ORANGE - Garrett

TAG: Flat gold tinsel
TAIL: GP topping dyed hot orange
RIB: Flat gold tinsel
BODY: Three "balls" of fluorescent dubbing, separated by ribbing. Colour flame
HACKLE: Flame cock
WING: White polar bear or bucktail
HEAD: Purple

TRINITY, ORANGE - Garrett

TAG: Flat gold tinsel
TAIL: GP topping dyed hot orange
RIB: Flat gold tinsel
BODY: Three "balls" of fluorescent dubbing, separated by ribbing. Colour orange
HACKLE: Orange cock
WING: White polar bear or bucktail
HEAD: Purple

WASHOUGAL OLIVE - McMillan

TAG: Flat gold tinsel
TAIL: Golden olive dyed calf tail
BODY: Flat gold tinsel
THROAT: Golden olive dyed calf tail
WING: White calf tail
HEAD: Black

WINTER'S HOPE, VARIANT

BODY: Flat silver tinsel
THROAT HACKLE: Purple & blue cock
WING: Yellow & orange calf tail
HEAD: Red

WITCH, BLACK - Brocco

TAG: Oval gold tinsel & fluorescent green floss
RIB: Oval gold tinsel
BODY: Black seal's fur
HACKLE: Pheasant rump dyed black
WING: White polar bear
COLLAR HACKLE: Teal flank
HEAD: Red

WITCH, ORANGE - Brocco

TAG: Oval gold tinsel
RIB: Oval gold tinsel
BODY: Orange seal's fur
HACKLE: Golden pheasant flank black
WING: White polar bear
COLLAR HACKLE: Bronze mallard
HEAD: Orange

WITCH, PURPLE - Brocco

TAG: Oval gold tinsel & deep purple floss
RIB: Oval gold tinsel
BODY: Purple seal's fur
HACKLE: Golden pheasant flank
WING: White polar bear
COLLAR HACKLE: Bronze mallard
HEAD: Red

THOR - Pray

TRANQUILISER - Kennedy

TRINITY, CHRISTMAS - Garrett

TRINITY, HOT ORANGE - Garrett

TRINITY, ORANGE - Garrett

WASHOUGAL OLIVE - McMillan

WINTER'S HOPE, VARIANT

WITCH, BLACK - Brocco

WITCH, ORANGE - Brocco

WITCH, PURPLE - Brocco

Arnold, Bob
Steelhead Water, Frank Amato Publications 1993.
Steelhead & the Floating Line, Frank Amato Publications 1995.

Bachmann, Troy
Frontier Flies, Frank Amato Publications 1998.

Bates, Col. Joseph D
Atlantic Salmon Flies & Fishing Stackpole Books 1970.
The Art of the Atlantic Salmon Fly, D.R. Godine 1987.

Buckland, John
The Pocket Guide to Trout & Salmon Flies, Mitchell Beazley Publishers 1986.

Buckland, John and Oglesby, Arthur
A Guide to Salmon Flies, The Crowood Press 1990.

Combs, Trey
Steelhead Fly Fishing, Lyons Press 1991, Paperback edition 1999.
Steelhead Fly Fishing & Flies, Salmon Trout Steelheader, 1976.

Dunham, Judith
The Atlantic Salmon Fly - The Tyers and Their Art, Chronicle Books 1991.

Francis, Francis
A Book on Angling, London 1867. Reprinted by The Fly Fishers' Classic Library.

Frodin, Mikael
Classic Salmon Flies - History & Patterns, Bonanza Books 1991.

Fulsher, Keith and Krom, Charles
Hair-Wing Atlantic Salmon Flies, Fly Tyer Inc. 1981.

Hale, J. H.
How to Tie Salmon Flies, London 1892 & 1919. Reprinted by The Fly Fishers Classic Library.

Headley, Stan
Trout & Salmon Flies of Scotland, Merlin Unwin Books 1997.

Inland Empire Fishing Club
Flies of the Northwest, Frank Amato Publications, 1998.

Jorgensen, Poul
Salmon Flies - Their Character, Style and Dressing, Stackpole Books, 2nd Ed. 1999.

Kelson, George Mortimer
The Salmon Fly, London 1895. Reprinted by The Fly Fishers' Classic Library.

Knox, Arthur Edward
Autumns on the Spey, London 1892. Reprinted by The Fly Fishers' Classic Library.

Lingren, Arthur James
Fly Patterns of British Columbia, Frank Amato

Mackenzie, Gordon
Hair-Hackle Tying Techniques & Fly Patterns, Frank Amato Publications 2001.

Malone, E. J.
Irish Trout & Salmon Flies, Coch-y-Bonddu Books, paperback edition 1998.

Mann, Christopher and Gillespie, Robert
Shrimp & Spey Flies for Salmon & Steelhead, Merlin Unwin Books 2001 & Stackpole Books 2001.

Marriner, Paul C.
Modern Atlantic Salmon Flies, Frank Amato Publications 1998.

Meyer, Deke
Advanced Fly Fishing For Steelhead, Frank Amato Publications 1992.

Morgan, Moc
Trout & Salmon Flies of Wales, Merlin Unwin Books 1996.

O'Reilly, Peter
Trout & Salmon Flies of Ireland, Merlin Unwin Books 1995.

Patrick, Roy A.
Pacific Northwest Fly Patterns, Patrick's Fly Shop 1948, Revised 1953, 1958.

Pryce-Tanatt, Dr. Thomas
How to Dress Salmon Flies, London 1914. Reprinted by The Fly Fishers' Classic Library.

Radenich, Michael D.
Tying the Classic Salmon Fly, Stackpole Books 1997.

Shewey, John & Maxwell, Forrest
Fly Fishing For Summer Steelhead, Frank Amato Publications 1996.

Stetzer, Randle Scott
Flies - The Best One Thousand, Frank Amato Publications 1992.

Supinski, Matt
Steelhead Dreams, Frank Amato Publications 2001.

Veniard, John
Further Guide to Fly Dressing, A&C Black, London 1964.

Index

Index

Index